The Few and the Many

The Few and the Many

A Typology of Elites

ERIC CARLTON

ACW4314

Published by
SCOLAR PRESS
Gower House
Croft Road
Aldershot
Hants GU11 3HR
England

Ashgate Publishing Company
Old Post Road
Brookfield
Vermont 05036–9704
USA

British Library Cataloguing in Publication Data

Carlton, Eric
  The Few and the Many: a Typology of Elites
  1.Elite (Social sciences)
  I.Title
  305.5'2

  ISBN 1 85928 194 X

Library of Congress Cataloging-in-Publication Data

Carlton, Eric.
    The few and the many: a typology of elites/Eric Carlton.
       p.   cm.
    Includes bibliographical references and index.
    ISBN 1–85928–194–X (cloth)
    1. Elite (Social sciences)   2. Elite (Social sciences)—Case
studies.   I. Title.
    HM141.C275   1996
    305.5'2—dc20
                                                            95–25475
                                                            CIP

ISBN 1 85928 194 X

Typeset in Sabon by Bournemouth Colour Press Ltd and printed in Great Britain by Hartnolls Ltd, Bodmin.

Contents

Introduction: Theories of Elites   1

    Definitions and Distinctions   1
    Elites and Values   7
    Elites and Intellectuals   9
    Elites and Ideology   12
    Elites and Aggression   15
    Elites and Personality Factors   16
    Elites and Social Democracy   17
    Elites and Ethics   21

1   Elitism by Birth: The Hindu Caste System   33

2   Elitism by Class: Social Differentiation in Classical Greece   45

3   Elitism by Selection: Byzantine Bureaucracy   59

4   Elitism by Race: Europeans and the Indians of Colonial America   72

5   Elitism by Moral Right: Europeans and Early Colonial Contacts   90

6   Elitism by Special Election: The Millenarian Phenomenon   104

7   Elitism by Conquest: The Tragedy of Cambodia   116

8   Elitism and Ecclesiastical Authority: The Church and Medieval Heresy   127

9   Elitism by Sex: The Gender Issue   143

10   Elitism by Party: National Socialism in Germany 1920–45   156

11   Elitism by Economic Status: The Western 'Models' Problem   169

12   Elitism by Culture: The Mass Culture Debate   181

13   Elitism by Education: The Status of Science Issue   190

Postscript   202

Bibliography   207

Index   218

'There are the good guys and the bad guys –
the problem is to know which is which.'

Burt Lancaster in *The Professionals*

Introduction: Theories of Elites

Definitions and Distinctions

In much modern writing – certainly in the social and educational sciences – élitism has not exactly had rave notices. The very idea of élite groups or organizations, whether self or other identified, arouses suspicions of superiority, authority and power which may be used to the detriment of others. There is a hint of conspiracy about the very term élite. It connotes something that is inimical to the public good rather than that which is desirable or beneficial. It evokes the notion of inequality: the image of a ruling few with élitism as a mode or method of domination. Indeed, in liberal societies, élitism is commonly a pejorative expression; when used, it sounds more like an accusation than a recognition of superior qualities. Or to put it more technically, 'élitist doctrines bring the normative dimensions of the élite to the fore and stimulate a polarizing, polemical style of discourse. ... The charge of élitism assaults those who approve ... any legitimate role of elites in society' (Marcus: 1983, pp.22–31). Elite and its cognates élitism and élitist, derive from the Latin *eligere* (to elect) whence, in eighteenth-century French, it came to denote quality – the choice of the best. This carried with it the related idea of 'distinction' with the normative implication of something which is *worthy* of choice.

In the social and political sciences, it came to be popularized by Pareto and Mosca, though mainly in the somewhat restricted sense of *governing* élites. With the gradual decline – or, at least, the blurring – of the older distinctions of social ranking, especially since the Second World War, there has gradually developed a certain uneasiness about any kind of fixed inequality although, as we shall see, such ideas are often applied inconsistently. There are some inequalities that we are all too ready to admit. We readily recognize those with natural gifts: good looks, strength, sporting prowess and the like, but are hesitant about such things as intelligence and learning capacities. And as far as the ability to govern is concerned, people have long been sceptical about those who presume to act as leaders. Even in the so-called cradle of democracy, ancient Athens, undemocratic as it was in so many ways, the people were in no doubt about the unreliability, dishonesty and downright ordinariness of most politicians.

Vilfredo Pareto (1848–1923) maintained that one should distinguish firstly between the élite and the non-élite, and then between the governing élite and the non-governing élite (Pareto: 1973). Elites were said to consist of individuals with the highest performance in their field. But with time superior elements develop in the governed masses and inferior elements accumulate among those that govern, and one élite is replaced by another. Thus social change is facilitated by this 'circulation of élites', with the alternation of conservative and progressive forces (which, presumably, become the next 'round' of conservatives). It has been argued that there is little actual evidence for this (e.g. Bottomore: 1964, p.274) but just a glance at the struggles of some of the early Greek city-states (*poleis*) will support Pareto's general thesis. He recognized that the pattern of circulation depended on the methods of recruitment and integration and that closure of an élite, often on the principle of heredity, would lead to the degeneration of that élite. Hence his conclusion that history is 'a graveyard of aristocracies'. Gaetano Mosca (1858–1941) was similarly somewhat disenchanted with liberal democracy as he knew it. He insisted that whatever the form of government, real power would always rest with an élite minority which he termed the 'ruling class' who were obliged to justify their position in terms of accepted political principles (Mosca: 1939).

Both Pareto and Mosca arguably derived these theories, in part, from Machiavelli (*The Prince*), who contends that political leaders must possess the cunning of foxes and the strength and determination of lions. For Mosca, in particular, the minority nature of the governing élite (or, as he called it, political class) gave it the advantages of tight organization and unity of action. These qualities were conspicuously absent in the masses who were incapable of concerted action. The fact that it was the minority who were always really in control meant *ipso facto* that democracy was a myth, a point developed by the German sociologist, Robert Michels (1876–1936) who proposed that sovereignty in any organization is the prerogative of the professional leadership. This constituted the 'iron law of oligarchy' (see Scott: 1990, p.xi). Much of Michels' work was concerned with labour organization, and he maintained that elected officials become divorced from their memberships by virtue of their specialist expertise, and the eventual divergence of their respective goals. As Michels puts it, 'Long experience has shown that among the factors which secure the dominion of minorities over majorities ... the first place must be given to the formal instruction of the leaders ... [this] special competence, this expert knowledge which the leader acquires [is] almost inaccessible to the mass ...' (Michels: 1962, pp.107–10). Increasing size and complexity of organization also prevent the masses from effectively participating in the political process.

Understandably some theorists see this as a direct attack on liberal traditions – a proposition that, if true, undermines the very idea of democracy. Michels writes of the 'disastrous floods ... [that] flow over the plain of democracy rendering [it] unrecognizable' (ibid., p.62). One critic, using the same simile, replies that if 'oligarchical waves repeatedly wash away the bridges of democracy, [men] will doggedly rebuild them .... There cannot be an iron law of oligarchy ... unless there is an iron law of democracy' (Gouldner: 1955, p.506). Be that as it may, it does not really destroy Michels' contention. Effective participation in the social process has taken place, for instance, in many non-centralized tribal societies, but these were invariably small scale. As soon as expansion occurred, possibly through coalition, as with the plains Indians in the nineteenth century in the face of white incursions, then élites form if only for the sake of temporary expediency.

Strictly speaking, the terms élite and oligarchy are not synonymous. Or, to be more precise, an oligarchy is a form of élite but an élite is not necessarily an oligarchy. The expression oligarchy does indeed mean the rule of the few but it is a term that is rarely used outside the political sphere. Thus to cite the example of classical city states once again, we find that one of the most popular forms of government was an oligarchy of the aristocracy (literally the rule of the best people). Even less is the term élite to be confused with that of class. Certainly, élite cannot be equated with class in the traditional Marxist sense that class is based on economic determinants. An élite may form for reasons quite other than economic ones and this would include, as in more modern Marxist theory, the notion of management and control of the means of production, besides the actual ownership of those resources. Similarly, élite may not simply relate (as Max Weber) to one's life chances, although Weber's extended criteria of educational skills are characteristic of élites. However, it is true that élites may determine the life-chances of others. Furthermore, the notion of class consciousness does not apply in the same way to élites. In theory, a class becomes a class-for-itself because it becomes subjectively aware of its objective class situation; an élite is an élite because it *is* an élite. It does not need some kind of educational or enlightenment process to be made aware of its situation. It does not need to realize its identity, or appraise the problem of inherent contradictions and oppositions. Its awareness of 'superiority', of difference, is always there. This is what makes it an élite. It certainly does not necessarily entertain visions of an alternative society. In fact, it might be argued that it is the *imperfections* of society that reaffirm the status of élites.

The issue of class and élites was very much brought to the fore in the writings of the American social analyst, C. Wright Mills. Though sometimes thought of as a neo-Marxist, Mills, influenced by Max Weber, argued that the expression 'ruling class' was really the conflation of two different levels of analysis, rule being a political concept, and class an economic concept. He also rejected the idea of class consciousness in relation to the American middle-classes in his study *White Collar* (Mills: 1951). He followed this with research in which he again relegated the concept of class to the background, and also proposed rather radical views on the matter of élites. In another very popular work (Mills: 1956), he argued that control of American politics was in the hands of relatively few dominant figures in the military and commercial sectors who were 'related' – not always self-consciously – in both policy and practice. This 'military–industrial complex' constituted the controlling force in the American economy. During the Vietnam War, this text, *The Power Elite*, became 'a key thesis in anti-imperialistic denunciations of the American bourgeoisie' (Calvert: 1982, p.187). But Mills' critics, notably Talcott Parsons, pointed out that status and power did not necessarily go together any more than class and élite. For example, American physicians enjoyed high status and often high incomes, but had very little power (Parsons: 1957). We shall see too that in other social contexts, for instance in the experience of certain religious functionaries, there may be high status and influence, rather than power, combined with relative poverty. Class, then, which, as a concept, is notoriously difficult to define or delimit, must not be confounded with that of élite.

The French social theorist, Raymond Aron, has argued that the abolition of class, in the Marxist sense, would not mean the abolition of élites. Indeed, he suggests that élites may have a positive function in that their conflicts may restrict the activities of the ruling power (Bottomore: 1964, p.192). Aron prefers the term 'leading strata' to that of élite. This has particular merits in the context of, say, the *ancien régime* in France which constituted a 'true ruling class' and comes close to Mosca's 'political class'. Paradoxically, it is both too broad and too narrow to substitute for élite: too broad in that, by definition, it involves, at least, a whole social stratum, and too narrow in that it again relates exclusively to the political arena. It is still not unusual to find the term élite used rather loosely to denote such a stratum. For example, when Prime Minister Major's first 'classless' Honours list was published, critics commented that 'six out of ten of all awards went to members of the traditional middle-class élite of senior civil servants, politicians and wealthy businessmen .... The entrenched élitism ... remains untouched. Nearly nine out of ten OBEs ... went to ... the top two classes' (*Sunday Times*, 2 January 1994). Again class is being seen as the basis of patronage and those duly honoured are *ipso facto* members not of a privileged group, but of an 'élite'.

One sometimes suspects that these semantic exercises are devised simply for the sake of being different. In some cases perhaps they are, but in general we can generously assume that social theorists are striving for greater clarity and precision. The assumption is that if we can name a thing, we can contain it conceptually. Unfortunately, neither life nor language is quite as simple as this. Semantics aside, there are a number of critical issues that arise in any consideration of élites and élitism. How are élites generated and how do they form? What is their basis (or bases) of recruitment, and what exactly determines the forms they take? Are they open or closed? Are they self-perpetuating? And to what extent are they linked or integrated? How responsive are they to external (public?) pressures, and how accountable are they to society in general? Will there – must there – always be élites, and if so are they desirable?

Seymour Lipset, in his comparative study of value patterns in British and American society, distinguishes between élites which form as the result of *contest mobility*, that is, upward mobility which is theoretically a prize that is open to all, and those formed by *sponsored mobility*, in which élite recruits are chosen by the established élite and *given* élite status (Lipset: 1971, p.322). Here, élite membership is being related to status, specifically the well-tried distinction between achieved and attributed status. Such ideas stem directly from Weber's work on bureaucracy which we shall consider later in the case studies. Weber maintained that the equalisation of social conditions was an important prerequisite for the growth of bureaucracy – arguably a particular form of élite – since 'recruitment of officials strictly on the basis of ability and qualifications could only be established when public office became accessible in principle to all citizens' (Bottomore: 1975, p.142).

One of the ongoing arguments in élite theory is that of the Pluralists versus the nonPluralists. To some extent our discussion has already touched on what is, in some ways, a rather sterile debate which assumes two extreme positions: that associated with Marxism, which assumes an all-powerful economic élite which exploits the masses in its own interests; and that associated with those who adopt a Pluralist position and contend that society consists of many 'contributory' élites. It is all somewhat reminiscent of the related argument about the possession and distribution of power. The traditional Marxist position was that of the 'constant-sum' whereby a few people hold and wield power at the expense of others. The 'amount' of power remains constant, and is used by the holders of that power to further their own interests. The opposing view, sometimes referred to as the functionalist view, maintains a 'variable-sum' position in which power is possessed by society as a whole and is used to further its *collective* goals. It is something which is held in trust, as it were, and directed by those in authority for the benefit of all (Haralambos: 1980, p.101).

Pluralists offer a very similar approach regarding élites. They regard the Marxist view, of an all-encompassing élite that dominates society, as a kind of conspiracy theory. Instead, it is argued that society is made up of many élites, educational élites, industrial élites, political élites and so on, which despite their differences function in complementary ways in order to sustain society. Interestingly, both sides in this debate are indebted to Pareto and Mosca, who were really in opposition to Marx in that they insisted that élitism was inevitable because the masses were incapable of making intelligent decisions for themselves. Theoretically, this is not the Marxist position, but in practice it has approximated to the Communist position. C. Wright Mills, supported by the American urban community researcher, Floyd Hunter, takes a compromise position. They opt for a conscious 'amalgamation' of élites to form one overriding élite, an interpretation that has been vigorously contested by the academic, Robert Dahl, on the grounds that the 'power-élite' position only indicates a *potential* for control, not actual control. If it could be shown that this hypothetical minority actually had the power to make key decisions and overrule all opposition to its policies, then – and only then – will its existence have been established. Whether, in fact, American society is characterized by an open democratic system, as Hunter claims, is still a matter of argument. It would appear to be reasonably commonsensical to assume that much depends on which city, in which circumstances and in what ways.

Elites undoubtedly exist. Yet again the real issues are how they form, how they cohere, and how they function; or, as one theorist suggests, in terms of agency, exclusivity and relationality (Marcus: 1983, p.10), how do they operate, in what senses are they separate, and how do they relate to one another and to the wider society? These are obviously complex issues that must be treated in different ways for different societies. Hopefully, these things will be made clearer in our case studies. As one authority puts it, 'indiscriminate use of the term "élite" has masked the value of élite analysis. If élites are simply those at the top of any hierarchy whatsoever, then the identification and analysis of élites is trivialized. After all, if all societies and all organizations, by definition, have an élite of top office holders, then the language of élite analysis tells us nothing' (Scott: 1990, p.xiii). So far, so good. But the same writer wants to know if such groups are characterized by 'consciousness, coherence and conspiracy' because this may tell us something about the exercise of power in society, the implication being that only then will we uncover something to our advantage.

Elite theory is more 'naturally' and easily applied to earlier societies that had well-established, and often unquestioned, hierarchical organizations. One thinks particularly of certain tribal societies in pre-industrial Africa such as the Dahomey and the Ashanti in the west, the Zulu and the Swazi in the south, which were technically despotisms but which all had their élite nobility. Even better examples are those many complex pre-industrial societies, India, China, Egypt and the like, some of which we will be considering in more detail. The former group have been reasonably well treated by ethnologists and anthropologists while the latter, as the province of historians, have been rather neglected by the social sciences.

As far as modern societies are concerned, it is probably true to say that élite research received considerable impetus from the upsurge of the fascist systems of the 1930s and 1940s and the continuing situation in the Communist bloc after the Second World War. In addition, decolonization, especially in Africa, led to the formation (or in many cases the re-formation) of liberated states which, in many instances, went over to some form of élitist rule, either as oligarchies or autocracies. The research that ensued was obviously strongly influenced by Pareto and Mosca, and, as we have seen, tended to bifurcate into the so-called Pluralists (Robert Dahl, Daniel Bell, et al.) and those that we might term the 'power élite' theorists (C. Wright Mills, Ferdinand Lundberg, et al.) Perhaps regrettably, these studies were largely confined to the question of power and the extent to which élites controlled a whole variety of institutions and constituencies. This issue has not yet been resolved. As one authority puts it, 'In mass societies with differentiated institutional orders, manifestations of élite organisation have a phantom quality which is a perpetual obstacle in [the] field of research ...' (Marcus: 1983, pp.18–19). In fact, Anthony Giddens has tried to cut through the debate by pointing out that in contemporary society some version of the Pluralist position must hold, because leadership is exercised by amorphous, differentiated groups rather than any kind of monolithic organization.

Elites and Values

Seymour Lipset (Lipset: 1971, p.323) following very much in the tradition of Talcott Parsons, maintains that value orientations dominate the issues in élite theory. Parsons asks how social life is possible, and concludes that it is value-consensus alone which integrates society. It constitutes the basis of social unity and provides the foundation for co-operation between members in their pursuit of common goals. Value-consensus is the principle which gives a society its singular identity (Parsons: 1951). In the same apostolic tradition, Edward Shils maintains that decisions made by élites are necessarily in line with the standards accepted by society as a whole. It is argued that the central value system legitimizes the existing distribution of roles and rewards to persons possessing the appropriate qualities which in various ways symbolize degrees of proximity to authority and praises the qualities of those who occupy authoritative positions in society. One can see obvious flaws in this argument but Shils, anticipating possible objections, qualifies this by saying that 'the value systems obtaining in any diversified society may be regarded as being distributed along a range ... running from hyperaffirmation of some of the components of the ... central value system to an extreme denial of some of [these same] elements ... [such as] the attitude towards established authority' (Shils: 1970, pp.416–18).

The values issue has been taken up by two of the most notable modern élite theorists, Harold Lasswell and Daniel Lerner, who state that their primary intention is to expose what they term the 'democratic fallacy'. They want to correct the view that governments are run by the governed. Governments, they emphasize, are run by the governors, who in democratic systems are believed to represent the governed. In such systems they are elected by the governed to whom they are also ultimately accountable. At least, this is the theory. It would be interesting to know just how many people believe it works like that. In the United Kingdom, certainly, the public appear to rate politicians on a par with estate agents and car salesmen. Yet they are not quite sure what other system would work better.

Lasswell and Lerner are also keen to counter what they call the 'pathetic fallacy', that is, the idea that the 'object of one's attention is necessarily also the object of one's affection' (Lasswell and Lerner: 1965, p.v.). Actually the reverse may be the case. Those who study élites do so because of the need to question methods and doubt assumptions. Political élites, especially, can often be shown to be unwittingly non-rational and quite often deliberately unethical, and become the victims of their own coercive ideologies.

There is some agreement that societies do indeed have a plurality of élites, and that these correspond with the 'valued outcomes' which humans seek to maximize. These, in turn, determine their institutional practices, which also include resource management. These valued outcomes, which in many ways are reminiscent of the psychologist, Abraham Maslow's 'hierarchy of needs', comprise – unsurprisingly – power, enlightenment, wealth, well-being, skill, affection, respect and rectitude, i.e. behaviour that conforms to certain ethical and religious standards. It is argued that élites will form as institutionalized responses to such aspirations, and that those concerned may well see themselves as upholders of a particular creed which is threatened, or a value system which has to be defended against attack. Such threats, especially in the political sphere, may well precipitate leadership crises within an élite and bring about some realignment of loyalties.

Elite self-justification – the cases élites make out for themselves – may represent 'an amalgam of realistic observations and collective fantasies ...' (Elias: 1956, pp.226–411). We shall be considering this when we look at certain psychological aspects of élitism, where we will consider whether or not there are possibly any predisposing factors underlying the pursuit of power. It is also worth bearing in mind that counter-élite figures, those who oppose the dominant hierarchy – as, for example, Martin Luther and the Renaissance Catholic Church – are themselves susceptible to the same pressures. They are just as likely to become élite personalities in their own right, and become leaders of movements which then generate their own counter-counter-élites. (Interestingly, the word hierarchy literally means priest-rule, and is therefore particularly appropriate in the context of ecclesiastical disputations.)

Elites and Intellectuals

Sometimes the terms intellectuals and élites are used almost synonymously. But it takes very little thought to realize that in actual cases this is far from the truth. Political élites have often comprised those who could hardly be considered among the best educated in the community (for example, the top Nazi leadership) and many rulers too have been notoriously ill-educated, though often politically shrewd and militarily gifted, for all that (Chingis or Genghis Khan would be one such example). Where they were educated but weak rulers, they often had enough administrative acumen to choose able subordinates, as was the case with Hirohito of Japan during the Second World War; unlike Mussolini whose stock of able military commanders was almost nil. There are surprising examples of strong rulers – however we wish to define 'strong' and 'weak' – who were effective and successful (= ruthless?), and who ignored the intellectual élite and nobility, especially in their choice of military commanders. We find this with Timur-Leng (Tamerlane) the Tartar, whose hordes ravaged the Middle East and Eastern Europe in the fourteenth century, and the Ottoman Sultan, Suleiman the Magnificent, who did likewise some two hundred years later.

The criteria for élite status vary from society to society, and sometimes, over time, within the same society. To the modern mind, these qualifications for élite status may seem unusual – even bizarre. Henry Selby, writing as an anthropologist, says that 'societies exist with élite classes made up of very strange types of people ... megalomaniacs in Kwakiutl society (an American Indian people of the Pacific coast region), paranoid misers of the Yurok (an American Indian people of California), dreamers of the Menominee (an American Indian people of Wisconsin) all formed élite groups' (Selby in Wilkinson: 1969, p.5). Among some of the most interesting examples are the Chuckchee of Siberia who selected what we might see as epileptics as their spiritual leaders (shamans). The spiritual world of the Chuckchee was peopled by daemonic powers that could kill at will, and which – so it was believed – could only be controlled by the shamans. Thus the person who aspired to be such a leader developed the requisite symptoms. These gave them the necessary credentials for 'office', so the expected became the experienced. It is intriguing to know how the image was maintained. Merit is always a critical factor for élites. A spiritual leader's reputation is usually based on success, so presumably their effectiveness and therefore their status, was maintained very largely on the negative supposition that if it wasn't for their intervention things would have been a great deal worse.

Regardless of the exceptions and the aberrations, we can say that, in general, there is a strong correlation between intellectuals and élites. Intellectual élites are rather difficult to define as they are often less organized, less cohesive, and frequently enjoy less power than other élites, except, of course, when they are part of the governing élite. Where the intellectuals are not themselves part of the élite, they almost invariably – especially in the modern world – play a key *in*direct role in the organization and day-to-day running of society. One has only to think of the scientific élite about which there are, admittedly, mixed feelings. Much of the ambivalence may be well founded, but we can take some comfort from the fact that it is not the discoveries of science that we have to fear, but the questionable application of those discoveries – decisions which are normally made by the 'governing élite', the politicians.

It follows from this that élites, and certainly intellectuals, are not necessarily 'nice' people. Cleverness and high status do not have to be consonant with morality. Indeed, the more sceptical among us might suggest that there is an *in*verse relationship between élites and ethical unimpeachability. One has only to look at the upper echelons of virtually any society, most particularly despotic societies where the élite are seen jockeying for position to ensure, as in, say, Soviet society under Stalin, that they are not the next to go (Conquest: 1990); or, to take a more extreme example, just glance at the executive of the Nazi SS. Many of these were academics, lawyers, economists and the like, many of high professional standing, who were deeply involved in the extermination programmes even to the point of commanding 'special action', or mass murder, units (Carlton: 1992). Perhaps one of the most abiding myths of civilization perpetuated by thinkers, certainly since Plato, is that goodness is somehow a product of greater knowledge.

Those who exercise authority at the subordinate level, the administrative élite or bureaucracy, often have a good deal of autonomy and may form a corporate view of what is 'wise', 'sensible' and, above all, 'practicable' for the state or organization. The technical complexity of modern systems means that the governing élite rely upon their expert knowledge, and they often have the power to implement, modify or even delay policies or schemes which have been initiated elsewhere (Bottomore: 1975, p.136). They embody the continuity principle of the system in that they often remain when the leadership has changed because their expertise is seen as indispensable.

It is here that we are back with the class issue once again. Does an intellectual élite constitute a separate class? Or does it merely recruit from a particular class? (Note the academic composition of the top officials in British Government.) Or – and this is a somewhat more contentious view – is the intellectual élite in some special sense relatively class*less*? Karl Mannheim argued that because intellectuals are educated in a milieu which encourages its members to think in terms of several perspectives, their conclusions are not so likely to be class-bound (Mannheim: 1956, pp.91–170). Writers such as Barrington Moore have also pointed out that it is radical intellectuals who are often extremely partisan in their views, and actually become – as, for example, Fidel Castro in Cuba – leaders of revolutionary movements (Moore: 1966). Other theorists have adopted a similar position, and have argued that the two most important left-wing revolutions this century, those in Russia and China, were not worker inspired, but intellectual *coups d'état* (for example, Lasswell and Lerner: 1965, p.80); though this point has been contested by Robert Brym who insists that we should distinguish between *coups*, takeovers by small groups often led by intellectuals, and large-scale revolutions where the proletariat are actively involved (Brym: 1980, pp.37–40). Brym has also argued that, in the political arena, it is only those with the time, money and education in democratic systems that can afford to indulge in electoral activities. This is by no means an original observation. Even as long ago as the Greek city-state (*polis*) it was well known that it was mainly the independent self-employed and the *un*employed that had the time to attend the Assembly and thus decide the fortunes of the majority of the community. In developing countries intellectuals have undoubtedly contributed to the socio-economic welfare of the citizens, but it must also be admitted that it is usually the educated strata that have been responsible for the continuing graft and political corruption in many of these states (for examples in Latin America, see Tomasek: 1970).

Elites and Ideology

There is some evidence, however, that it is proletarian indifference, inertia, or downright resignation concerning their inability to change things, that enables members of the intellectual élite to take the lead so frequently in reform movements. How is this done? One might paraphrase Max Weber and argue that no regime or movement can rely exclusively on 'knowledge' as a source of legitimation in order to maintain itself. They require some popular 'belief (ideology) by virtue of which persons exercising authority are lent prestige' (Weber: 1957, p.382). In Weber's original statement, it was not 'knowledge' but 'coercion' that was in question. And it is worth noting that there is often, in fact, a considerable overlap between intellectual and military élites. Though functionally distinct, and not infrequently in opposition, the élites in both systems can usually be counted among the educated of society (Andreski: 1970).

Ideology adds a special – perhaps convenient – justification for social arrangements. In agrarian societies, where law-making and the wide recognition of traditional myths and the exercise of ceremonial power were combined, ideology obviously had a particular potency. Indeed, as Hannah Arendt has pointed out in her writings on totalitarianism, ideology may constitute a form of total explanation by the application of a single idea to the various realms of reality (Arendt: 1958). Where it does not, or cannot, supply the necessary legitimations, ideology can have a reinforcement function. In this capacity, it will simply constitute a further validation of policies and values which have been primarily determined by non-ideological factors such as, say, the decision of a governing élite to go to war. In some circumstances it will be coercive, in others it will merely act as a motivational inducement, and in this way may bridge the gap between incredulity and expediency.

Coercion is usually only a means to an end. The purpose of any takeover, no matter what the regime, is to supplant – even destroy – the old élite, and introduce what it conceives as a new order. Once all effective opposition has been eliminated, it will try to legitimize its takeover and rule by persuasion. Might is easily transformed into right. This may be done by recasting those institutions that shape public opinion, altering educational practices, rewriting the law and changing the office-holders. This happened, for instance, when the Soviets seized power in 1917, and the use of terror quickly gave way to an apparent consensus – at least, a consensus of acquiesence. Mosca put it succinctly: 'ruling classes (i.e., governing élites) do not justify their power exclusively by *de facto* possession of it, but try to find a moral and legal basis for it, representing it as a logical and necessary consequence of doctrines and beliefs that are generally recognized and accepted' (Mosca: 1939, p.70). Interestingly, such revolutionary changes are often followed by a further evolutionary change; the élite itself may undergo considerable alteration. Either through purges or political expediency, or a combination of both – again, as in Stalinist Russia – the old élite is displaced by a new élite; or in Pareto's terms, the 'lions' gave way to the 'foxes'. This usually results in an increased centralization, and thus depersonalization of power which, of necessity, must be further 'promoted' and legitimized.

Legitimation can be seen, then, as a 'grounding' for the normative order of society. And legitimations, whether resting on time-honoured traditions or on appeals to emotional chauvinism, justify how a society *ought* to operate. They are inextricably linked to the problem of meaning. Every society that has persisted for any length of time, particularly if it has developed a modest degree of complexity, has also evolved some interpretation of its own way of life. Ideological frameworks, therefore, provide symbolic meaning systems for those involved. In many instances, they supply the moral imperatives that are required if members of a society are going to meet their communal obligations. It is belief, intellectualized as ideology, which can provide the essential self-evidence for the institutionalized social order (Carlton: 1977, pp.20–2). As such, it is a potent force, for good or ill, in the hands of the governing élite.

Ideology comes in many forms. Religious beliefs and constellations of political principles may all constitute ideologies. Conservative ideologies obviously are those which support the social status quo, and are indispensable to governing élites. Revolutionary ideologies, on the other hand, as in modern Islamic fundamentalism, act as unifying and dynamic aids to those who aspire to become élites in some future new order. Conservative ideologies, by definition, tend to explain and defend existing institutions, especially those concerned with government, whereas revolutionary ideologies attack the existing social order. Ideology, then, is a belief system, and as such is a particular configuration of ideas and attitudes in which elements are bound together by some dominant form of constraint. This may be religious or secular, although in some systems, for example, god-king systems such as those which have obtained in places such as ancient Egypt and pre-colonial Peru, the secular and religious spheres are often impossible to distinguish.

One last cautionary word about ideologies at this stage of the discussion. It is difficult to take seriously any crude conspiracy theory of ideology. No one doubts that ideologies can serve to further the interests of a dominant minority, but this does not exhaust their function or meaning. Conspiracy theories, or interest theories, as they are sometimes called, do not explain *how* and *why* the ideology in question has come to be accepted and believed. Ideologies *can* be contrivances, and can act as agencies of exploitation, but there is ample evidence – certainly where powerful religious ideologies are concerned – that the ideologies did condition social relations, and were really believed by exploiters and exploited alike (Carlton: 1977, p.25). Because an ideology either implicitly or explicitly defines the field (that is, the class, race or group of persons), only those of that class, race or whatever who possess, or are held to possess, those 'superior' qualities can be justly known as an élite. It is when the claim to possess the required characteristics is challenged, and the self-definition of the élite is questioned that problems arise. The would-be or erstwhile élite – and this again is particularly true of certain types of exclusivist religious organization – becomes alienated from the wider society when its self-definitions are not recognized by others.

Gerhard Lenski suggests that we should make a distinction between 'materialistic élites' and 'ideological élites' (Lenski: 1966, pp.60–8), a distinction that we have partly anticipated. Takeovers by materialistic élites often come in the form of *coups* where one exploitative bunch are simply replaced by another; a palace revolution rather than a social revolution. With ideological élites, the changes are likely to be much more substantial. Whatever the form of the élite, it is still probably true that the distinction of rewards, either in material or status terms, will be a function of the distribution of power rather than the needs of the system; though, as Lenski points out, without an exploitative élite in many historical societies, there probably would have been no economic surplus to distribute. The surplus itself was a function of the ambitions – and ruthlessness – of the élite. Such a situation produced its own reactions, not least that of increased instability as everyone vied for a share of the pie. In modern societies, on the other hand, these conditions are more likely to generate popular resistance, either from an established priesthood, such as Buddhism in Cambodia and Islam in Shah-ruled Iran, or by movements which are supported and armed by outside agencies with whom they share a common ideology. In the face of this threat, the élite either collapses or becomes more repressive, thus possibly sowing the seeds of its own future destruction.

Elites and Aggression

Broadly speaking, then, regimes – and this really means their élites – collapse either because of external threats such as war, or internal disturbances such as *coups* or, more seriously, revolutions. Natural disasters such as earthquakes and climatic changes may also play their part in creating conditions that invite incursions from outside, as was almost certainly the case with the earthquake on the island of Thera (Santorini) in the Aegean which brought about the downfall of the intriguing Minoan civilization in ancient Crete. But for all practical purposes, natural disasters can be discounted. The downfall of the vast majority of regimes – and no regime lasts forever – can be safely attributed to human agency.

As a very general rule, the more despotic or oligarchic the state, the more likely it is to wage aggressive war; and the more constitutional it is, the more the likelihood is that it will be reluctant to embark upon expansionist adventures. But again, this is far from being an invariable rule. Athenian society was notoriously aggressive at particular times in its history, not unusually against weaker, smaller states, and Athens is still regarded by many as the original model democracy. The options open to an élite that is successful in war are limited, but the choices available to a conquered élite are virtually non-existent, if, indeed, it is allowed to continue at all (Carlton: 1992). However, if it favours collaboration with the conqueror, it may, in its own way, become more ideologically assiduous than the dominant power. This is what happened in the Vichy regime in France during the German occupation (see Dank: 1978).

As for *coups*, we very frequently find that these begin among the military. Either there is a split among the military élite itself, or it begins with the disenchantment of the younger, more 'progressive' members of the officer corps (see, for example, Gutteridge: 1969). Rarely do *coups* originate among the rank and file, as did the Sepoy uprising that precipitated the Amritsar massacre in India (Carlton: 1992, chapter 3). Similarly, few actual revolutions survive without the support of the military. For example, the revolution in Iran in 1977 would probably never have got any further than excitable street demonstrations had it not been for the fact that the Army deserted the Shah and his ruling élite and came out on the side of the people. And last, but not least, such social revolutions need that one crucial ingredient to tip the scales and consolidate the whole operation, a persuasive ideology proclaimed by a new and dynamic religio-political élite. 'By themselves, rebellious intellectuals are no threat to a political élite. They lack numbers and resources .... However, in conjunction with others, they can provide the catalytic agent, the counter ideology which is necessary for every successful social revolution' (Lenski: 1966, p.71).

Elites and Personality Factors

The whole question of the rise and fall of élites raises the issue of personality as well as structural factors. But there are reservations: many social scientists and historians are rather sceptical about introducing such ideas, presumably because it is extremely difficult to assess to what extent or in what ways personality variables play a significant part in the social process. Certainly as far as rulers and what are rather loosely called charismatic leaders are concerned, one feels instinctively that they must be important, but exactly *how* is still a matter of debate. No one doubts the influence of Alexander, Caesar and Napoleon on events, but it is impossible to know what would have happened without them, or what shape history would have taken if they had died sooner or later. The 'great man' theory of history has some cogency, yet even the actions of great men are conditioned by the *Zeitgeist* or temper of the times which perhaps generates or certainly allows such policies and practices. The historical situation has to be right. Yet regardless of the obvious unknowables and uncertainties, perhaps personality variables need, at least, *some* consideration.

It can be reasonably assumed that élites take on the identity that is expected of them, *qua* élites. Certain behavioural patterns are considered appropriate, therefore élites' self-presentation will assume forms that will be socially acceptable, at least to some. Every élite – and, presumably, every member of an élite – must choose a public image (situated identity) and the choice of that image will depend upon what other people are supposed to think. Not unusually, misjudgements are made in this respect. Note the recent (1994) scandals regarding believed moral infringements of the British 'back to basics' policy, and the equally salacious whispers about Presidential high-jinks in the USA. In such cases, officials will offer protective excuses for these and possible future failures. Some social psychologists contend that people are more likely to overplay their hand and use these self-handicapping strategies when they are vainly trying to maintain an image of self-competence, possibly established on the basis of some past success (Schlenker: 1985). They also suggest that there are several well attested tactics of self-presentation, particularly *ingratiation* – a common ploy of those aspiring for political office, *intimidation* – not an unknown characteristic of those already *in* office, *exemplification* – designed to elicit perceptions of integrity and worthiness, and *supplication* – when all else fails, an appeal is made based on dependence and sympathy (Jones and Pitman: 1982). One can see all these tactics at work especially in the political arena where self-monitoring is cultivated as all part of the art (see Tetlock's research on the campaign statements of recent US Presidential candidates: 1981). Although we must admit that we are prone to adjust our behaviour to particular situations, self-presentation can be an unconscious as well as a cynical exercise (Goffman: 1959) .

Elites and Social Democracy

Among the many ways in which élites can be categorized, one of the simplest is the distinction that should be made between appointed and self-appointed élites – the latter often attracting more disapprobation than the former. However, this distinction frequently breaks down in practice. This happens particularly where appointed élites, even when appointed with public approval and/or election, as, for example in certain Trades Unions, can become entrenched and constitute a seemingly irremovable hierarchy, a situation that hardly accords with the ideals of social democracy. Consequently, for many people élites of any kind have come to be seen as bad news, although one sometimes suspects that those that complain most bitterly about élites and élitism would happily become key figures in any new élite. It is always salutary to ask, especially of oneself, whether the kind of regime one would like to live under, is the same as the kind of regime one would like to control. Are we all covert totalitarians at heart?

Perhaps one of the most impassioned and vigorous defences of social democracy is to be found in Sir Karl Popper's *The Open Society and its Enemies* (1945, 5th edition, 1966). The book was written when totalitarianism in its various forms was proving militarily successful in state after state. (It is worth noting how many states turned to some form of dictatorship in Europe between the Wars; see Lee: 1987.) Popper, like Freud and his successor, Erich Fromm, argued that the appeal of totalitarianism was its apparent ability to liberate people from taking responsibility. Freedom was a burden from which they wanted to be emancipated. It is a somewhat tenuous hypothesis, but it is almost certainly true that many (most?) people find the responsibility of decision-making – as Sartre has argued – too much for them (Sartre: 1957), perhaps because they can't bear to be wrong: '[we] fear death, fear ... the consequences of our own actions, fear the future ... [and] the unknown' so we press for assurances from religion and from political philosophy (Magee: 1973, p.88), neither of which can any longer be said to be characterized by unchanging certainty.

Democracy, in one form or another, has a long and chequered history. Although the Athenians are said to have invented democracy, their system of government was both more *and* less democratic than anything that we understand by the term: more, in the sense that the Athenian constitution was a form of radical democracy in which the people of the Assembly (*ekklesia*) were the executive – the final authority on all matters of state; and less, insofar as the franchise was limited to citizens only, that is, free males of eighteen years and over. This automatically excluded women, resident aliens (*metoikoi*), and, of course, slaves who may have comprised over 25 per cent of the population. Procedures were such that some of Athens' intellectuals grew impatient with the system which was open to abuse by gifted demagogues who were sometimes able to sway public opinion on various critical issues. So much so, in fact, that Sokrates argued that the state should be run by specialists, not amateur politicians. These sentiments are attributed to Sokrates – whom Popper calls a friend of democracy – by his distinguished pupil, Plato. As far as we know, Sokrates wrote nothing, and it is possible that Plato is 're-interpreting' the ideas of his teacher in terms of his own reactionary dispositions. After all, it was Athenian democracy that condemned Sokrates to death on the rather nebulous grounds of 'impiety', something which Plato regarded as unjust, and something he was not prepared to forget.

Popper regards Plato as a 'sincere' anti-egalitarian who in his famous treatise, *The Republic*, set out a blueprint for a carefully stratified society ruled by wise, highly trained, 'guardians'. Whether it represents Plato's ideal or whether it was simply a theoretical exercise is difficult to know, but Popper and others have argued that it really provides one philosophical basis for totalitarianism. Aldous Huxley's *Brave New World*, written in 1932 (and still in print) during the rise of the European dictatorships, is a remarkably prescient satire of utilitarianism. It is also an extension of Plato's work, except that whereas Plato is 'constructing' a society that he believes is appropriate for human beings, Huxley concentrates on the means whereby human beings can be fashioned (pre-conditioned) to fit a particular kind of society. Plato undoubtedly had a deep aversion to popular government, and definitely favoured some form of merit-based élitism. But whether, as Orrin Klapp argues, he actually 'despised the masses' (Klapp: 1973, p.67) is open to debate. If he did, he probably felt that he was justified, especially considering the recent history of Athens and the cruelties of the devastating Peloponnesian War with Sparta (431–404 BC). He disliked majority government, but likewise hated tyranny and even distrusted the sorts of oligarchies found in many Greek states. For Plato, education was everything. Only those who were disinterested in economic rewards (the 'guardians' were not to have their own property), and who were worthy specialists in the art of government, should control the state.

Many might regard Plato's amalgam of rigid censorship, more freedom for women, the abolition of the family and controlled eugenics as well, as all rather revolutionary, although others see it as the symptoms of the arrested development of an impossible Utopia. For some, it has all the earmarks of the worst kind of fascism; for others, it has many anticipations of the more objectionable aspects of Communism. In attacking those intellectual leaders such as Plato and Marx, as opposed to the common self-seeking of so many political leaders, who have threatened the 'open society', Popper acknowledges that they may do so with the highest motives. They are sometimes people of considerable ability whose main ambition is the betterment of society as they see it. For Plato, this was a return to an albeit mythical past, whereas for Marx it was some kind of ephemeral future. Intellectual movements of these kinds necessarily involve a certain degree of utopianism. Such ideas are not only the product of élites, but are held to foster a climate of élitist thought which, it is felt, has a limited place in a democratic society.

Insofar as all societies require rules and general recognition and observance of such rules and conventions, to that extent some kind of ruling élite seems inevitable. It is conceded (for example, by John Wilson: 1966) that this is not necessarily odious to the egalitarian since this is the parallel of any class of experts, doctors, economists, lawyers, and the like. But the egalitarian tends to distrust ruling élites more than professional élites because of their capacity to *enforce* compliance with their wishes. Egalitarians argue that it should be the task of ruling élites to be aware of public opinion, and to reflect the wishes of the people rather than override them. In short, the fear of egalitarians is that élites will come to see themselves as superior people who have a right to control the destinies of others. Interference by government can be tolerated, otherwise there would be social chaos. But the public voice must be heard, otherwise it is tantamount to treating the public as inferiors. The egalitarian assumes an intrinsic equality, and therefore that any exercise of power of an élite only exists as a mandate from the people who can withdraw it as and when it is necessary. Experts are there to advise and not to dictate.

Egalitarians maintain that there are certain general principles that all élites should observe. First of all, élites should be functional rather than privileged. That is to say, they should be *qualified* as élites, and not occupy their positions by some kind of 'right' or inheritance. They should, too, be prepared to give the people what they want rather than what is thought to be good for them. The underlying premise is that 'nobody has the right to impose his values on anybody else' (Wilson:

1966, p.177). Neither must the public be coerced, bribed or indoctrinated into accepting the élite's values by any calculated system of rewards and particularly punishments which can only be counter-productive in the longer term. And, most important of all, an élite must be prepared to face the consequences of its own actions. If, for example, it is a scientific élite, members must be answerable to the people for any misjudgements which affect the community at large, or if it is a political élite, members should be liable to investigation and even impeachment if this is deemed necessary.

Much of this argument assumes that an élite is a kind of self-seeking caste that dominates – or threatens to dominate – the abject masses. True, élites tend to be internally homogeneous, unified and self-conscious bodies somewhat like exclusive clubs. They are also largely self-perpetuating, and members may be drawn from select segments of society: the wealthy, the learned, the powerful – in short, the privileged few. To this extent élites will be essentially autonomous, and answerable to few – if any – others for their decisions (Putnam: 1976). This even applies to members of political élites in democratic societies who, though theoretically subject to a parliament, senate, or whatever, tend in practice to have things much their own way. Wilson's 'conditions' for the functioning of élites seems like a counsel of perfection; an ideal that some may think worth striving for, but which may never actually be realized.

There are, however, some theorists who see élites in much more positive terms, as 'effective and responsible minorities'. They are socially significant groups who are 'ultimately responsible for the realization of major social goals and for continuity of the social order' (Keller: 1963, p.4). In other words, an élite is a group of people set aside from others by distinctive gifts or skills and by the ways these are utilized in the service of society. This echoes the view of Aristotle, Plato's pupil, who saw the state as an instrument that was designed to serve communal needs, because the state exists – or should exist – in order to produce the 'good life', and for this it requires extraordinary people, people of virtue and integrity who value justice above personal interest and ambition. Such ideas have been endorsed by many, including the sociologist Karl Mannheim who, unlike Marx who regarded the presence of élites as a passing phase, actually supports the proliferation of such groups who have a positive role in democratic societies. He felt that in the modern world there was a welcome trend away from the exercise of arbitrary power by individuals, to the exercise of 'institutional power' by élites which is thus legitimate and more limited.

It is all too easy to intellectualize the subject of élites in such a way that they become abstract entities that are unlocated in the real world. A case study approach has thus been adopted to avoid this. We need to see how élites really work in specific social contexts. In this way, we can distinguish between the less influential 'segmented élites' and what Suzanne Keller calls 'strategic élites', that is to say, those whose 'judgements, decisions and actions have important and determinable consequences for many members of society' (Keller: 1963, p.20). We will – hopefully – also see not only how élites interact with the non-élite, but also note, as the sociologist Raymond Aron has suggested, the conflicts both between and within élites. Indeed, if we are prepared to regard the history of politics, in particular, as the study of élites, it follows that social change is largely the consequence of changes in the composition and structure of élites. History can then be seen not, as Marx, as the history of class struggles, but as the interminable struggle between élites.

Whatever else history does or does not suggest, it certainly indicates that élites are here to stay. It would appear that ever since the agrarian revolution when it was discovered that by cultivation it was possible to maintain a settled society, it was also found that by producing a surplus, it was possible to maintain craft and ritual specialists who could pursue their various activities on behalf of the community. Hence a more and more sophisticated division of labour, and the beginnings of control by experts (élites). By extension, it also led to the state, and the conception of the 'social contract', an act of voluntary participation and co-operation with the state which in turn, would protect the people's interests. In contrast, conflict theory holds that states were born not out of co-operation, but as a consequence of conflict and conquest. Forms of organizations were forced on people, as were also the administrative systems (bureaucracies) to ensure order and the collection of taxes. Social contract theory is thus regarded as a metaphor rather than a description of a historical process (Prewitt and Stone: 1973, p.10). We are never likely to know, but it takes very little thought to realize that these theories are not mutually exclusive. Elites and élitism, then, are substantive facts, no matter what brought them about or whether they are sustained by coercion, the requirements of the system, or simply public apathy.

Elites and Ethics

What about the normative implications of élites? Everyone knows that they exist, and even, in some senses, that they are necessary, but are they actually *desirable*? Popper, as we have seen, has serious reservations about this. In commending democracy, he argues that it is to be preferred to other possible forms of government because it allows conflicts in society to be resolved by rational means. The people can change their rulers without recourse to violence. Yet, at the same time, even such a dedicated democrat as Popper concedes that democracies do not always choose the best policies. Popper's view of democracy is much like Woody Allen's view of sex ('sex without love may be an empty experience, but as empty experiences go it's one of the best'). Popper maintains that of all the imperfect systems that humans devise, democracy is probably the best protection against arbitrary repression. For him, the guarantee of freedom is the key factor. While readily acknowledging that some people are intellectually superior to others, he is generally hostile to the idea that they should be empowered to rule because (a) selection of élites may be particularly difficult, and (b) they too can make mistakes, and (c) 'virtuoso rulers will naturally select obedient drudges as their successors' (Quinton: 1976, p.161) – a point that one might feel is open to debate; *subordinates*, yes, but hardly successors. Popper hedges his bets here a little. With all his reservations about élites, he admits that, theoretically (and, at times, actually) people in a democracy are free to give power to an oligarchy or an autocrat. Furthermore, he does not directly tackle the issue, very much a concern of the Greeks, that democracy could degenerate into a tyranny of the majority. Perhaps it is for this reason that, paradoxically, he seems to be distrustful of public opinion which he regards as anonymous and even irresponsible. Democracy, with all its faults, is just the best of a bad bunch.

Other writers on political philosophy such as Bertrand de Jouvenel (*On Power*) and John Rawls (*A Theory of Justice*) write in a not dissimilar vein. Writing during the Second World War, de Jouvenel is particularly concerned with the abuses of power, and concentrates on the distinction between what he regards as legitimate and illegitimate (assumed) authority. Rawls, on the other hand, presents us with a critique of utilitarianism as a basis for social morality. As a consensus theory, utilitarianism contends that the maximization of human welfare is the greatest possible social good and is thus, according to its critics, concerned with majority welfare to the detriment of social minorities. Rawls asks, instead, for a particular application of 'fairness' which does not discriminate against selected segments of the population, but which gives a qualified distribution of rewards to all members of the community. There need be no distinction between, say, public and private ownership, providing that whatever the system, there is no repression or discrimination. Laws which favour the privileged are unjust, especially if they are detrimental to the life-chances of the disadvantaged. Rawls, whose ideas have been extensively criticized (Gorovitz: 1976, pp.287–9), is by no means an unqualified egalitarian, and his particular conception of liberty would therefore seem to moderate the justifiability of some form of circumscribed élitism.

For a more full-blooded qualification of untrammelled élitism we must turn to writers such as Friedrich Hayek, and his natural ally, Michael Oakeshott. Strictly, an economist rather than a political theorist, Hayek, an Austrian *émigré* for much of his life, has been categorized as anti-liberal although an unbiased study of his writings would almost certainly verify that he was certainly liberal – albeit of a rather conservative kind. For Hayek, to be liberal is to advocate freedom from arbitrary repression. For him, then, good government is less government. Democratic systems, for all their virtues, may be far from liberal in all sorts of significant respects; political freedom need not be a condition of individual freedom. Such a position can be variously seen as that of 'true' unrestricted individualism or as that of pioneer spirit Reaganism, or, indeed, Thatcherite conservatism – a label he would disavow because, for Hayek, conservatism is, by definition, inherently non-progressive and antidemocratic.

Hayek's view of democracy is somewhat unconventional, but, like Oakeshott, what he has to say usually has an unwelcome but provocative edge to it. For example, he maintained that liberalism is prepared – or should be prepared – to accept majority rule as a method of making decisions (democracy), but not as an authority for what the decision *ought* to be. This normative emphasis is certainly élitist in tone, and although he is a great advocate of individual freedom, he is always conscious of the ignorance of the masses which makes their vulnerability to domination that much more feasible. He believes that the coercive power of governments should be strictly limited, but appears to doubt the capacity of the people to achieve this. Indeed, he argues that the value of any particular freedom is not arrived at by some kind of consensus or majority rule. The implication being that the masses (*contra* Aristotle) do not know what is in their own best interests; the obvious inference being that this should best be left to the experts, in effect, to an élite.

Hayek's contemporary, Michael Oakeshott, has spelled out the same sort of message, and applied it to just about everything from political theory to cookery, taking in morality along the way. As a professional political philosopher, Oakeshott is careful to qualify what he means by philosophy. He insists that it is not a body of knowledge in the sense that, say, physics is a body of knowledge. And it is certainly not an ideology of some kind. It is rather an aid to understanding; as a discipline it should be diagnostic and interpretative. He sees philosophy as a *method*, a way of looking at things. Philosophy is therefore also a history of how others have looked at things, and so Oakeshott prefaces his own ideas by recalling certain prior arguments in political theory. He reminds us that Hobbes stressed that individual purposes could be successfully fulfilled by obedience to the *de facto* power of the state, while Locke argued that the state must conform to principles dictated by what he saw as the rational law of nature. Rousseau, on the other hand, tried to transcend this dichotomy by formulating a principle which allowed for a measure of rational self-interest, but which was not exclusive to individual wills, namely, the General Will (Greenleaf: 1966). It was a concept which Rousseau later qualified, possibly because he was unable to show just how this might be realized in practical situations.

Oakeshott, who has also been labelled as a Tory apologist, is undoubtedly a conservative in the broad sense of the term. Like Hayek, he is a seasoned campaigner for liberty and has turned a hyper-critical eye on all such prior – and often respected – arguments. Yet, in his own way, he is a traditionalist in that he suggests that if people have organized themselves in certain ways in the past, domestically, religiously, politically and so forth, these arrangements must have *something* to commend them. They must have a certain validity. He argues that we should not endorse iconoclasm for its own sake and modern does not necessarily mean best, so we must give due respect to traditional values and procedures. He, therefore, repudiates imposed patterns of change, emphasizing, as Popper – who advocates 'piecemeal social engineering' – that change should be gradual, tentative and 'natural'.

It follows from this that he is impatient with ideologies which he sees as deterministic because they tend either to be related to forms of inevitable historical processes, as can be found in certain kinds of Marxism, fascism and even religion, or they are grounded in a believed 'natural order' – an ideal often associated with such philosophies as egalitarianism and the somewhat mythical notion of natural rights. In both cases, there is a tendency among the relevant political groups to try to implement such ideas by radical means. He argues that abstract principles – often formulated as ideologies – can never be gathered in advance of actual political activity. He says that 'they are not the product of autonomous and antecedent reflective effort, but are the outcome of meditation on [and] abridgements of a form of politics that already exists. Practice is prior to doctrine' (Greenleaf: 1966, p.42). As Oakeshott himself graphically puts it, 'So far from a political ideology being the quasi-divine parent of political activity, it turns out to be its earthly step-child' (Oakeshott: 1962, p.118).

Although both Hayek and Oakeshott recognize the value of experts, they are quite opposed to élites that are motivated by totalizing ideologies. Their distrust is based upon the assumptions that:

1. *Ideologies tend to be too inflexible*. They often claim to be absolute and to have a permanent validity, and their very rigidity means that they are not always adaptable to the ever-changing realities of actual situations.

2. *Ideologies are inadequate guides to political activity*. Ideologies are abstractions. Therefore, they can never provide a complete understanding of social activity, and can never be a sufficient guide to political action. The various Communist states would bear this out. None of them ever adopted Marxian doctrine in its pristine form. All of them *adapted* rather than adopted Marx's teaching. The different states that were governed according to Communist principles (and those, of course, that still do) have all been run on similar but not identical lines. There have been many different shadings – indeed, it might be argued that the forms are not yet settled.

3. *Ideologies are not politically realistic*. Indeed, it is argued that they are unfailingly too idealistic. Oakeshott, in particular, insists that success in politics is 'unavoidably sporadic'; it is only achieved – if this is even the correct term – from day to day, and is therefore never complete or unqualified. Politics is not about utopianism, the attempt to set up permanently impregnable societies *à la* Plato. On the other hand, it is not about whims or hunches either. There has to be discussion, bargaining and eventually some kind of settlement – this is what politics is really about. He would have entirely agreed with George Woodcock at the 1967 Conference of the British Trades Union Congress when he reminded the audience that in the realm of industrial relations 'we proceed by a series of shabby compromises …. There is no other way in industrial disputes where men have afterwards to go on working together'. Or, as Oakeshott expresses it, politics is the 'politics of repair'. It is the art of choosing the least evil of the available courses of action. If we were to ask by what criteria such choices are made, we can assume that the answer would be given in pragmatic terms.

In fairness, it should be pointed out that Oakeshott is not wholly anti-ideology. He says that ideologies may 'reveal important hidden passages in the tradition, as a caricature reveals potentialities in a face' (Greenleaf: 1966, p.43). One thinks of the disturbing strain of anti-semitism in Germany and Austria long before the radical ideologies of the Nazis. What is really happening here is that Oakeshott is damning with faint praise. In rejecting ideologies as the sole criteria for political activity, he is really suggesting that insofar as ideologies have anything to say, it has been said before, albeit in a somewhat different form. They are the conscious or unconscious plagiarizing of others' ideas, of which they are little more than caricatures or bad copies.

The underlying contention here is that social practices and procedures, and certainly rules of conduct, are most useful – and, by implication, more acceptable – when they are *familiar*. Nothing is absolutely sacrosanct, and everything is open to question, but, at the same time, prudence demands that change should be cautious. All activity, especially political activity, should only proceed by careful examination of existing arrangements. Only then should there be amendments, corrections and modifications, because it is only in this way that society can be made more coherent. Take, for example, the reforms in Britain in relation to slavery, early in the nineteenth century. Despite all the agitation for change, all the protests were disregarded until public opinion was ready for it, and – perhaps more to the point – when technology had advanced to the stage where slavery was no longer necessary. Add to this, the fact that, as far as the United Kingdom was concerned, slavery was colonial slavery which was being practised by others a very long way away (and therefore affected no one at home directly), and we have most of the necessary ingredients for reform. Or, to take a more up-to-date example, consider the case of homosexual law reform. The real reason that this came about – for good or ill – was not because people recognized arguments of principle, but because of what was actually being practised by the authorities. It was nothing to do with equality or natural rights, or justice for all. The police had already been told to take things easy before the Act was passed (amusingly, it was a Private Member's Bill), and the attitudes to homosexuality had already changed so much that it was now given formal legal recognition. What was almost *de facto*, now became *de jure*. It is not simple to explain exactly why public opinion was now ready for change, but the change in the law did give a certain coherence to this particular situation.

A basic precept behind much of Oakeshott's thinking on all sorts of issues is the simple distinction between what he calls technical and traditional knowledge. This is particularly pertinent to the subject of élitism because élites usually form on the basis of certain qualities or special knowledge that they are known or assumed to possess. Technical knowledge is *theory*, and traditional knowledge is *practice*. Technical knowledge can be precisely formulated as rules or instructions, written down, learned by rote: for example manuals on 'How to drive a car' or 'How to play the piano', which expound method and elaborate standards. By comparison, traditional knowledge seems incomplete and imprecise. But is it? All the manuals in the world will not give anyone road sense, or substitute for the hands-on experience of the pianist, until they actually put these instructions into practice. No one does these things until they do them. Of course, skills may be learned from those already versed in the art. It's like a child acquiring ideas, say, about tennis by watching the experts who often make it look so ridiculously simple, although the technique of the truly great player may, in fact, be unlearnable because it involves the combination of so many 'uncapturable' qualities. It's all very reminiscent in academia of postgraduate courses for teachers and social workers, as if one could learn to teach or learn casework skills. These things can only be acquired in the process of doing them. The taught techniques will not make up for lack of experience. A person will only teach when they teach, or learn the delicate art of dealing with clients when they actually deal with them.

It is held that the 'rationalist' (that is, theoretical/ideological) approach must take account of existing arrangements; it is defective if it ignores traditional knowledge. The rationalist wants rationality ('streamlinedness'). He is said to repudiate circumstantial complexities. He abhors the untidiness and wastefulness that he finds in existing arrangements. But what is the result? Not uncommonly, chaos. Modern history is replete with examples: the post-war Labour government's ill-conceived ground-nut scheme in West Africa; the attempted economic rationalization of the ill-fated Chinese commune system; even the political instability of the recently quasi-democratized Russian states. Rationalism must fail if it disregards existing conventions. It cannot successfully bound ahead of what is considered 'right' by consensus; contextual norms must be observed. Conduct cannot be governed by contrived principles which are set down independently in advance of the undertaking concerned. Reliance on predetermined 'rules' may well be misleading. One has only to glance back at the ideological blunders of governments of every hue. It can be seen in the United Kingdom. Labour's comprehensivization of schools involving the abolition of the 11+ selection procedure which was implemented without sufficient research, and whose merits and demerits are still being debated by educationalists. Or the Tories' unlamented 'poll-tax' scheme which came to a well-deserved if ignominious end, only to be replaced by another which many hope will meet a similar fate.

The rationalist who shapes our political destinies is almost invariably a member of an élite. They will not necessarily reject experience out of hand, or always proceed on an *a priori* basis, but they will have a tendency towards administrative reductionism in that they try to reduce the complexities of actual situations to rule, that is, to technical knowledge only. As Oakeshott acerbically put it, 'And book in hand ... the politicians of Europe pore over the simmering banquet they are preparing for the future; but like jumped-up kitchen porters deputising for an absent cook, their knowledge does not extend beyond the written word – they have no taste' (quoted by Greenleaf: 1966, p.53).

Rationalistic panaceas may also imply coercion. In totalitarian systems the idea is enough. The vision has often been taken as sufficient to warrant its forcible implementation by governmental power. For the extremist – whether of the right or the left – time is of the essence. 'The man in a hurry' (as Hitler is said to have been) cannot indefinitely endure the status quo. He wants to see his ideas materialize in his own lifetime. Presumably, élites are often similarly impatient, witness the radicalism of the early Soviets under Lenin – schemes which later had to be modified. There is, too, probably some justification for the assertion that rationalistic panaceas make a particular appeal to the politically immature: those with little experience who are seeking a quick way out of their difficulties, and succumb to the temptation to take political short-cuts. These may take the form of simple schemes or propositions which are then mechanically employed to achieve the desired objective. In the United Kingdom economy, for example, for ever imperilled by the vagaries of the market, it may be 'nationalization' that is the key to a better and more equitable society, while, for others, the clarion call is for more 'privatization'. Both are heuristic devices which are seen as the guarantee to future prosperity, but are both fraught with problems. After all, every system brings with it its own evils. Where the politically immature have assumed or seized power, there are always special dangers. In the French Revolution, for instance, we find that, at first, theory played a minor part. The actions of the revolutionaries were most often prescribed as practical solutions to immediate problems – not the result of clearly preconceived ideas. Interpretation came later. They began with a rationalist ideology which was modified along the way, and actually implemented on a day-to-day basis. In their uncertainty, the uninitiated may call upon all sorts of 'political cribs', as Oakeshott terms them, anything from the writings of Mill to the 'thoughts of Chairman Mao'.

It is probably true to say that, by and large, people not only look for simple solutions, they also want *precise* solutions. Thus over the years rationalistic panaceas have tended to proliferate. They are often based upon supposed 'certain knowledge' of what the ideal standards are, or of what human nature really is, or of what the future course of events should be. There is a propensity to confuse slogans with policies: 'Liberty, Equality and Fraternity', the 'Rights of Man', 'Racial Purity' and so on, sound very persuasive, but mean nothing until they are defined. And even then they may be morally questionable and of doubtful practical use. Their mere repetition does not constitute political knowledge.

Writers in the Oakeshott type of conservative tradition tend to occupy an uncertain middle ground. They favour pluralism; no leader, government, faction or corporation or élite should have a preponderant power. At the same time, they are inclined to be nervous about mass society. Thus no party or class, no association or union, indeed no majority, should enjoy unlimited power. All concentrations of power have, by definition, corrupting tendencies. Instead, power should be diffused, 'A coherence of mutually supportive liberties' (Oakeshott: 1947–48, pp.489–90 quoted by Greenleaf, 1966). Any kind of collectivism is suspect. More power is too much power. Moderation is the thing. Not too much government, not too much law, in fact, not too much anything. Governments must sometimes intervene in the economy, but when the running of the economy and political control of the economy are in the same hands, the distinctions are blurred and lost. Then we have what C. Wright Mills calls a coincidence of interest, the government supported or sponsored monopoly – a situation which is a denial of true freedom.

Traditionalists of this kind do not advocate a crude and uncritical individualism. This is felt to be inconsistent with an effective social democracy. But they do believe in the unfettered life, and are against attempts to enforce conformity. Changes may be independently premeditated but they should never be precipitately imposed on society. The individual should therefore resist inordinate constraint. A person should pursue his own interests while, at the same time, trying to accommodate the interests of others – really, a kind of qualified hedonism. Only in this way could an individual both achieve and express that individuality.

Entrepreneurialism is admired. There is applause for the late Medieval merchant adventurers, self-determined individuals, who went out and, as it were, took hold of life and bent it to their own particular designs. There is praise too for Protestantism because, as Talcott Parsons argued, it constituted a breakthrough to a more rational mode of thought. Complementarily, there is criticism of the mass man, the anti-individual, the other-directed person whose thinking is done for him. Wasn't it Shaw who maintained that people dread freedom because it brings responsibility (possibly echoing Shakespeare who says in *Hamlet* that responsibility brings about a paralysis of the will)? This is the person who doesn't *pursue* happiness, he just wants to enjoy it. This sums up the anti-individual, certainly for Oakeshott. He displays no ability or inclination; he has denied his own freedom so often that he no longer has the capacity to make decisions for himself. The anti-individual seeks protection in submission to others, and welcomes uniformity of beliefs and conduct. He rejoices not in liberty of choice but in equality and solidarity. The mass man is content to be an anonymous unit in an egalitarian community. In Sartre's existential terminology, he is guilty of *mauvaise-foi*, bad faith, in that he has not even been true to himself.

Such attitudes, it is argued, readily lend themselves to exploitation by others who fool the people that their choices are really their own. In effect, little changes. Even in politics, the 'chosen' follow an already patterned mandate and it is often notoriously difficult to determine exactly what really is being planned or proposed. Does one ever get a straight answer? (It was Malcolm Muggeridge who, when referring to the late John Kennedy's press conferences, spoke of the charade of non-questions and non-answers.) In these conditions government élites grow in power and, instead of acting as custodians or referees, they assume the role of moral guardians and directors.

It is time to ask how valid these criticisms really are. Do they have any real cogency, or are they simply the expressions of a world weary, political agnosticism? It has to be admitted that in some ways, these arguments are very persuasive, but they do beg a number of questions and are open to certain objections.

To begin with, it is necessary to clear up one possible source of confusion. Anti-rationalism doesn't mean anti-rational. The liberal tradition, as outlined, is all in favour of rationality, but is opposed to the kind of rationalism that wants to reduce the criteria for human action – political or otherwise – to certain kinds of prescriptive formulae. Furthermore, it is not anarchic; it does regard collective action and general rules as necessary for the orderly running of society, but these must conduce to individual liberty. The obvious objection here is that freedom means different things to different people, and even to the *same* people in different situations. Few would surely espouse unlimited individual freedom – a situation which could only lead to chaos. Conflict would be bound to occur when everyone exercised their freedom at another's expense. There has to be some kind of imposed order; the 'natural' harmonization of human interaction is still a long way off.

The cautious approach to social problems and political change also needs to be examined. Going with the tide may be all right in a stable society but what of, say, Germany in the 1930s? This poses a real problem for traditionalism. Did Nazism not need a *radical* rejection? The counter-argument is that the evils that befell Germany were due to the imposition of a rationalist-type ideology, but even so could it have been neutralized by democratic, traditional, liberal procedures? Surely today there are critical issues in society that really should be resolved as soon as possible: problems of the environment, starvation, medical aid for disease in the Third World, and the innumerable matters concerned with poverty and the exponential increase in the world's population. And that's only the beginning. Traditional solutions, as per Oakeshott, just won't do any longer. The matters are too urgent and too immense for the tentative efforts of piecemeal engineering.

Ernest Gellner has argued that a conservative is either a knave or a fool. Why? Because existing social arrangements and standards of justice diverge, and if one cannot see this one is a fool, and if one is not prepared to see them brought into line, one is a knave. The conservative can defend his position – albeit rather weakly – by either implausibly maintaining that the ideal *is* the real, that this is the best of all possible worlds, or by insisting that the alleged ideal was not valid in the first place. The conservative might reply that the status quo cannot be confidently categorized as wrong because there are no objective criteria whereby it can be condemned. Oakeshott, for one, does not pretend that this is the best of all possible worlds, yet denies that we can know *why*. But what can the conservative say about demonstrably evil systems other than recourse to some kind of extreme relativism? This seems to betray an embarrassing cynicism in that it denies validity to anything but the purely pragmatic.

A further comment should be made about the place of traditional knowledge, especially in the politico-economic sphere. Valuable as practical knowledge is, it can be shown that theoretical knowledge also has a place, for instance, in the impact – admittedly qualified – of Keynesian economic theory. But it is in the sphere of science and technology that theory really comes into its own, and is only verified by practice. In some ways, the theory–practice issue is a false argument; in fact, the two go hand in hand in the organization of real affairs.

One of the main difficulties with this kind of conservatism, and one which is especially germane to our present discussion, is the contradictory position that it appears to adopt regarding élites. On the one hand, it evinces an obvious distrust of groups, unions, associations and especially governments that threaten to imperil the freedom of the individual. Yet, on the other, it is equally uneasy about the 'tyranny from below', the uninformed, possibly ill-educated masses who presume to dictate to their 'betters'. It leaves the impression that those who adopt this position really constitute a broadly based, critical élite themselves, albeit an élite-in-themselves rather than an élite-for-themselves.

In the social sciences, where élites are inclined to be *persona non grata*, there is a tendency to see élites everywhere. Many hostile sociologists, in particular, 'are ready and eager to detect guiding élites in ... dubious circumstances' (Mennell: 1980, p.79). Social networks in modern communities are usually so complex that élites are sometimes difficult to identify unless we are thinking of ruling élites which by any reasonable standards must be seen as inevitable (Giddens: 1991, p.336). But if we are prepared to blur the distinction between an élite and an interest group, and extend the concept of élite to any of those often discordant choirs of authoritative voices, whether in the arts, sciences or morals, that tell us how we should think on a wide variety of issues, the term élite takes on a new, if more amorphous, meaning. Administrative élites of government and industry, and professional élites such as lawyers, doctors, teachers and so on, are easy to identify, although once identified their actions may be difficult to anticipate, and even more difficult to understand or control.

CHAPTER ONE

Elitism by Birth:
The Hindu Caste System

There are a number of interesting theoretical issues that are not yet resolved about the caste system:

1. Should we talk about *the* caste system or caste systems as a type? Is the caste system peculiar to India or can we speak of societies that, say, practise some form of apartheid as being caste systems? In other words, are there features of the 'true' caste system as it is found in traditional India that are not to be found elsewhere?
2. How does a caste system originate? What pre-disposing factors have to be present to generate this rare/unique social phenomenon?
3. Is it just an unusual form of social stratification, or is it essentially a carefully contrived method of social control?
4. Exactly what kind of phenomenon is it? Is it really based on *economic* – or more specifically, occupational – factors, or is it, as is often supposed, actually an aspect of *religion*? Or could it really be about race? Or perhaps some combination of these?

It is probably as well to begin with a definition. What do we mean by 'caste'? The word 'caste' denotes a race or breed, whereas the related term 'casto' (from the Latin *castus*) suggests purity or chastity. But it would be unwise to make too much of this; after all, the word itself is just an expression that Europeans have used to describe a system which was novel and foreign to them. In this sense it is both an imposition and an approximation. It normally refers to a form of social organization found in India. It is based on rigid ranking according to birth involving hereditary restrictions on occupation and marriage, the whole system being underpinned by religious sanctions. According to one authority (Ghurye: 1933), caste has the following basic characteristics, though not all have equal importance:

1. A segmental division of society into distinct groups with membership determined by birth, and rules to ensure their separation and perpetuation.
2. A definite hierarchy of social precedence headed by the Brahmin caste.

3. Restrictions on social intercourse based on notions of ritual pollution (for example, in relation to dining).
4. A variety of civil and religious disabilities arising from this system,
5. Restrictions on occupation.
6. Endogamy, that is, the necessity of marrying within one's own caste.

This categorization would still be very generally accepted, although some scholars would put more emphasis on some factors than others, and some would include additional ones, especially race and the issue of social closure, meaning that access to wealth and prestige is closed to certain social groups.

It was once usual to think of the caste system in terms of five main gradations (varnas) which some regard as a Brahminical model (Thapar: 1976, p.38):

● Brahmins, the priests
● Kshatriyas, the warriors and aristocracy
● Vaishyas, the merchants and cultivators
● Shudras, the peasants and labourers, plus
● the Outcastes or Untouchables, later known as the Scheduled Caste who were traditionally subject to well-defined strictures.

This, at least, was the formal pattern, but over the years this was modified in all kinds of ways. Occupational statuses changed, and various combinations and permutations came to be recognized. Until caste as a system – though not as a practice – was outlawed in 1955, certain features persisted, especially those related to ritual contamination. These five orders are really somewhat artificial. The actual system was enormously more complex than this. The effective or operational unit of caste activity was the *jati* (sub-caste), and even these were internally divided. One authority points out that 'there are thought to be some 3 000 castes in India .... Some derived from tribal or racial elements, some are occupational ... some are territorial, some religious and so forth' (Hulton: 1951, p.2). Indeed, a local region might easily contain twenty to thirty castes or sub-castes that ranged across the spectrum from Brahmins to the most servile labourers. Theoretically, a person could not change caste, although there was mobility *within* castes.

How, then, did all this arise? The short answer is that we don't know in detail; scholars have not arrived at a generally agreed scenario. It is notoriously difficult to arrive at any consensus about such remote, ill-documented events. Presumably we must either look for the answer in terms of historical circumstances – which is bound to be speculative – or in terms of some factor or factors that are to be found in Indian society, but are not found in the same form elsewhere.

The early mythological history of India is recorded in the Puranas and Brahmanas written between *c*. 1,000 and *c*. 600 BC, which tell how the first king, Manu (the self-born) was the hermaphrodite son of the god Brahmin, the creator god of the divine trinity (*trimurti*) including Vishnu and Shiva. During the lifetime of the tenth Manu who ruled the Earth, the great flood is said to have occurred. The god Vishnu warned him of the impending disaster, and he alone survived together with his family and the seven sages of wisdom when their boat lodged on a mountain-top above the flood waters. Whether this was an actual remembered event, or whether it is just another version of the older Mesopotamian flood-legend about the hero, Uta-Naphistim, is still a problem. There is evidence from the discovery of inscribed seals that there was some contact between India and Mesopotamia in the remote past.) What we do know from the Rig-Veda, a collection of over a thousand hymns dating from *c*. 1500 BC, and from the findings of modern archaeology, is that there existed a high civilization (*c*. 2500–*c*. 1500 BC) known as the Indus Valley civilization based on Mohenjo-daro and Harappa in modern Pakistan (Wheeler: 1968). Interestingly, its script which is clearly syllabic, consisting as it does of at least 400 signs, has not yet been deciphered; therefore all we know about this culture is its physical remains. This came to an end with the invasion of the Aryan (*Ariyas*) peoples probably from the Caucasus area. These warrior nomads brought with them a culture which was inferior in certain respects, but superior, especially in military technology, to that of the Indus Valley people. They settled not only in India but also in Iran and as far afield as Asia Minor, Greece and Italy (philologically Indian Sanskrit can be shown to be structurally related to Greek and Latin).

The Aryans were apparently quite unlike the indigenes physically, being taller and lighter skinned, hence the term *varna* (caste) which really means colour. They patently saw themselves as a superior people, and reduced the indigenes to a kind of servitude, and echoes of the invasion and its aftermath can be found in the Rig-Veda. Aryan settlement involved a clear division of labour. Crafts and trades were carefully categorized, and village property – presumably largely appropriated by the new dominant power – became family (private) property. Statuses became crystallized around specific tasks such as, say, chariot-making which had a high priority, and more menial tasks which were not so highly rated. Status was therefore related to function. Elders and army leaders became the royalty and aristocracy of the new society, and priests sometimes became priest-kings. Eventually, these categories hardened into caste, and caste into a hierarchy of privilege from which the indigenes, the dasas, were largely excluded.

It is not really possible to understand caste without knowing something of the Brahminical teachings which underpinned its operations. The Brahmins, as the self-appointed highest caste, were the literati of Indian society, and thus the accepted interpreters of the sacred books. Their principal doctrines were those of *samsara*, the transmigration of the soul, and *karma*, the retribution in each life for the sins of the previous incarnation. This endless cycle of death and rebirth were all part of the pursuit of salvation which could only be achieved by faithful adherence to *dharma*, the fulfilment of caste obligations. These included ritual duties such as paying due respect to certain animals (note the low status attributed to leather workers) and those concerned with cleansing from pollution. There were also social obligations which consisted largely of negative prohibitions and strategies of avoidance relating to such things as types of food, and the preparation and cooking of food. It was also a duty to avoid alcohol – an interesting issue insofar as in more recent times non-caste (outcaste) distillers are known to have made a great deal of money and risen in the socio-economic hierarchy by an 'alternative' route because high-caste people were forbidden to distil liquor.

By the enforcement of such rules, the Brahmins were able, perhaps unselfconsciously, to maintain a rigorous pattern of social control. 'Every caste tended to imitate the customs and ritual of the topmost caste .... Thus separate village communities were integrated and maintained in a larger social and political system ... by a religious system of values expounded and interpreted by a priestly caste' (Bottomore: 1962, p.120). The ideology plus its attendant sanctions was such that people obeyed because they believed that their eternal destinies were in jeopardy. The poor and the powerless presumably clung to the hope of something better in the next life. The system promoted the promise of post-mortal mobility, and encouraged the idea of life-after-death compensation. It is significant that although some of these ideas have weakened in modern times and that, for example, 'untouchability' as a legal status has been formally abolished by the Indian Constitution, actual social relations have been slow to follow suit. People are probably still more influenced by custom than by legal precepts.

The heyday of the caste system coincides roughly with the European Middle Ages. At this time, the real distinction was between the Brahmins and the others who effectively worked for them. Among the lower castes, distinctions do not seem to have been quite as rigid. Caste status was apparently modified by economic status, especially where highly desirable skills such as engraving and gold working were concerned. The system could always be conveniently adjusted to suit the requirements of the nobility. For example, women, in general, occupied a modest place in Indian society, but the more talented – and certainly the more attractive – might well become highly regarded courtesans. Others might be given by their parents or chosen as temple slaves. Temples were centres of education and girls might begin as temple dancers, though not unusually they became prostitutes whose earnings went towards the upkeep of the temples and their priests. Numbers of people became slaves out of poverty or – more specifically – the poverty of their parents, yet slavery never became a major institution.

Brahmins, in theory, were semi-divine beings, and their élite status is evident from the royal patronage and privileges they enjoyed. They were the priestly class, yet their power was also political and economic. Many owned land and were exempt from tax. Some even acquired sufficient surpluses to enable them to indulge in a certain amount of commercial activity, although their trading had to be limited to their homeland and confined to certain commodities only. Some of the law codes, which were written from a Brahminic point of view, also exempted Brahmins from torture and execution, though not all the texts agree on this. For very serious crimes, it does seem to have been possible to confiscate their property, and send them into exile. There were, of course, many types of Brahmin, civil servants and the like, besides those given over solely to religious pursuits who, although of high status, were often little better off, economically, than low caste people.

Essentially, the Brahmins represented the conforming, traditional socio-religious culture. But they were challenged by various heterodox cults, some of which were influenced by other systems, Islam, Buddhism, and so on, which presented the public with a syncretistic alternative to the conventional faith. The attraction may have been cult activities which took orgiastic forms with strong sexual overtones, but their devotees also questioned Brahminical teaching about such practices as pubertal marriage, especially for girls, and the strictures on widow re-marriage (Thapar: 1976, p.240). Brahmins were sometimes brought into disrepute by schisms among themselves, especially over religious doctrine. There are echoes of the West in their arguments as to exactly how salvation can be found, whether by knowledge or devotion or by sheer passivity – disputes that certainly played into the hands of their chief rivals, the Buddhists. And this is not to mention the different emphases of Vedic religion from those of later Hinduism.

The profile of Brahmin élitism was, in certain respects, not unlike that of the higher clergy in the Western Church where there were often conflicts between the ecclesiastical and secular powers on matters of authority. The Brahmins claimed a higher rank as it was they who were the interpreters of the holy laws which it was incumbent on the monarchy to observe and obey. Yet, in a sense, each was dependent on the other, though Brahmins may have had an edge where it was believed that they could invoke the necessary supernatural (magical?) sanctions. Weber maintains that nowhere else did priests command such power.

There is some suggestion that lower castes were treated with some disdain by the Brahmin élite. According to Brahminical theory the whole created order was characterized by an inherent inequality, 'the rank order of the cosmos was eternal because every animal or god and every man – according to the caste of his birth – were souls whose positions resulted from the merits earned and the sins committed in a previous life' (Bendix: 1960, pp.172–3). Therefore existing inequalities were the cumulative merits or demerits of previous incarnations. There were no *common* rights or duties because all humans were different. Each category (caste) had its own *dharma*, and every person had to act in accordance with their *dharma*. Such a view implied an almost infinite pluralism – and more than a hint of fatalism. In effect, the doctrine was that no matter how awful one's condition, everyone got what they deserved.

In the quest for salvation, reformed Brahminical teaching emphasized the need for austerities, even to the point of asceticism. It stressed not only escape from sinfulness, suffering and imperfection, but also from this whole transitory existence. Brahmin theory taught that salvation only comes when the soul is liberated from the 'wheel' of retribution and rebirth. Only in this way can the individual become one with the Brahman, the divine principle. But this fervent pursuit of asceticism – an ideal believed to be beyond the capacities of the common man – further distanced the Brahmins from the laity, who lacked Brahminical self-assurance, and had to put their trust in the conscientious fulfilment of the ritual obligations. They just had to follow their own way; in Hindu theology, no priest could intercede on their behalf. Indeed, in Weber's view, the very ethos of the Brahmin intelligentsia was detachment – a complete indifference to the world of mundane affairs.

Over time, emphases changed. Religious orientations oscillated from one prominent deity to another, partly as a 'counter-reformation' in response to the impact of Islam. Sects formed, and the ordinary illiterate members had to look for guidance among mendicant Brahmins who acted as gurus within their 'parishes'. Gurus, who were often endowed with charismatic attributes, were able to give religious instruction and function generally as confessors and counsellors. In its own way, this diversification of role undermined the status of those conventional Brahmins that possessed high social rank. They had little time for their more proletarian counterparts, especially those uneducated gurus of lower castes – 'mystagogues of the masses' – that had infiltrated their profession. Yet both types, in receiving gifts and respect – even adulation – from their people, constituted élites within their respective communities, and enforced their own kinds of discipline.

Weber took the view that Indian asceticism was both *irrational*, in that it stressed in form the redemptive value of the ecstatic experience, and *extraordinary* in that it deprecated the world and enjoined believers to disregard ordinary affairs. Probably only a tiny percentage of the people ever saw salvation as an intellectual problem, and only a minority became the adherents of any sects; popular religion was ritualistic, eclectic, and non-affiliated. It was directed towards the fulfilment of caste obligations, the hoped-for avoidance of ill-fortune, and simple, mundane aspirations for the good life.

The relative stability of a Brahmin-cum-aristocratic dominance of Indian society has been questioned by some scholars (for example, Bernard Cohn, 'Recruitment of Elites in British India' in Plotnicov and Tuden: 1970). It has been argued that from about 1500, Islamic influence had become so strong among upper-class Hindus, including Brahmins, that their life-styles (and ideologies?) had changed considerably. It is further maintained that Hinduism had become so interiorized by Islam that even the sects were not immune to its attractions. This is perhaps surprising considering how rigid the caste system was reputed to have been. But surely the thesis that India was not a unitary society, existing changeless through time, will surprise no-one. It is perhaps apposite that when Hinduism as a religion was introduced into Cambodia in the first century AD it was *not* accompanied by the practice of caste divisions. At the height of the later Khmer civilization there, we see a highly stratified society, but not the closed groups associated with India. Possibly the early migrants wanted to escape from the rigours of caste. And even when caste beliefs were exported to Sri Lanka (Ceylon) – for that seems to have been the sequence – not all the Hindu prescriptions were adopted, the main neutralizing factor being that this was predominantly a Buddhist society. For instance, although the idea of pollution through eating habits remained, the Sinhalese did not practise the intricate food taboos and cooking restrictions that had evolved in India. Marriage preferences have usually been good indicators – and regulators – of strata relations, yet exceptions have always existed. In Sri Lanka, a high caste man could take concubines from a lower caste without incurring very much opprobrium, and even casual liaisons were entertained (although the reverse, sexual contacts between high caste women and low caste men, were not tolerated) but it highly doubtful whether intimacy extended to common meals (Roberts: 1982, pp.37–8).

Caste status was exhibited in attitudes, values and beliefs as well as behaviour. Elite Brahminic status was particularly expressed in terms of such superior attributes as purity, honour and intelligence which, as we have seen, warranted deference and respect from others. But the idea that caste was so rigidified that it was not subject to alteration or variation is not borne out by the facts. That such a system works at all is due to what may seem to us as a strange kind of consensus. As one writer puts it, 'In caste systems, as in all plural systems, highly differentiated groups get along despite subjective definitions of the situation because they agree on the objective facts of what is happening and what is likely to happen – on who has the power, and how, under what circumstances, and for what purposes it is likely to be exercised. They cease to get along when this crucial agreement changes or is challenged' (Gerald Berveman, 'Stratification, pluralism and interaction: a comparative analysis of caste' in de Reuck and Knight: 1967, p.55). The European liberal ethic assumes that all people are born equal, but as Edmund Leach rightly points out (de Reuck and Knight: ibid., p.15), this is a judgement, not a fact. Social systems different from our own rest on different assumptions. Feudal systems have presupposed that people are born unequal, and the traditional Indian caste order was just such a feudal system in which people knew their 'proper station'. To know one's place in society, and not to aspire to anything else, least of all to join the ruling élite, was the unspoken basic tenet of the caste system. In this sense, it was possibly the closest approximation to a realized 'Brave New World' except that, in this case, it was a Brave Old World. Huxley's utilitarian blueprint is a satirical solution to the problem of social stability. For by a careful process of pre-conditioning, people never question the élite or the system, or their place or future within it.

What then is the basis of caste? Is it race, is it economic or cultural factors, or is it essentially a religious phenomenon? And is it really possible to distinguish these?

Let's take the argument for race first. There seems to be little doubt that this is a factor worth considering. The Aryans, a Caucasoid people, took territory occupied by peoples that were apparently smaller and darker skinned, some of whom are known as Dravidians. The indigenes were no match for the invaders who tolerated them as serfs and labourers in the service of the new dominant culture. Their low stratum position eventually placed them as Shudras below the 'twice-born' of the upper three caste categories. However, it seems quite accidental that the conquerors were light-skinned. Their obvious military superiority owed more to their chariotry than to their pigmentation. The 'read-back' method is open to all sorts of flaws; it's a little like attributing the Muslim conquests in the seventh and eighth centuries to the assumption that Islam was a superior kind of religion. (This becomes a different argument if we attribute military victory to the greater fervour and fearlessness of Muslim believers.) In the case of India, we cannot even take for granted that the Aryans had a superior culture. There is no evidence of a high Aryan culture in their original homeland – wherever that was. Indeed, if the Indus Valley culture is anything to go by, apparently rather drab and depressingly regimented, it was almost certainly more 'civilized' – in the commonly understood sense of the term – than that of the invaders who were probably nomads from Southern Russia. The new élite, then, were only an élite in a specific, limited sense. They had more military muscle, though, with time, this became transmuted into a generalized social superiority.

What must not be done is to confuse the idea of colour and that of caste, and then compound this with emotive arguments about racism. We are surely all aware of the situations where blacks have been unjustly dominated by whites. But there have also been many situations in which whites have oppressed whites, and reduced them to permanent servitude. And there have certainly been many instances in which blacks have oppressed blacks; one has only to think about the Zulu *vis-à-vis* the subordinate tribes in the early nineteenth century, or the Matabele in one-time Rhodesia, or the Lovedu in the Transvaal at about the same time to see that relatively closed systems operated in these societies as well. As this does not take account of those circumstances in which – to use current distinctions – blacks and coloured, have oppressed each other. The Africanization policies in some newly decolonized African states where Asians have been forced to leave, as in Uganda, bears this out. It will be interesting to see what transpires in South Africa in the longer term now that black Africans have a near monopoly of power.

Can the term 'caste' therefore be meaningfully used about non-Indian situations? This has occasioned a great deal of debate among scholars and there is still nothing like a consensus on the issue. Some are academically – and one sometimes suspects, ideologically – convinced that the term caste should be extended to other societies, particularly the United States and pre-1994 South Africa. But is this valid? There are some similarities with the Indian situation, but there are also a great many differences. For example, in these societies there are mechanisms which confirm the *social* and *economic* inferiority of the underprivileged groups (poor whites as well as ethnic/indigenous groups), but unlike the Indian experience there is little or no *psychological acceptance* of their situation. In fact, as we are all well aware, in these and similar societies there have been active protest movements and liberation organizations trying to change matters to their advantage. Revolts have occurred in India too, but they were of quite a different order, and were usually directed against colonial authorities, not high-caste countrymen.

There was a complex of factors in the caste system which is peculiar to the Indian situation. Where else does one find such an emphasis on purity and pollution with all their implications and ramifications? Where else is such stress laid upon the prospect of rebirth as an avenue – indeed, *the* avenue – of social mobility validated by religious sanctions? Certainly not in South Africa or the United States. Social mobility and economic advancement may be difficult in other societies, but it is not impossible. If we insist on using the term caste in some broader sense, it would be better to think about, say, ancient Sparta where a tiny minority of true-born Spartiates held down an indigenous population of serf-like helots, or the oppressive system that operated in early post-conquest Spanish America, or, for that matter, the situation in modern Indonesia. Given all the qualifications and ambiguities, it is probably wiser not to apply the word caste to any other system of stratification, no matter how 'closed' it may be. To use it in any other way can never be more than a metaphor or – at best – an analogy.

Another question we must sort out is to what extent caste was primarily religious or economic. Marx argued that caste is related to what he termed the 'Asiatic mode of production'. In other words, he saw it as essentially an *economic* phenomenon which would naturally disintegrate under the impact of industrialization. Weber, on the other hand, maintained that caste is really a *religious* phenomenon. He acknowledged that it had strong economic, that is, occupational, implications but insisted that its manifestations were mainly informed by underlying ideological imperatives. This question is directly related to the source-of-stability issue. Again, Marx argued that the degree of institutional stability in Indian society was a function of *economic factors*. Work was centred on an hereditary division of labour and carried out by caste-based occupational units. N.K. Bose has qualified this by contending that the roots of stability really lie in the co-ordination of inculcated *cultural ideals* which encouraged the organization of production in terms of self-contained local units. De Reuck and Knight (1967), however, conclude that the basis of stability was *political*, and that the 'secret' was in conformity not consensus. It was maintained by sanctions, not by negotiation and agreement. The initiative was always with the élite. There was a strong inculcation, even among the lower orders, of the norms of self-respect and this, they say, ensured a kind of dignity amidst the denigration.

So do other societies compare? Obviously, all societies have control mechanisms to facilitate conformity to norms and adherence to the rules.

No matter what society we think of, control mechanisms are there to ensure compliance and to maintain social stability. But other conquered-states situations did not involve the imposition of a caste system. Admittedly, there was often very clear differentiation, but not the inviolable rigidity of caste. This form of control was particularly effective because it was buttressed by ideological sanctions. At the present time it still exists not as a legal but as a perceived reality, although evidence suggests that even this is succumbing to political and economic expediency. The changing value systems in India indicate that the society is moving from one of ascribed status to one of achieved status (note, for instance, the popularity of certain personalities in the burgeoning cinema industry regardless of their class origins. 'Stars' have become part of the new economic élite).

The literature on caste is understandably replete with examples of the disadvantages of the caste system. It is argued that:

1. It inhibited the extension of meritocratic skills.
2. It inculcated attitudes of resignation.
3. It retarded economic development by confining talent and restricting resources, particularly by unnecessary ritual prohibitions.
4. It militated against sexual equality (though note the freedom of sexual expression in certain traditional Hindu cults).
5. It perpetuated Untouchability (it is interesting that, twenty years after the 1955 Act outlawing such practices, the prejudices still remained. One survey at the time showed that some 90 per cent of one-time outcastes still lived outside village boundaries).
6. It did nothing for the indescribable poverty in Indian society.
7. It promoted social divisions and forms of élitism purely on ascriptional grounds.

Given these negative factors about caste, it seems only fair to ask if the caste system had any virtues. One feels that, since it existed for over 3,000 years, it must have had some positive advantages. These might be summarized as follows:

1. It ensured the continuation of certain hereditary skills.
2. It limited unnecessary competition (Gandhi once suggested that it could be offered to the world as the best remedy against heartless competition and the social disintegration that comes from avarice and greed); it might even be argued that the caste system relieved the burden on the ordinary Hindu to prove himself, as his position was irrevocably fixed.

3. It had useful integrative (village/*jati*) functions in that it aided the stability of family life, and gave identity to its members (Bottomore: 1962, p.132); indeed, Weber suggests that caste did not invariably prohibit people of different castes working together, and that some mixing of caste groups was even more evident outside the workplace.
4. It reinforced national and ethnic bonds by inhibiting social revolution.
5. It encouraged reverence for life (traditionally — for good or ill – it was against the destruction-of-life principle; for example, bird-trapping, fishing, even oil-seed crushing were once proscribed by caste rules).

What appears to us as a system that is grossly unjust, may well have not seemed unjust to the Hindu at all. The Brahmin was simply being rewarded for his exemplary behaviour in a previous incarnation. Admittedly, the élites enjoyed more privileges than others, particularly immunity from tiring manual labour. But, in general, this was regarded as justified where members of the Brahminic order actually did possess scarce and socially valued skills. So even where there was *systematic inequality*, the prestige of the élite was not entirely explained by high-caste birth. Differential rewards could be at least partly explained in terms of functional importance. If it was only those of high-birth who could be trained as administrators and so forth (perhaps an unfair ascriptive privilege) then, once they were proficient (achieved status), their value to the system was beyond dispute (Johnson: 1964, pp.544–8).

To conclude, we should distinguish between organic and organizational adjustment to changing situations. Like so many bureaucratic systems, the Indian élite had a high survival value and the ability to continue over time without very much adaptation to changing external circumstances. Broadly speaking, bureaucratic élites – especially those that are held to be born to the task – tend to depend for survival on their internal coherence rather than having to justify their existence in terms of their service to society (LaPière: 1954, p.311).

CHAPTER TWO

Elitism by Class: Social Differentiation in Classical Greece

In general, we know surprisingly little about Classical Greece, certainly less than may be commonly supposed. Almost all we know is about Athens, mainly through the surviving work of Plato and Aristotle, the playwright Aristophanes, Plutarch, Xenophon and particularly Thucydides. We know something too about Sparta, Corinth and some of the larger island states, but really only smatterings about the numerous other city-states. Therefore, in this discussion we are going to concentrate on Athens and Sparta where we can be reasonably confident of the facts.

During the Greek Classical period (508–323 BC), that is from the reforms of Kleisthenes until the death of Alexander the Great, Athens was a radical democracy. And by that is meant that the Athenian constitution was, paradoxically, both more and less democratic than anything that *we* understand by the term. *More*, there was no executive, as such, neither was there a Senate or Parliament in anything like our sense of those terms. Ultimately decisions were either taken or ratified directly by the people (*demos*) at the Public assembly (*ekklesia*); and *less*, insofar as only a minority within the state was actually enfranchised. It would follow, therefore, that this should have been a state without élites, but, as we shall see, this was not, in fact, the case. Elites did exist, and in a sense, *had* to exist, although their activities were sometimes called into question by an enquiring and suspicious public.

Athens was the principal town in the 'county' of Attica. The term usually employed is that of city-state, although, strictly speaking, Athens was neither quite a city nor a state. It was a *polis* which effectively controlled Attica, and certain other city-states (*poleis*) beyond its borders. There were scores of autonomous city-states in Greece, in the Aegean islands and on the coastal areas of Asia Minor (*Ionia*) and the Black Sea, which began as colonial settlements from the mainland and were still 'related' to their mother cities. City-state organization arose for a number of reasons, not least because of the topography of mainland Greece (*Hellas*) which fostered separated and often fiercely independent communities (compare, for example, the clan system and the terrain in traditional Scotland). Their development coincided with the decline of the monarchy as an institution in most of Greece during the eighth century BC. This was followed in many states by oligarchic government in the hands of the traditional aristocracies (literally, the rule of the best people) who were virtually synonymous with what the Greeks called the *eupatridai* (the well-born ones). Sometimes oligarchy or some more popular form of government gave way to *tyrannoi*, popular leaders who seized power unconstitutionally and ruled either by consent or coercion.

In Athens, in the early sixth century BC, there was so much social unease over the oppressive behaviour of the large landowners that a leading official, Solon, was charged with instituting a number of very important socio-economic reforms which ultimately pleased very few, least of all the aristocracy, especially when he recommended the cancellation of debts. He established a system of four classes of citizens based on crop returns. These economic criteria made more citizens eligible for public office, but excluded the lowest class from any office at all. He thus eliminated the birth qualification and substituted a property qualification. These reforms gave institutionalized articulation to the class divisions within the society, and the previous ascription-based status distinctions of the nobility began to give way to the achievement-orientations of the wealthy.

Towards the very end of the century, Kleisthenes introduced much more radical reforms. This was the real beginning of Athens as a democratic state. Very soon afterwards, the Greeks came into direct conflict with the Persians, the great power of the time, who controlled the Greek states in Asia Minor. The Persians sent a punitive force to the mainland which was unexpectedly defeated at Marathon by the Athenians and their allies (490 BC). Ten years later, the Persians launched a full-scale invasion which was equally unsuccessful against a coalition of Greek states (480–79 BC) including Sparta. Thus there began in Athens – whether consequently or coincidentally, we are not sure – a period of unprecedented cultural achievement. Artistic and architectural as well as political developments took place in a 'golden age' of less than a hundred years. It still seems incredible that so much talent could have found expression in such a relatively brief period of time in the principal town of an area no larger than a modest English county. Not that this period was without its problems. The Athenians felt it was time to flex their military muscles, and their campaigning seasons continued with the customary inter-state warfare – a fratricidal hobby of the Greeks. There were also ongoing difficulties with the Persians abroad that had to be dealt with so, all in all, there was rarely a year when the Athenians were not fighting someone somewhere or another.

Gradually, the Athenians built up a modest but appreciable empire. Athens had the most powerful navy in the Aegean, perhaps in the whole Mediterranean world, while Sparta had the most invincible army on land, a situation that had ominous possibilities. In order, ostensibly, to counter the still possible Persian threat, Athens formed a league of allied states each of which made contributions to a central fund housed on the island of Delos. But as the possibility of a further Persian invasion diminished in the mid-fifth century, Athens had the monies transferred to her own treasury, and then used them to initiate a huge building programme to beautify the city – hence the wonders of the Athenian Acropolis. Of course, there were protests from some of the allies, but the Athenians, under their leading politician, Perikles, insisted – albeit unconvincingly – that it didn't matter what they did with the money providing they kept their part of the bargain and protected the allies from Persian attacks. There was much grumbling among the allies but there was no concerted revolt for by this time they had become dependants, and their tax had become a form of tribute.

The key factor in any consideration of class and social differentiation in Athenian society was that of citizenship. The total population during the Classical period is quite unknown; scholars, as usual, differ considerably in their estimates. An informed approximation puts the figure at 250 000 to 300 000, of which the full citizens comprised less than 20 per cent. Attica covered an area of about one thousand square miles, but a very high percentage of the population occupied the walled city itself, an area of barely one square mile. This included the commanding Acropolis (high town), the Agora (market place with its public buildings), and the hill known as the Pynx where the citizen Assembly met to discuss public issues. A citizen was a male of 18 years or over born of both an Athenian father and an Athenian mother. Within the citizen body, there were still classes based on economic criteria, but all were enfranchised; all were allowed to speak at the Assembly, and all were theoretically equal before the law. Strictly speaking, females were not full citizens: they were not allowed to participate in the political process, they did not attend the Assembly and were not allowed to vote. This was not because of a fear or distrust of the fair sex (although to judge from the myths and plays, that did exist) so much as a compliment to the males. These small, autonomous states often struggled to survive both economically and militarily. They could not afford mercenaries or a professional army to protect them, and therefore had to rely on their own citizen militias. The basic education in many states including Athens consisted largely of developing athletic and military prowess. Small wonder, then, that those who were prepared to fight and possibly die for the state should claim the exclusive right to order its affairs.

Wealth counted for a great deal, but breeding was still important. Most Athenian males were small farmers, artisans and labourers. Commerce, especially for the upper classes, was still not quite respectable. If the dialogues of Plato are anything to go by, however, the most shaming thing was to have to work for somebody else; Athens was very much the ancient equivalent of the enterprise society. There was a certain mobility within the citizen ranking system, but a poor labourer could hardly aspire to the aristocracy. Political and military merit were acceptable, though neither age nor cultic pretensions conferred any special privileges. The military orders, in particular, betray something of the nature of the ranking system. The highest order, the cavalry, was largely composed of the sons of well-to-do families who could afford the right kind of training for their offspring. Lower orders served as heavily-armed infantry (*hoplites*), at least those who could manage the expense of providing their own accoutrements of war, and the lowest class of all (*thetes*) might act as lightly-armed infantry, or, more commonly, as oarsmen in the navy. By and large, the Greeks did not use slaves for this purpose; military service was a high honour, and on campaign slaves were normally only employed as body-servants. Anyway, it didn't pay to train slaves as warriors, as this might have dangerous possibilities.

The distinction between citizen and non-citizen is probably best exemplified in relation to resident aliens in Athens. Resident aliens or metics (Gk. *metoikoi*) – a rather anomalous category – were not, strictly, foreigners insofar as they were likely to be fellow Greeks who for various reasons had migrated to Athens. They constituted an appreciable proportion of the Athenian population during the Classical period, and many were engaged in entrepreneurial activity of one kind or another. They were bound to observe Athenian law and to meet the customary financial obligations, including a special tax for people of their class. They had no political rights, and their legal status was such that they had to be represented in court by a citizen who acted as a patron. It is a sign of their differential status that although the statutory penalty for the murder of a citizen was death, the murder of a metic only merited exile. They also had educational disadvantages: although allowed the privilege of exercising in the gymnasia with Athenian youths – a critical element in Greek pedagogy – they could not join them for ephebic training (a kind of conscription that lasted for two years), yet were permitted to serve with the military. They were normally not allowed to own personal property, though they could own business premises. They could purchase household goods, and could actually own their own slaves. Some metics did very well in Athens, and were probably treated as well there as anywhere else in Greece. They were prominent in a number of industries; indeed, a few became quite prosperous as bankers, factory-owners, and so on, if such terms can be broadly applied to a pre-technological society. They seem too to have enjoyed reasonable relations with citizens; they received equal pay and were even allowed to intermarry, but the children of such unions were always regarded as metics.

But things could go wrong. There is a well-known incident which points up just how sacrosanct the status of citizen was in Athens. It was not uncommon for the city to be short of bread, and in 445 BC a special gift of grain was made from Egypt; it was taken for granted that this was for distribution among citizens. During the proceedings, a large number of metics were found posing as citizens in order to get a share in the allocation. Citizenship was inviolable, and the courts could be extremely severe about presumptions of status. The culprits were immediately arrested and struck off the city's register and sold into slavery. It should be pointed out, however, that this seems to have been a particularly serious one-off economic issue; there is no evidence of general metic-oppression as part of state-policy.

A much more important division than that of citizen and non-citizen was that between free and unfree. The unfree in Athens, as in so many complex pre-industrial societies, were of course the slaves. We are not at all sure about the size of the slave population: it may have been as high as thirty or thirty-five per cent of the total population. All we can now do is to make inferences from particular known incidents. For instance, during the Peloponnesian War between the Athenians and their allies and the Spartans and their allies, which dragged on (on and off) from 431 to 404 BC and eventually involved most of the Greek world, we know that some 20 000 chattel slaves took advantage of the Spartan invasion to desert the mines where they were working. This probably means that although slaves were employed in all kinds of capacities from household servants to police, the majority were chattel slaves, branded and chained, that laboured in the silver mines at Laurium where life was certainly 'nasty, brutish and short'.

It is thought that most slaves were foreigners; evidence suggests that the Greeks generally became increasingly unwilling to hold other Greeks as slaves. People became slaves as war captives (though rich prisoners were often ransomed) or by purchase at slave markets, or occasionally through debt. Healthy male slaves fetched a good price, approximately equal to the cost of their keep for a year. Often males of warrior age were at a premium because in war it was not that unusual to kill the male captives, who could be a menace, and sell the women and children into slavery. Generally speaking, slaves were privately owned. Possibly most families didn't have any, but those with a little land might have one or two. Many were employed in rudimentary factories, shield-making, fish-curing or whatever, and they received comparable pay, part of which – predictably – went back to their masters. Among the wealthy citizens there were those who held vast numbers of slaves; a well-attested example is that of Nikias, perhaps the richest man in Athens in the late fifth century, who rented 2 000 slaves at a daily rate to the mining industry.

The key difference between slaves and citizens was not one of occupation but of rights. Slaves had no rights of any kind, they had to be legally represented by citizens, and were not allowed to marry or cohabit without the master's permission. But even here there were anomalies. Slaves were allowed access to the religious cults, and it became a joke among visitors that they couldn't tell a slave from a free man in Athens. In other words, some Athenian slaves were rather 'uppish' – especially those in the liberal professions – and considered to be too well treated by their owners. Also, there was a system whereby some slaves were able to buy their freedom, and 'friendly societies' (*eranoi*) were set up to enable slaves who were earning to put a little aside for the purpose.

Athens was by no means alone as far as the institution of slavery was concerned. It was a given fact of life everywhere. For instance, after the disastrous Athenian invasion of Sicily (415–413) – really the turning point of the Peloponnesian War – the Syracusans took enormous numbers of Athenian prisoners, some 7 000 of whom were condemned to a brief existence in the quarries, and the remainder were profitably sold into slavery. What is so interesting about Athens is that in this most go-ahead of Greek states where there were thriving industries (especially pottery), where there was an expensive patronage of the arts, and, not least of all, a politically aware radical democracy, there was also probably the most extensive system of slave-holding in all Greece. Ironically, democracy went hand-in-hand with repression.

To show just how radical this democracy was, it is necessary to outline briefly how the system worked. The whole citizen body constituted the Assembly which met 40 times a year, though just how well attended it was we have no idea (a quorum may have been 6 000). These meetings, in turn, were organized in ten sets of four, and each of the four followed a pre-set formula as far as general topic areas were concerned. This was 'led' by a council of 500 (the *Boule*) consisting of 50 men from each of the ten tribal *demes* (wards) of the state. Each councillor was chosen by *lot*, and was not allowed to serve more than twice. This body itself was divided into ten steering committees (*prytaneis*) each of which served for a tenth of the year, and comprised five men from each of the ten *demes*, also chosen by lot. These committees chose a new Chairman every day, again by lot, and in effect he became – in a highly qualified sense – a 'king for a day'. He could be overruled, as Sokrates discovered on the one fateful day that he occupied the Chair, when some naval commanders were condemned to death by the Assembly, much against his advice, for failing to rescue some of their drowning men.

There was, therefore, a continuous turnover of personnel, and what with councillor duties and other work in the various Athenian courts, policing and guard duties, distribution and taxation, officiating at shrines, and other sundry activities, virtually every male had an opportunity for public service at some time or another. This, at least, is how the system was supposed to work, but we can safely infer that the path of true democracy did not always run smoothly. The 'Upper House' known as the Archonate and the King's Council (for retired archons) had, by Classical times, lost much of their traditional influence. So, in theory, the Assembly was the final authority on all matters of public order in the state. '*De jure*, the Athenian citizenry was sovereign, and *de facto* no group or official could dictate to it, check it, and review or revise its actions. But it could be influenced by trained rhetoricians and swayed by gifted demagogues and openly led by exceptional charismatic figures such as Perikles, but no person or group could order its policies' (Carlton: 1977, p.169). These popular 'leaders' did not always emanate from the aristocratic élite. For example, Kleon, a tanner (or tannery owner?), had a particularly 'hawkish' reputation before his death in the Peloponnesian War. But they usually did so. Alkibiades, an able and personable aristocrat and a remarkably persuasive orator, was the main advocate of the catastrophic Sicilian expedition, and previously he was the principal instigator behind the Assembly's decision to condemn the entire population of the island of Melos to death and slavery in 416 BC. It took an exceptional politician to change sides more than once in wartime, and not only talk his way out of it on each occasion, but actually get himself elected by both sides as a *strategos* or military adviser (Ellis: 1989).

There were probably more boards and committees in the Athenian system than would seem necessary to get things done. Perhaps the idea was to share responsibility, and reduce opportunities for graft and peculation. The ballot system seems to have been designed to minimize the possibilities of corruption. In all, there were probably some 700 paid officials – paid, admittedly, at quite modest rates – besides all those who served the state on a purely voluntary basis. In the fourth century, citizens were actually paid a pittance to attend the Assembly, presumably to defray loss of earnings for those who had work, although Aristophanes the satirist – perhaps exaggeratedly – insisted that the poor could just about make a living this way. Many, perhaps most, Athenians saw their system of government as a fairer way to distribute the burden of civic duties, and they tended to have a healthy suspicion of those who actively sought office for its own sake. Some of the intellectual élite disputed the wisdom and efficiency of such a system, and others actually despaired of its outcomes. Sokrates, for example, argued that if he wanted a ship's pilot he would need *trained* personnel, yet the ship of state was in the hands of those without any semblance of expertise. Another anonymous writer contended that the 'mob' were quite happy to take the credit when things went well but were quick to blame others, whom they had appointed, when things went badly ('The Old Oligarch' in Claster: 1967).

Some offices were hereditary, especially those concerned with the care of shrines, as at Eleusis for instance, but such positions were rare. Elections were mainly confined to military appointments, possibly on the assumption that war is too important to be left to the politicians. There were sixty or so officers needed for any one year, including the ten-strong board of generals. On the whole the task of military leadership fell to the aristocratic élite, although there were some notable exceptions; so much depended on the whim of the Assembly. It, therefore, becomes debatable as to exactly who ran the show. Ostensibly, it was the people who had the last word on state affairs. In this sense, it was sometimes a kind of 'tyranny from below', a dictatorship of the proletariat. Yet we find that behind the scenes the aristocracy still exerted considerable influence in certain areas of public life. There was also, of course, the intellectual élite, such people as the Sophists, writers and other philosophers; many of their ideas are still with us, although we are not at all certain just how much influence they had in their own day. The intellectual élite overlapped with the artistic élite; architects such as the designers of the Parthenon, Ictinus and Callicrates, and sculptors such as Phidias and his school. It should be noted, however, that the state was not always that kind to its artists and intellectuals, and some (Phidias and Sokrates are notable examples) were victims of what now appear to be rather contrived accusations. The Athenians were very liberal about some things; witness, for instance, the bawdiness of the Old Comedy, but they could be equally *un*forgiving about other matters of which they disapproved or possibly didn't fully understand.

But when we think of Greece, especially Athens, we think particularly of political democracy. Politics is, after all, our main concern here. Yet it is as well to remember that even in democratic states there was an incipient political élitism, an impatience with the unwieldy and sometimes incompetent democratic process, and a nascent trend towards oligarchy. So much so, in fact, that when those with oligarchic tendencies got half a chance, they were sometimes even prepared to engineer revolutions to achieve it. On the strong island city-state of Samos, for example, just off the coast of Asia Minor, an oligarchic *coup* was organized by a group known as 'the three hundred'. They arranged the murder of a 'virulent' democrat and tried to seize power, an act they thought would bring them favour with the Persians who controlled most of Asia Minor, and, better still, bring them Persian money – a move that has all the hallmarks of the arch-plotter, Alkibiades. But it was put down by a force of Athenians who considered Samos to be within their sphere of influence. At much the same time (411 BC), a more powerful group of oligarchs, 'the four hundred', took over Athens itself, but were divided among themselves; some wanted a moderate oligarchy, but others favoured rule by a more restricted élite. Among their motives, besides that of seeking power, was the desire to bring an end to the war with Sparta, itself a highly unusual oligarchy. There were the customary assassinations and counter-assassinations, and eventually most of the plotters fled to Sparta. Order was restored, and one of the principal – and bravest – revolutionaries, Antiphon, who stayed in Athens, was brought to trial and executed.

It is instructive to compare the much-applauded radical democracy of Athens with the state organization of their traditional enemies, the Spartans. By general Greek standards – if such an expression makes sense where there were so many different autonomous states – Sparta was unconventional economically, politically and even architecturally. It was sited in a vast fertile valley in that part of Greece known as the Peloponnese, and was not the typical walled city, but a collection of connected villages constituting a kind of county town. Unlike Athens, it was poor in public buildings and one contemporary writer, Thucydides, said that if posterity were to judge Sparta by its architecture it would be hard to believe how powerful this state had once been. Its people, sometimes referred to in Classical literature as Lacadaimonions, were of a different stock from the Athenians, having reputedly entered the land as warlike invaders, perhaps from the Balkans, from the twelfth century BC onwards. The records are very sparse, but tradition has it that in the eighth century these people took over the land to the south-west known as Messenia, and used this as a source of manpower and extra produce. This necessitated keeping the Messenians and the non-Spartan indigenes in permanent subjection, so, to this end, certain important reforms were introduced in the following century which greatly modified the nature of Spartan society at a time when Sparta was developing something of an hegemony in southern Greece, and had established a league of loosely confederated states.

The constitution which evolved, and the social institutions which it necessitated have been both abhorred and admired by contemporary and modern writers alike. Plato may have, in fact, based his 'ideal state' blueprint, the Republic, on certain aspects of Spartan life and practice. Henceforth, Sparta and her allies, on whom she did not impose her own constitution, seem to have dedicated themselves – out of a variety of motives – to the eradication of tyranny and democracy. 'Both were distrusted. (Like Sokrates, the Spartans regarded one as potentially disruptive as the other.) All this was mainly achieved by alliances rather than military conquest – though possibly with the help of a little intimidation at the margins' (Carlton: 1990, p.47). The reforms instituted by the Spartan government harked back to a more archaic – and heroic – age. In this she was 'admired but not imitated, an inspiration to political theorists, and a comfort to those who found democracy distasteful' (Andrewes: 1976, p.66).

Sparta had a complicated – and some might think, 'untidy' – four tiered system of political organization. It consisted unusually, of a monarchy with two hereditary kings who held office simultaneously, somewhat like early Republican Roman consuls. The kings represented the continuity principle of the Spartan state and, in theory, this dual monarchy was supposed to lead to a more balanced exercise of power which, by and large, obviously worked. The kings had ritual as well as military duties, and were also largely responsible for the administration of Sparta's dependent territories. But their power was effectively limited. The real executive power was the Ephorate of five men elected annually by the Spartan Assembly who supervised the entire working of the state. Again, in theory, the kings and the Ephors were supposed to work together, but, in practice, relations were often a little uneasy, especially when the Ephors decided to exert their full authority on matters of policy. At the third level, there was the *Gerousia*, a Council of thirty elders of which the kings were *ex officio* members. All, except the kings, were over sixty years of age, and were elected for life by the Assembly. Lastly, there was the Assembly itself which consisted of all full citizens, the Spartiates themselves, who were over thirty years old, that is, men of trained warrior status. The Assembly does not appear to have been responsible for legislation nor, *un*like the Athenians, did its members debate issues; its task was rather to consider and approve the recommendations of the executive.

In effect, then, Sparta was a monarchy, an oligarchy (the Ephors), and technically also a gerontocracy (the rule of the aged – the *Gerousia*), yet it also had a form of limited democracy in that the full citizens enjoyed complete constitutional equality, though not necessarily equal status. Viewed in this way, it all seems a little lopsided, but it stood the test of time, perhaps because anybody who was anybody in this highly élitist system, had the opportunity – indeed, the obligation – to contribute to the workings of the state.

Spartan élitism is clearly evidenced in its almost caste-like social structures in which each level is characterized by a stark demarcation of function and status. The élite itself were the Equals (*homoioi*), the Spartiates themselves, who may never have numbered more than 9 000. Within the ranks of the Equals, certain gradations were recognized – an inevitability in a warrior society. As we have seen, a man was eligible to join their ranks at the age of thirty when his extensive military training, much longer than that of the Athenians, was completed. At the same time he was given a parcel of land (*kleros*) and extra *kleroi* with the enlargement of the family. Although officially out of the army, in practice, he always had to be available for further military service when necessary. If, as happened, a man failed to be elected to the Equals he was literally 'blackballed' and normally remained an inferior for the rest of his life.

The warrior ideal of 'excellence' (*arete*) seems to have been completely endorsed by Spartan women who constituted the breeding machines of the state. Older men would sometimes invite young warriors to mate with their wives for this very purpose; needless to say, the children were reared in the name of the *social* father – the biological factor being almost irrelevant. Any man with three sons was exempted from military service, and a man with four sons was excused all 'state burdens'. Although girls in this strongly patriarchal society enjoyed more freedom than in many other Greek states, including Athens, it was boy children that were at a premium. They were commandeered by the state at the age of seven, housed in barracks, and subjected to the most rigorous training programmes which included extremely ascetic living conditions. They were sparsely fed, went barefoot summer and winter (even in snow), and had few clothes. Younger boys were put in the charge of older boys on a kind of proto-Public School 'fagging' basis. Some sexual inversion between them may have been encouraged; we are not absolutely sure about this. What is certain is that there was a considerable emphasis on youth and beauty, and that homosexuality was probably an indulgence rather than the *de rigueur* practice that some modern writers have suggested. Exclusive homosexuality was actually a subject of ridicule; by law, Spartan males had to marry at twenty. Such conditions – one might almost say, privations – were calculated to produce hardy warriors in order to maintain Sparta's military supremacy. The system obviously met with some success as the Spartans had the most invincible army in Greece for the best part of three hundred years.

At the second level were the non-Spartan citizens of semi-autonomous communities known collectively as the *perioikoi* (literally, the living-around ones). These people were able to exercise a certain amount of self-government, but were finally subject to the dictates of the Spartan élite. The *perioikoi* were themselves divided into several classes and were involved in numerous occupations. Their political interests, however, had to be confined to the administration of their own particular communities. They were allowed no say in the affairs of the sovereign state, although Spartan officials did sometimes intervene in *their* local concerns. They had to hold themselves in readiness for military duties in which they often acquitted themselves with distinction. But, ultimately, they 'had to accept any decisions the parent state might make for them, and providing they were politically unambitious they could lead a moderately uneventful existence' (Carlton: 1990, p.48).

The lowest rung in the hierarchical ladder was reserved for the helots (*helotes*). These are believed to have been the descendants of the indigenes of the territory originally taken over by the Dorian tribes from whence the Spartans derived. They were not slaves in the normally accepted sense of the term; they were not normally bought and sold, but allocated by the state to Spartan masters. In effect, they functioned as state serfs. They were allotted lands to cultivate and had to pay half their produce to their masters. They could be punished and even executed without trial, and there is some evidence – admittedly not too reliable – that Spartan youths were sometimes encouraged to kill the odd helot as part of their military training. Certainly the murder of a helot did not occasion any undue disquiet, and it is highly unlikely that a Spartan would be prosecuted for such an act.

Dominant as the Spartans were, they were very much a minority compared with those they controlled; so they were extremely apprehensive about the possibility of Messenian rebellions and helot uprisings. Their secret police, the *Krypteia*, kept a vigilant eye on things, but this did not prevent occasional disturbances. In the 460s the helots took advantage of a serious earthquake in the Peloponnese to stage a rebellion that took five years to suppress. It was unwise to allow helots to be armed, so normally they were not allowed to serve with the military, although they were employed as body servants by their masters while on campaign. During the Peloponnesian War, the Spartans, as a brutal precaution against possible insurrection at a time when they could least afford it, cynically liquidated some 2 000 helots after pretending that they were going to set them free (Thucydides, p.313).

Sparta can be confidently classified as a militaristic society. Many Spartans were able to live as absentee landlords, leaving the care of their lands to their serfs, and concentrating their attentions on military affairs. They did what they did best and, until they were defeated by the Thebans in 371, on land they were the best there was. They required strong forces to keep their non-Spartan communities, and especially their serfs, in subjection, and they also needed them to maintain their military pre-eminence in mainland Greece. Their rivals, the Athenians, had naval supremacy for much of the Classical period, and had thriving trading relations at home and abroad. The Spartans found it difficult to compete on these terms. They felt their position to be under threat, so they responded in the only way they knew. They didn't fight for booty; in many ways, they were a very conservative, almost ascetic, people. The contest was partly ideological: they favoured oligarchy over democracy, and ideally wanted this to be adopted by other Greek states. But perhaps more than this, their rivalry with Athens was about status, retaining their name and their reputation in the eyes of others. They didn't succeed. Their empire – if such it can be called – was very shortlived. They eventually won the war with Athens, but lost the peace. They proved to be just as oppressive as those they supplanted. Their cultural insularity and their insistence on the purity of their 'breed' meant that their numbers gradually declined in relation to their rivals. The élite became smaller and smaller, yet the élite of the élite, the ruling oligarchy, still retained its power. It was not until the middle of the third century BC, that any significant change took place. In the end, they were defeated not so much by their enemies as by demography.

If there are lessons to be learned from this phase of Classical history, one of them is surely that if interpretation is to begin with the study of institutions and values, the city-state, *as a system*, set up a conflict of ideals which was never quite resolved (Davies: 1978, pp.168ff.). Whether governed democratically or oligarchically, the pressures of dissension were always at work. The ideal, as Aristotle – a keen advocate of distributive justice – observed, was for the citizen to enjoy the freedom to participate in deliberative or judicial office. But that this so often failed to live up to expectation is all too obvious. Where the city-state system was 'unsuccessful', there was often a tendency to subordinate other city-states or to use them to further sectarian interests. And where this was not happening, there were dispiritingly frequent disputes *within* the city-states themselves. Isokrates, a famous Athenian orator, speaking at the Olympic Games of 380, said, 'Instead of fighting for their land against others, citizens fight each other inside the city walls. More cities have been taken prisoner than before we made the Peace [with Persia]. So frequent are revolutions that men who live in their own cities are more despondent than those punished with exile; the former fear the future, the latter expect to return at any moment. So far are cities from "freedom" and "autonomy" that some are under tyrants, others under Spartan governors, others are in ruins, others are under barbarian [that is, non-Greek] masters' (quoted by Davies: ibid., p.169).

The problem, then, is not just the conflict between ideas and ideals, but between ideals and practicality. Any system can work given the will to make it work and the Greeks found that, whatever the system, some kind of élitism was inevitable. The Greeks, in general, distrusted monarchy and positively deplored tyranny, but even democratic states harboured those with oligarchic tendencies, possibly because they came to tire of proletarian mismanagement and were fearful of mob rule. It could be argued (as Aristotle) that some states replaced the proportionate equality of oligarchy with the numerical inequality of democracy – a system of the lowest common denominator. (For an opposing view which emphasizes the undue influence of Plato et al. on a view of Athenian democracy, see Wood and Wood: 1978.) Yet in every city-state some form of élitism was unavoidable. All city-states, democratic or otherwise, had their key figures, their own dominant personalities, acknowledged leaders who possessed the wealth, expertise, or sheer 'personality' and prestige to get things done.

CHAPTER THREE

Elitism by Selection: Byzantine Bureaucracy

If we make the not unreasonable assumption that very rarely in any society is there enough for everyone, it follows that communities must either share the little they have on a more-or-less equal basis, the sort of thing that frequently happens in simple pre-industrial societies, or goods – and presumably other benefits – must be allocated on the basis of selection. Distribution can be made according to a number of criteria, birth, class, age and so on, and not least on the basis of some kind of valued expertise. In pre-industrial societies, especially of a complex type, this usually meant the specialisms of designers, craftsmen and artisans. It particularly meant the literati, the scribes, the educated, who looked after the administration of affairs, in short, the bureaucrats without whom the whole system would grind to a halt. If anything, this is even more true of modern industrial society. Whether we like it or not, the very complexity of modern government and business organizations requires – though they do not always *get* – smooth and efficient administration.

The very term bureaucracy now has somewhat pejorative overtones. It connotes a superfluity of overpaid officials and inept clerks beavering away anonymously and perhaps indifferently in flimsily partitioned offices. Above all, it suggests – possibly a little unjustly – slowness of operation, clicking machinery, rules and forms, and above all red-tape. And yet much of this activity, modernity finds indispensable. In the social sciences, the term bureaucracy has certainly been overworked. One modern authority defines it as 'a centrally directed, systematically organised and hierarchically structured staff devoted to the regular, routine and efficient carrying out of large-scale administrative tasks according to policies dictated by rulers or directors ...' (Kamenka: 1989, p.157). This echoes the 'ideal-type' or model bureaucracy elaborated by Max Weber many years ago. For Weber, an idea-type was not a representative or typical type, nor was it an average or extreme-instance-of-the-case type, but a 'pure' type insofar as it is just a mental construct. The ideal-type corresponds to an idea, not to reality. It is constructed by abstracting certain elements of empirical reality and – depending on the bias of our interests – forming these into an inherently coherent system. As convenience-constructs, models are necessarily simplifications of the real world. As such, they provide a limiting case with which actual social phenomena can be compared. An ideal-type is simply an analytical tool, so it follows that many such models can be constructed in relation to the same phenomenon. Weber fully recognized that no models are 'true' or 'untrue', only useful or not so useful insofar as they help us to arrive at some understanding of social events.

Because Weber's ideas are so fundamental to the issue in question, perhaps we should consider them in a little more detail. His ideal-type of bureaucracy involves other theoretical issues which we should note, namely his views on rationalization, types of authority, and social differentiation. Weber saw the world as becoming more and more ordered or, as he termed it, 'rationalized'. Governments were becoming increasingly centralized, and business enterprise more subject to planning and control. And he regarded the growth of bureaucratic organization as a key feature of this process. Related to these ideas were his views on authority. He proposed a typology of authority consisting of:

- *traditional authority*, where authority is validated by custom and long-revered social norms,
- *charismatic authority*, where authority is vested in a leader, by virtue of his office, or, more typically, his personality, and
- *legal-rational authority*, which is characteristic of developed societies, and is inextricably linked to the function of élites.

These categories are not mutually exclusive, and obviously overlap in particular instances. For example, Nazi Germany had a charismatic leader whose regime had its own totalitarian rationality, but which also made an atavistic appeal to native or 'folk' norms and values.

As far as social differentiation is concerned, Weber took exception to what he regarded as Marx's rather narrow views on class. Instead, he proposed a three-tier conceptual scheme of class, status and power. His idea on *class* was similar to that of Marx though with more emphasis on 'life chances', that is, access to scarce resources that determine differences/similarities in one's personal biography. Life chances are related to social mobility, opportunities that are made or sought to improve one's position in the social hierarchy through wealth, marriage, social achievement, and so on. *Status*, on the other hand, while often linked to class, is very much bound up with honour and social esteem, and may have nothing to do with wealth at all (for example, certain religious functionaries actually make a virtue of poverty). *Power* is closely associated with both class and status, and implies the ability to carry through one's intentions – perhaps against resistance – by force or coercion if necessary. Weber thought of power mainly in political terms, in other words, in terms of élites of one kind or another.

Weber saw ideal-type bureaucracy as a type of organization governed by certain principles on whose features we can elaborate:

1. Officials have fixed duties, and the authority to carry out assigned functions (although the means of compulsion at their disposal was strictly limited); their conditions of employment are seen as legitimate and governed by clearly defined rules.
2. Every official's responsibilities and authority are part of an hierarchy of authority.
3. Officials and other administrative employees do not own the resources necessary for the performance of their assigned functions, but they are accountable for their use.
4. Official business and private affairs are strictly separated. In fact, the *im*personal nature of bureaucratic organization is considered to be one of its principal virtues.
5. Offices cannot be appropriated by the incumbents as though they were private property, but an office, once established, tends to continue. (In practice, of course, offices were often bought and sold, for example Roman tax-gathering concessions where lessees frequently exceeded and abused their mandate; not that the Roman authorities worried too much as long as they were paid their dues.)
6. An educational system facilitates the training of experts to take up their position in the existing hierarchy. It is thus a meritocratic system which includes special examinations. This may be an indication of democratization in that all social strata are theoretically able to qualify for office. (Again, in practice, the system may work to favour certain strata only, for instance, in Imperial China, mandarins' sons were given preferential treatment, though by the fourteenth century this privilege was also bestowed upon military officers' sons who were given a special quota of places.)
7. Those that are ruled cannot replace this bureaucratic apparatus because it rests on the basis of expert knowledge (always a problem for revolutionary governments who have 'purged' the previous administration).
8. A money economy, though not essential, Weber saw as very important to a highly developed bureaucracy. The economic surplus that was gathered as income in complex (often riverine) pre-industrial civilizations such as Egypt, Mesopotamia, and so on, made possible the establishment of treasuries and officials to operate systematic budgets to maintain the state. This, in turn, brought

increasing centralization of funds and concentrations of power which necessitated new allegiances and dependencies. So, for example, in many earlier societies, a soldier once owned the implements of his trade, whereas in developed systems he is supplied from central arsenals. Thus his affiliations to district, city-state or whatever are overruled by a new allegiance to a central authority.

9. In industrialized societies, technology brings an elaborate division of labour which is conducive to bureaucratic systems of administration. The rational organization of free labour is a particular characteristic of capitalism.

10. The relative permanence of an administration – especially in modern societies – is aided by its command of the storage and retrieval of information, all of which has boundless possibilities for the problem of control.

Bureaucracy, then, is very much a feature of mass societies, although not invariably so. This applies as much to democracies as to autocracies and oligarchies of various kinds. Wherever systems are centralized there must, of necessity, be some form of bureaucratic organization. Bureaucracy certainly tends to minimize the differences between 'Capitalism' and 'Socialism', as both present a very similar organizational face. Indeed, bureaucracy may actually become more extensive and thus more powerful with the levelling of social and economic differences, as they did after the revolutions in France and Russia. This point is made particularly well by Milovan Djilas concerning Yugoslavian communism under the late Marshal Tito. Implicit in his criticism – and he writes as a communist – is that the state merely substituted one form of stratification for another. Djilas argues that communist states are not based on the favourite Marxian dictum concerning proximity to the ownership of the means of production, but to proximity to the nexus of power (Djilas: 1957). In such circumstances, the lesser bureaucracy may act as a convenient buffer between the people and the Party machine, as in earlier autocracies they often functioned in a similar way in relation to the autocrat and his subjects. (Note that in the 'Great Terror' trials in Soviet Russia in the 1930s, the élite – many of whom were executed or exiled to Siberia – were blamed, often by respected intellectuals who could not bring themselves to believe that either Stalin or the Party could be at fault.)

In capitalist systems, bureaucracy may tend to strangle private-profit enterprise with its customary proliferation of rules and regulations. It may also both generate nepotism and similar forms of corruption, and/or encourage 'investment' in a Party machine as happened with the industrialists in Nazi Germany, or – for that matter – the brewers in the United Kingdom who are known to have made generous contributions to Conservative Party funds.

Weber contended that bureaucracies welcome a poorly-informed Parliament. This could also apply to the ruler himself. After all, a monarch's edicts have often been 'derailed' by administrative experts as with Frederick of Prussia and the proposed abolition of serfdom. It can also apply to a well-informed *demos*. Even when the people are the so-called masters of the situation, as in Classical Athens where there was no bureaucracy, public opinion could be manipulated by a skilful and articulate élite. Perhaps 'the rule of the people' is always something of a meaningless abstraction.

Before we look at a particular form of bureaucratic organization, there are two further disadvantages worth considering. In given circumstances, bureaucratic systems can lead to a *realignment of the focus of responsibility*. This is very evident when a regime collapses and is supplanted by another. Someone has to be blamed for the actual or supposed injustices perpetrated by the failed or defeated government. Only in this way can the new regime justify its takeover of power. In a very general sense, we see this in British politics after a General Election where one party has been supplanted by another. The country's deplorable condition is invariably ascribed to the mistaken policies and overall mismanagement of the previous government which will have been much-maligned during the run-up to the Election itself. Condemnation of Party A will be accompanied by high-sounding, but suitably qualified, promises from Party B. But when the new government is installed it will inherit the same efficient (or otherwise) administration as before. The bureaucracy is left virtually unblemished to serve its new masters.

A variant of a more extreme kind can be found after the fall of the Nazi regime in Germany in 1945. Key figures in the regime were rounded up, and many – though by no means all – who were held to be responsible for war crimes were tried by the courts. But although about ten per cent of the German people had originally been affiliated in some way or another to the Party, Nazis suddenly became unsurprisingly scarce. It was as though hardly anyone had ever heard of the Party and those that had, had predictably protested their deep anti-Nazi sentiments. More to the point, the blame for the war, the atrocities, the Holocaust (for which only a tiny minority have ever been prosecuted) was 'them', those that were in charge, those that led the German people astray. Hitler and his cronies were those who were really culpable; the ordinary German had been incapable of doing anything about it. Gerald Reitlinger expresses it well when he writes of the SS being the 'alibi of a nation' (Reitlinger: 1981). When the Nazis were defeated, many of the officials who had served the regime were reinstated – after all who else had the know-how to run the country? And the well-tried industries, Krupps, Bayer, Siemens and I.G. Farben (who made the Zyklon B for the gas chambers) and the like were soon back in business. The old bureaucracies were there to serve another élite.

Complementarily, another problem with bureaucracies is that they can lead to *a complete diffusion of responsibility*. This is something that hardly needs to be laboured. When any enquiring individual is confronted by the infuriating anonymity of the Tax Office or some other monolithic organization such as the British Departments of Health and Social Security or Department of Education and Science, his temerity will commonly be rewarded by complete frustration. Out of the multiplicity of minions who work there, let him find any *one* that is responsible for his problem, or even knows that he actually exists. Like it or not, it is impartial, dispassionate considerations of this kind that are said to give bureaucracies their impersonal efficiency. The trouble is that the more bureaucracies succeed in eliminating the personal, emotional and the irrational from their official affairs, the more de-humanized they become.

One further issue: in the 'trade' there is some debate as to whether bureaucracies should be seen in structural or historical terms (Kamenka: 1989, pp.73–5). The structural approach emphasizes the need of societies to solve certain essential tasks, such as public works, the collection of revenues and especially the problem of defence. A more historical orientation lays stress on the specific cultural contexts in which the particular bureaucracies have to operate. It is assumed that these singular socio-political factors will determine the kinds of administration that are necessary to any given sets of circumstances. Obviously, these two approaches are complementary, and can be illustrated from our brief study of Byzantine civilization.

The history of Byzantine civilization is traditionally dated from AD 330, the year that Constantine, the new master of Rome, completed the five-year project of having the small but strategically placed city-state (*polis*) of Byzantium transformed into the fortress city of Constantinople (modern Istanbul). The original city-state situated on the Hellespont (Dardanelles), gateway to the Black Sea, is believed to have been founded by Greeks from Megara in the seventh century BC. The Greeks came to regard its harbour as a vitally important factor in their attempts to protect their corn supplies which came from the lands around the Black Sea. With the demise of Greek ascendancy, and the predominance of

Rome, Byzantium still remained a relatively modest city until Constantine, who was seeking a site for an administrative centre for Rome's Eastern empire, realized its very real advantages. His ambition was to create a capital that would rival Rome itself. He introduced Roman law, built and stocked libraries and museums intending that his new capital should become a centre of art and learning, but – in very many ways – its culture remained obstinately Greek. Constantine wanted to popularize the minority Christian faith by which he felt he had been helped to power, although now matter what faith any of his citizens followed, it was his intention that their main focus was on the divinely-approved Emperor. With characteristic incongruity, Constantine also initiated the citizens to some of the more questionable aspects of Roman life, notably 'bread and circuses', the customary palliative for mob unrest.

The subsequent history of the city, until its conquest by the Ottoman Turks in 1453, was as chequered in its own way as that of Rome itself. In 395, with the power of Rome very much in decline, the city of Constantinople, now well-established as the capital of the Roman East, became severed from the Western Empire which was now suffering increasingly from periodic barbarian invasions. Eventually Rome was forced to succumb in 410. Constantinople too had to deal with similar incursions, especially from the Vandals, and eventually arrived at the anomalous solution whereby barbarian generals and mercenaries were engaged to defend the Empire against other barbarians, particularly the Huns. During these early centuries, the general situation in Byzantium was not helped by the divisions caused by persistent theological disputations. It seems as though as soon as one heresy was dealt with, or one doctrinal question resolved, others arose. Eventually, in the sixth century, one of the Eastern Empire's greatest rulers, Justinian, together with his singularly ambitious wife, Theodora, went some way to restoring a semblance of stability to affairs.

Impregnable as the city was believed to be, it was still beset by would-be conquerors from the north (the Avars) and from the east (the Persians). Despite these, and the periodic famines and occasional earthquakes, the city continued to survive, although early in the seventh century internal dissension resulted in an unpopular *coup d'état* and the subsequent takeover by a new dynasty. What looked like a new beginning actually ushered in one of the darkest phases of Byzantine history. When the Empire was weary of war after repelling its known enemies, it was set upon by a new power from the south. Hordes of fervent Muslim tribesmen ravaged the Middle East from the mid-seventh century onwards. They crushed Sassanid Persia, captured Jerusalem and invaded Syria and Egypt. They then moved westwards to Spain and the

Balkans, but were held at Constantinople (677). The city was saved by its seemingly unassailable walls. The eighth century too was taken up with yet more wars against the Arabs, including the great siege of 717–18, and with the interminable bloody squabbles within the hierarchy itself. The ninth century was no exception, although then the enemies were the Bulgars and the ascendant Muslim Saracens. Revolt and regicide continued to be among the favourite pastimes of the upper echelons of Byzantine society, and in 867 a slave boy – who was probably a court catamite – murdered his benefactors and became emperor. Under his rule and that of his immediate descendants (misnamed the Macedonian dynasty) the Byzantine Empire reached the peak of its power and magnificence.

In addition to the monarchy, the two great institutions of the Byzantine state were the Church and the military. The monarchy, as we have seen, was often subject to *coups* and internecine squabbles, and the Church was likewise riven by acrimonious controversy, but the military – by no means immune to dissention – had to provide the bulwark against the state's many enemies.

No state can withstand every assault, and decline can be traced from the early years of the eleventh century when Constantinople was ruled by a series of weak and ineffectual monarchs. Corruption became more widespread, and very gradually areas of the Empire were taken over by other powers, especially the Normans. In retrospect, the turning-point of Byzantine fortunes was possibly their failure to meet the challenge of the Seljuk Turks in 1071, a people that had already overrun Asia Minor and who came, not out of imperial ambition, but simply to ravage and despoil, leaving wastelands in their wake. The Crusades too, launched ostensibly to free Palestine (Israel) from Muslim control, came as a mixed blessing to Constantinople. The Crusaders had similar aims to the Byzantines *vis-à-vis* the Muslims, but some of their leaders obviously coveted the city for themselves. They helped to repel the Turks, yet indirectly exacerbated the Eastern Empire's relations with the West. Trade suffered as other states came to compete with Constantinople in terms of commercial enterprise. Consequently, the Empire came to rely more heavily on Italian, especially Venetian maritime assistance in both its mercantile and military activities though – as it turned out – not always to its advantage.

The strife within the royal household did not improve as the Empire grew weaker. In the late twelfth century, the Emperor Andronicus, who had seized the throne by assassination, grew impatient with the influence of the Italians, and initiated a massacre of their merchants within the city. This kind of despotism couldn't last, and mercifully he only reigned for two years. But the Venetians had the last word. In 1203, a Crusade that was destined for Palestine was diverted, on Venetian insistence, to Constantinople where there were richer pickings. The city was taken and sacked and many of its treasures that were unappreciated by the ignorant soldiery, such as its priceless store of ancient manuscripts and works of art, were destroyed. The western princes, their religious 'mission' now forgotten, divided the spoils, destroyed the administration and took over the trading concessions. The Empire broke up into numerous autonomous states, and new rulers commanded a much reduced rump state still based upon the city. The standards of the new monarchy were – if anything – worse than before. Emperors came and went, some deposed, others murdered. The rot could no longer be arrested.

Like nature, power deplores a vacuum. The leaders of a flourishing Serbian state were now threatening Constantinople, but the real danger in the Middle East of the fourteenth century was the Ottoman Turks who took much of what had once been part of the Eastern Empire. Constantinople, almost incomprehensibly, was able to withstand the pressure for the best part of a century, perhaps partly because the Turks also had problems further east with the Tartars. But once Tartar expansion had begun to falter at the beginning of the fifteenth century, Turkish hopes revived, and under their Sultan, Mahomet II, they successfully besieged the city in 1453. Under Turkish domination, Byzantine civilization, as such, effectively came to an end.

The very longevity of the Byzantine state, according to one notable authority, 'was almost entirely due to the virtues of its constitution and administration. Few states have been organized in a manner so well suited to the times ...' (Runciman: 1975, p.61). What is, in fact, so surprising is that it survived at all considering its paucity of really competent rulers. If we are looking for the secret of its success, there is little doubt that its viability was largely attributable to the efficiency and dedication of its bureaucracy. Yet, to a large extent, the bureaucracy was at the mercy of the ruler in the sense that he (only very rarely was the ruler a woman) had the authority to change the composition of the bureaucracy. The Empire was an absolute autocracy. The ruler made the ultimate decisions. Ministers and officials could be dismissed at will. The ruler controlled all legislation, all finances and all military affairs. What is more, the Emperor was also head of the Church. He could convene Councils of eminent theologians to discuss contentious doctrinal matters and, if necessary, pronounce a resolution to the issue.

However, the monarchical system was elective; his right to rule had to be approved by the Senate and the Army, and (theoretically) the people; on occasions, public clamour worked wonders. If a ruler proved to be incompetent or very unpopular, his continued rule could be disputed, and a successor put in his place. There was thus a *de jure* constitutional check on his absolutism, but in practice there were all sorts of variants. For example, the Emperor had the power to 'co-opt' other Emperors to succeed him, and sometimes several Emperors reigned at any one time. Indeed, by the tenth century, an admired military leader might become an Emperor-regent by marrying into the royal family. And if a usurper claimed the throne, and he had the power to enforce that claim, his 'election' could be legitimized on a *post facto* basis. On the other hand, there were limited religious sanctions that could be brought to bear. The Patriarch of Constantinople, the city's leading churchman and the Emperor's nominee, could require certain assurances from an Emperor-elect, usually that he would promise to observe and safeguard the sanctity and traditions of the Church. There was, of course, always the possible threat of excommunication if these vows were not kept, but experience has shown that such threats – whose efficacy was, anyhow, quite unprovable – were not always recognized, and might well be ignored. However, it always paid an Emperor to hold – or, at least, declare that he held – orthodox religious views. Life was much easier that way. After all, in theory, we are dealing here with a particular kind of theocracy, however much the history of the ruling house would seem to belie such a view.

The Senate, which was at its most influential in the sixth and seventh centuries, was quite unlike its early prototype, the Roman Senate in that it was a large, amorphous body of prominent people, consisting of all present and past office-holders and people of rank above a certain level, together with their descendants. Although its power was not clearly defined, it did represent the views of the upper, advantaged classes of the state. It is quite clear from the records that relations between the Senate and the monarchy were not always that harmonious, but even when the Senate lost much of its power, it did retain a certain symbolic importance.

The administrative machinery of government was quite complex. Courtiers and officials were carefully graded according to the criteria of birth and function. When the Empire was at its peak – and, for simplicity of analysis, that is what concerns us here – there were eighteen ranks, the three highest of which were reserved for members of the imperial family. Also included within this ranking system were those of the patrician class who might or might not have specific administrative duties. The senior court of officials were also the chief administrators, and the most important of these was the Master of the Imperial Chanceries who was responsible for running the entire machine, and took orders from no-one but the Emperor. He was personally answerable for the sovereign's safety and this meant authority over the imperial guard consisting largely of Normans and 'barbarians' (that is, soldiers of Russian or Norse origins).

In this he was assisted by a Lord Chamberlain who was not uncommonly a eunuch. He also had charge over the Byzantine equivalent of a secret service which employed a veritable army of spies intent on rooting out any suspicion of disloyalty or subversion. In the eighth century, for instance, eight Emperors were deposed in the space of 21 years. Obviously, special vigilance was essential. He also acted as foreign secretary which again necessitated the recruitment of large numbers of informers both in neighbouring states and in the outer reaches of the Empire. It is estimated that in the Eastern regions alone there were some 10 000 at work in this vast intelligence network, which must have been a considerable drain on the exchequer (Rice: 1967, p.86).

Rather more important than the Senate for all practical purposes was the Cabinet. It really constituted a special body of high officials, chosen by the Emperor, to advise him on any matters concerning the Empire. As time went on, and the Empire was becoming more under threat from external invasions, the military came to be disproportionately represented by the addition of admirals and praetorian prefects. It is interesting that, regardless of the august nature of this body, every member was obliged to stand during the deliberations. This was actually a special favour, as it was usual for people to prostrate themselves in the presence of the Emperor, a practice known as *proskynesis* introduced by Alexander the Great after the fashions of ancient Persian court protocol.

At its height, the Empire was sustained by a very carefully graded hierarchy of officials, each with their own particular dress and insignia of office. The majority were poorly paid, but senior officials often sported large estates and lived in some style. Praetorian prefects were appointed to govern the main regions (prefectures) into which the Empire was divided. They did not control the military garrisons, but they were responsible for the upkeep and payment of the troops, a charge which was obviously levied as taxes from the populace. They also had jurisdiction over the district sub-divisions (*themes*), and could appoint or dismiss their respective officials who had charge of the fiscal, commercial and legal affairs of their districts. As the Empire diminished in size, so many of the *themes* came under the control of petty autocrats, nominally owing allegiances to the Emperor, but in fact rulers of semi-autonomous states. There were, in addition, city prefects (*eparchs*) – almost like town mayors – who were responsible, especially in Constantinople, for the judiciary and the maintenance of law and order.

The legal system of the Empire, although amended in various ways by different rulers, particularly the Emperor Justinian, remained essentially based on the old code of Roman law. Under Justinian's rule which ended in 565, North Africa, Italy and southern Spain were temporarily recovered from the Slavs and the Persians, and a vast system of fortifications was begun. Administration of the provinces was tightened and the law more precisely codified. Indeed the Justinian Codex is still highly respected by jurists today for its elements of jurisprudence. Admittedly, its prescriptions and those of later rulers may strike us as somewhat barbarous, especially considering that they were drawn up by ostensibly religious men. But then the cruelty of disfiguring and maiming was obviously not within their particular range of sensibilities. There were civil courts and ecclesiastical courts, though these eventually merged to become regional courts on which both church dignitaries and laypeople could be represented. The highest court, the Imperial court, was the ultimate court of appeal, and its decisions were regarded as final. The compositions of these courts changed over time, not least because of the charges of corruption and peculation that were made particularly in the later days of the Empire.

A somewhat novel feature of Byzantine society – although it was prefigured in the rivalries that characterized the Roman games (*ludi*) – was the division of the city into Blue and Green factions. It may have begun as a geographical phenomenon, but it developed into a kind of lifestyle cult with all sorts of social ramifications. Each faction recruited from different sections of the community; and their rivalry, which seems to have been quite divorced from class considerations, had ecclesiastical, commercial and certainly political implications. They could also be mobilized as a police force and as a militia during emergencies, an expedient which was not always to the city's advantage, especially in times of dangerous social unrest. They were sometimes involved in riots which threatened and sometimes actually overthrew the government. But, menacing as they could be, they persisted until the end of the Empire. As with the earlier Romans, this form of factional division also had a recreational dimension. Each had their own athletes together with their often unruly supporters competing in the games – a central feature of Byzantine life.

The Emperor and his court could not, of course, exist without two fundamental prerequisites, the continued strength of the economy largely based upon overseas trade, and the maintenance of an effective military force made up of a navy and a regular army plus militia and mercenaries. Most of the work of the Byzantine bureaucracy was therefore necessarily concentrated on the viability of these institutions.

As in the Rome of earlier days, one of the principal tasks of the state was to keep the masses happy, and this meant keeping the masses fed. Much of the wheat had to be imported, either from the Black Sea area or from the famed granaries of Egypt. There were issues of free bread to the people, so wheat and its distribution was a crown monopoly. Where people were deemed to be able to purchase bread, it was often sold at a subsidized price. This was controlled by a body of officials who were charged with ensuring enough supplies were received and stored ready for the winter, that the allocations were equitable, and that abuses were kept to a minimum. If, as did happen on occasions, these supplies from the customary sources dried up, it was not unknown for the city to confiscate the harvests of farmers in their subject territories elsewhere (for example, Thrace and Macedonia). When times were bad, free distribution of corn and other goods had to be cut, but the royal largesse was still usually maintained for the customary festivals.

The people were subject to a range of taxes administered by treasury officials. They included land taxes, import and export taxes, and taxes on certain kinds of consumer goods especially wine. Entrepreneurs had to pay licences to set up businesses, and there was meticulous government control of all commercial life including the fixing of prices and wages, and the issuing of permits for overseas travel and trade. This all required a more and more extensive bureaucracy which had to be financed and this, together with the unsurprising extravagance of the monarchy, meant that despite the vast revenues collected, the state was often faced with economic crises. The exactions were sometimes so onerous on the rural population that they refused to submit. Again the state drew on the experience of their Roman predecessors. They employed tax contractors who were inclined to force extra payment from the citizens while returning to the government the minimum agreed. This way everyone was happy – except the public. Despite all the abuses, however, the system survived for a thousand years largely due to the industry and conscientiousness of the vast majority of its officials whose very livelihood depended on the continued viability of the state.

CHAPTER FOUR

Elitism by Race: Europeans and the Indians of Colonial America

One of the most famous observers of indigenous Americans, George Catlin (b.1796), was educated as a lawyer but gave up the bar after two years in 1823 and began a lifelong career as an artist and amateur ethnographer. In 1831, he commenced a series of expeditions to various Indian tribes, spending long periods with them, learning something of their languages and culture, and making copious notes and sketches which later became the basis of several books and his 'Indian Gallery' collection of paintings and artefacts. In his diary he records that contrary to the advice of friends – and, by implication, the wishes of his family – he set out in 1832 to visit the 'Far West ... with a light heart, inspired with an enthusiastic hope and reliance that [he] could overcome all hazards and privations of a life devoted to the literal and graphic delineation of the living manners, customs and character of an interesting race of people who are rapidly passing away from the face of the earth'. He said that he was 'lending a hand to a dying nation who have no historians or biographers of their own ... [and was] snatching from a hasty oblivion what could be saved for posterity ...' (Catlin: 1989, p.3). He went on to say that even in his day the term of their (Indian) national existence had nearly expired, and that some three-quarters of their country had fallen into the hands of Europeans in just 250 years. He roughly estimated that some 12 million had died in this period, 'victims of whiskey, the small-pox, and the bayonet....' (Catlin: ibid).

These diaries, letters and portraits are a poignant reminder – if we need to be reminded – that these peoples, whom Catlin and so many others have seen as noble and proud, were already near to extinction, a state of affairs brought about almost entirely by the policies and practices of insurgent Europeans. Whether or not we can justly refer to this as genocide, is still an open question. Much depends on how the term is defined. Generally, we may say that genocide can be:

1. *Accidental*, where certain infectious diseases such as measles, chicken-pox and so on (to which invaders have a relative immunity, but which kill entire populations that do not enjoy such immunity) are introduced – a common occurrence in the days of colonization, particularly in Polynesia and the Americas.

2. *Incidental*, that is to say, as part of a larger policy of repression where conquered peoples are overworked and underfed and generally ill-treated in ways that rapidly reduce their numbers, a practice that was particularly characteristic of the Spanish in their exploitation of the Americas, or
3. *Methodical*, where there is a systematic attempt to liquidate entire populations, effectively a policy of outright genocide which was found pre-eminently in Nazi-dominated Europe (Carlton: 1992, p.146).

Does the wholesale depletion of the Indian tribes of North America come into any of these categories? The answer, insofar as our studies take us, is both yes *and* no. Let us take the last-mentioned possibility, of *methodical liquidation*. First, the evidence suggests that there were undoubtedly massacres on both sides. For example, in 1854 there was a misunderstanding over quite a trifling issue between some Lakota tribesmen and a detachment of soldiers under a Lieutenant John Grattan. This escalated, quite unnecessarily, into a full-scale confrontation. As usual, pride and honour were at stake. No one was prepared to back down, and what came to be known as the Grattan Massacre occurred. There was only one survivor of this inexperienced command, and even he died two days later. Grattan himself was found with twenty-four arrows in him, and was only identified by his pocket watch. But against this must be set the many occasions when the military or the settlers took often unjustified revenge on the Indians, such as the massacre of the Cheyenne at Sand Creek by the Colorado Volunteers because these tribesmen and their allies (the Arapaho and the Commanches) had made the migration routes unsafe for settlers in the 1860s (Taylor and Sturtevant: 1991). In the settler expeditions to Utah early in the nineteenth century when the Europeans were in conflict with the Shoshones there was ill-treatment of white prisoners, the burning of military forts and settlements, and, on the other hand, extensive destruction of Indian villages. Many deaths were caused by the enforced treks of Indians to new lands, often in the most appalling conditions. But there seems to have been no overall or concerted policy of extermination on the part of the whites which compares with, say, the Turkish persecution of the Armenians at the time of the First World War or the Nazi 'final solution' programme in relation to the Jews during the Second World War or, for that matter, Saddam Hussein's more recent atrocities against the Kurdish population of Iraq.

The first category, *accidental extermination*, on the other hand, is much more relevant. Probably more Indians died of 'European' diseases than military action. For example, it may well be that smallpox, accidentally introduced by white fur-traders, was the principal cause of the near obliteration of the Mandan peoples of the Upper Missouri. Indeed, it was probably the same frightful disease that spread to neighbouring tribes and killed some 25 000 within less than six months (Catlin: 1989, p.490). The other category, *incidental extermination*, is also relevant, but in a rather different way from that in which it is usually conceived. The Indians of Middle and South America were often worked to death in various ways by their Spanish overlords, particularly in mines, sweating for silver and gold. In North America, this was not the case; in fact, it could be argued that here the indigenes died of neglect. Regardless of well-intentioned schemes for their 'betterment', most Indians initially objected to reservation life far away from their homelands, and certainly did not always take kindly to white attempts at re-culturation. After the mid-nineteenth century, except for the Cheyenne/Sioux uprising and occasional forays against the whites by Apaches such as Cochise and Geronimo in the far South-West, many Indians, though disgruntled, settled down as best they could on government-allotted lands, and were only too prone to ease their resentment with cheap, white-supplied, whiskey.

Are we to conclude from this that the gross ill-treatment of the North American Indians was fundamentally the result of the European perception of the 'native'? If we can, are we talking of racial or cultural factors – or both? And if so, how did these affect policy? It is necessary to look briefly at these matters, and tackle the question of definitions and distinctions, and then go on to examine the issue in terms of two quite different tribal groups before arriving at certain conclusions.

Race is a very emotive issue; and making distinctions in terms of race is fraught with definitional problems. These come in two main forms, the first being differentiation between one group and another on the basis of a *variety* of possible criteria, religion, language, colour and so on, usually to their detriment, and this we shall term *racialism*, a phenomenon which seems to be as old as society. It can certainly be seen in archaic societies such as Egypt and Mesopotamia, and in classical societies such as Greece, although rather less so among the Romans except in their attitudes towards northern European peoples. *Racism*, on the other hand, is a relatively modern phenomenon. By this we mean the irrational belief – though often perceived as rational – in the debased qualities of certain groups or peoples, and the utilization of these beliefs as a basis for discrimination. The key difference between these terms is that racism as an ideology holds to a belief in the *inherent* – and ineradicable – inferiority and superiority of certain peoples (for example, Jews *vis-à-vis* Aryans). Such beliefs were undoubtedly present in the Americas in earlier days, and is one of the reasons why seclusion in reservations was thought more suitable for the indigenes than assimilation into 'civilized' society. But having said that, we will find that even this belief, and its operationalization as a policy, was subject to all kinds of qualifications and anomalies in practice, mainly because some Europeans were unsure as to whether the differences were really due to race, or whether it was more a matter of culture.

The race question can be studied from a *biological* standpoint, but this has a limited value because, scientifically speaking, race has very little meaning where so many people are impossible to classify. This does not apply so much to the American Indian situation, but even here there were important differences in physical characteristics. Catlin (1989, p.83) even toys with the idea that the Mandans might be descended from a Welsh colony founded by one Madoc/Madawe because so many of them bore a remarkable resemblance to Europeans. Race can also be looked at from a *psychological* point of view, that is in terms of personality formation, and from a *structural* perspective which is concerned with power relationships and their consequential pressures and tensions. But for the purposes of this discussion what concerns us is the *social* significance of race, that people attach meanings – real or assumed – to physical and cultural differences in ways that make them socially important.

A cautionary word: racial issues should not be confused with those that arise from the desire for political power. Problems in modern South Africa, for instance, are often interpreted in racial terms, but arguably they are really about political power. The whites have now abrogated their position of authority but few doubt that the conflicts between blacks will remain. Similarly, in the colonial period in the USA Indians became involved in the Europeans' struggle for dominance, some supporting the English and others the French. It had nothing to do with race or colour, or – for that matter – culture. It was white against white for control of the land. The Indians naturally thought they could play one lot of Europeans off against another, but they could never have benefited no matter who won. Neither should conflicts over religious ideology be confused with those arising from nationalist aspirations. The seemingly interminable troubles in Northern Ireland are a classic example of political ambition disguised as a desire for national self-determination.

The ancestry of the American Indians can almost certainly be traced to Asiatic peoples who crossed the Bering Strait in a series of migrations between 15 000 and 5 000 years ago. Other intrepid voyagers probably also arrived from the Pacific before the time of Columbus, and it is now generally assumed that some expeditions of Norsemen also found their way to the Americas in pre-Columbian times, though without any significant impact on the Indians they encountered. Whether there were any visitors from the Old World in ancient times, Egyptians or Phoenicians or whatever, is still very much a matter of speculation, although it has to be admitted that there is some uncorroborated evidence to this effect (see Irwin: 1964).

The term 'Indian' was first used by Columbus who thought that he had discovered the East Indies. (This text abjures the term 'native American' – all people born in the USA are native Americans.) It has come to denote all American natives, although we now know that we are dealing with a very wide variety of cultures using about two thousand quite distinct languages (Driver: 1964). Despite this, it is clear that the vast majority of Indians, regardless of culture, belong to the same general physical type. These cultures ranged from nomadic tribesmen to those who subsisted by hunting and fishing, to others who had created advanced cultures in Middle and South America such as the Maya, the Incas (technically the term used for the ruling family) and the Aztecs. The level-of-culture issue highlights the fact that the mode of subsistence tells us little about the nature of the people themselves. There was no direct correlation, for instance, between cultural levels and what we should regard as behavioural norms. 'Low' culture Plains Indians might be very restrictive and set a high moral tone, whereas intermediate agricultural communities such as the Tupinamba in eastern Brazil were cannibalistic, and the 'high' Aztec culture had the most extensive system of ritualized human sacrifice known to history.

By the time the Europeans arrived in appreciable numbers in the sixteenth century, the Indians occupied the entire American continent. They had settled to a life which seems to have been relatively unchanged for several hundred years. The advent of diverse Europeans – all in conflict with each other, and all seeking a share of the spoils – changed the face of the Americas for ever. Yet it would be a mistake to think it was Europeans who alone brought unrest and hostilities among the indigenes, although in various ways they did exacerbate them. There had been long-standing enmities between many tribal groups for as long as anyone could remember. But these tend to be overlooked or, at least, minimized in retrospect by those writers who, understandably, feel a genuine sympathy for the Indians because of the way in which they were treated by the in-comers. For example, it is highly speculative to write that 'the traditional Indian attitude of dignity and aloofness, which stood in marked contrast to the noisy, quarrelsome behaviour of the whites with whom the Indians came into contact, seems to have derived from a training that began in the indulgence shown by Indian parents to faults committed by their young ones .... The Indian parent did not attempt to establish his authority by harsh or compulsive means ... [avoiding] attitudes or actions which might antagonize ...' (Washburn: 1975, p.13).

This is the sort of causal sequence that is quite impossible to verify. It would certainly not apply to all societies that tended to display similar characteristics of aloofness and independence, some of which were ascribed by observers to extremely *strict* discipline (for example, the ancient Spartans).

Or again, consider the rather dreamy romanticizing which portrays Seneca youths who wandered 'the woods or onto a mountain to commune with the spirits, wait for a vision, ponder [their] dreams' in order to establish 'a relationship with the supernatural', in short to find themselves (Wallace: 1972, p.38). This was written about what was a part of the uninstitutionalized puberty rites of one of the leading tribes in the Iroquois' Confederacy which, as we shall see, was not only expansionistic but could also display extreme cruelty to its enemies, sometimes torturing its prisoners for days on end, also as part of their religious rites (see also Wallace: 1972, pp.104–7).

In general, it can be said that the American Indian believed in reciprocity. A gift or favour demanded in return something that was socially equivalent – something that was both psychologically and economically satisfying to the original giver. This very much extended to land, an issue which has long vitiated white–Indian relations. It follows that there was also a belief in retributive justice, a wrong had to be repaid *in kind*. With no independent judiciaries this meant personal or family vengeance in accordance with tribal custom. Extreme measures might also be taken in intra-tribal disputes, such as the instance in South Carolina in 1748 when the Cherokees demanded the death of a fellow Cherokee for the murder of an Englishman, and threatened to destroy his whole settlement unless he was brought to justice. Needless to say, he was duly executed by members of his own clan.

We can see something of the same attitudes in the Indian approach to war. The like-for-like principle is still evident. Warfare was very much a fact of life, and young males were reared – at least in most tribes – to be warriors. But it is highly doubtful if war was conducted primarily in the interests of 'ecological harmony' although it may well have functioned – in John Collier's extravagant prose – 'towards the shaping of a virile, structured, unafraid, truly noble personality' (Collier: 1948, p.102). Inter-tribal warfare was limited, relatively small-scale, and not usually attended by gratuitous massacres until warfare with the whites began. It was often little more than attacks on villages by enemy raiding parties, sometimes for spoils, sometimes to redress some wrong or to avenge a previous attack. This was very common as many tribes had their own sworn enemies. When the Europeans came, war often involved massacre and counter-massacre. Indians butchered white settlers who were felt to have no right to their lands, and this was often followed by the revenge of the military, not infrequently on a disproportionate scale once the Europeans had mustered enough force. Until that time, the initiative lay with the Indians who carried out devastating attacks on their settlements. For example in 1622, 350 out of the tiny English population of Virginia were killed. The English declared perpetual war on the natives; and again in 1644, Indian resentment reached a peak and there was another massacre when 500 whites were killed, though by this time their population had increased fourfold and was beginning to thrive.

Ironically, the coming of the Europeans, if anything, actually increased warfare between tribes and for many, changed their forms of political organization. There were two main reasons for this. The first was the pressure of land appropriation by more and more white settlers which forced tribal groups to move and thus infringe the rights of their neighbours. The confiscation of Indian lands by whites was the most frequent cause of discontentment and strife. In the very early days, there was enough land for everyone and the land allotments were agreed by negotiation. Tribes were often willing to cede land for much-prized trade goods. But with the greater influx of immigrants, the situation changed. The Europeans could usually find some convenient justification for changing the original terms of the agreement to their own advantage. The second reason was the fact that during the period of the colonial wars, various tribes took different sides, hoping – vainly – to improve their standing, and therefore enhance their prospects when their 'patrons' were eventually victorious, a hope that never materialized.

One particular cultural feature associated with war which ideologically set the Indians apart from the Europeans was what the whites considered to be an inordinately superstitious attachment to the spirit world. After a death – especially a violent death – many Indians had an inexplicable fear that the departed wanted to take others with them into the next life. This may account in part for such practices as the feud and the torture of prisoners as a form of ritual retaliation. In some tribal groups, especially those with a strong hunting tradition, many believed in personal guardian spirits who mediated their 'messages' through fasting (and visions?) and particularly dreams. The rather different beliefs of the agriculturally-orientated tribes, on the other hand, reflected the specific social needs of the typical agrarian society (Underhill: 1971, pp.10ff.). When foreign cultures undermined these beliefs, there is evidence that the societies themselves began to disintegrate. Indeed, the emergence of Indian prophets *after* colonization had begun, and the later introduction of such rituals as the Ghost Dance, can be seen as attempts to revitalize the indigenous traditions.

As a more bizarre demonstration of faith in their conception of the Great Spirit and also as an exhibition of potential and actual warrior prowess, we have only to look at the extraordinary rituals of the Mandans, one of the Plains societies. George Catlin describes in graphic detail how groups of braves ran skewers through their arms, legs and chests, and were then suspended by ropes so that pain from the wounds would be apparently unbearable. Yet this was done without protestation or complaint, even with a kind of serenity. After this, there were further rituals in which the 'victims' were compelled to run a specified course in their already weakened state, watched by other members of the tribe. And, if this were not all, were expected to offer one or more fingers for ritual amputation, though not those needed to use their bows for hunting and war. For this, there was no anaesthetic and no follow-up medical treatment; their recovery was left to the Great Spirit. Such practices seemed incomprehensible to Europeans. Little wonder that the white 'bearers of civilization' saw the indigenes as that much different from themselves.

Another distinguishing feature of the Indians was their attitude towards trade. Traditionally, trading seems to have taken place with little thought of gain. There was a great deal of barter, but much trade took place in the context of ceremonies and diplomatic exchanges. At first, tribespeople tended to disparage the profit motive of the whites, and many refused to engage in the bargaining and haggling that characterized European trading procedures, at least with those who they considered their friends. But European influences became all-pervasive. The Indians quickly appreciated the superiority of the white man's artefacts, especially the advantages of metal weapons and utensils, and, not least, the gun for hunting and warfare. These commodities were highly desirable and they were often willing to barter at disadvantageous rates to obtain them. They learned quickly. Soon they were trading them on, at an appropriate mark-up, to people of other tribes. Many were also attracted by European dress, and some observers have noted that by the mid-eighteenth century, Indian women were often virtually indistinguishable from their white counterparts. It was this growing dependence on such 'necessities' that increasingly 'bound the Indian in an ... often vulnerable relationship with the white man' (Ewers: 1958, p.70).

The advent of the Europeans, then, with their new commodities, particularly arms, their exploitative mentality, and their direct and indirect destruction of much of the wildlife on which Indians depended for survival, led to a serious disruption of normal inter-tribal economic and political relations. Some tribes were only too willing to accommodate the white man and his ways, while others were rightly suspicious of European motives and tried to distance themselves from white influences. Yet others, with eyes to the main chance, were happy to indulge in a little entrepreneurialism and acted as middlemen in trading activity, especially in the burgeoning fur-trade. Most difficult were probably those who were carefully selective in their relations with the whites: those such as the Iroquois and, further north, the Blackfeet, who remained generally aloof, but who were pleased to trade for guns with which to tyrannize neighbouring tribes. (It's rather like some modern non-European societies who want to take advantage of Western technology, especially arms technology, but do not want also to be influenced by Western values and culture.) It is probably true to say that although many mourned the loss of the traditional culture, some tribes – particularly of the Plains – reached the peak of their power, albeit temporarily, as a direct consequence of white influences (Washburn: 1975, p.80).

Although Europeans, by and large, acknowledged that in theory the Indians – especially the large confederacies – should be regarded as independent powers to be treated according to European protocol, in practice things were quite different. They took advantage of their own increasing numbers and developing power to ensure that the tribes remained submissive and, where possible, co-operative. Forts were built in Indian country, admittedly often at the request of tribes who required protection from their enemies, and gifts were given by the 'Great White Father' to his 'children' to ensure compliance, including specially stamped medals which helped to maintain the fiction of mutuality and equality. True, some lands were purchased from the Indians, but not infrequently territory was just claimed by right of conquest. Respect for the Indians had its limits: even the laudable policies of the Quakers in Pennsylvania were neutralized by the influx of new non-Quaker settlers, who took it as unquestionable that they had proprietary rights to the land.

The more powerful Indian nations resisted white pressure, but the smaller tribes could do little else but comply. Among the larger confederacies were those of the Creeks in the south-east and the Iroquois in the north-east. By 1770, the Creeks were perhaps the most powerful confederacy in North America, and were in a position to negotiate on favourable terms with the Europeans. But although they had previously taken sides with the British against the Spanish, as their strength increased they tried to maintain their independence by adopting a principle of neutrality. Even when the French virtually destroyed their near neighbours, the Natchez, they still stayed their ground (much to the chagrin of the British) and actually incorporated some of the remnants of the Natchez people with their confederacy. Their neutral stance, however, was confined to the contending European powers, not necessarily to other Indian tribes. They continued to attack other Indian tribes, and then receive them into their confederacy, a policy of absorption that stemmed from pre-colonial times and which actually increased with the disruption caused by the advent of the Europeans.

The Creeks were protected on most sides by buffer zones occupied by other tribal groups including their traditional enemies, the Cherokees. Their most vulnerable area was to the east where their own depredations had brought them into direct contact with the British with whom they developed amicable trading relations; although they had particular problems with the aggressive settlers in Georgia who had little or no respect for Creek territorial rights. The Creeks were anxious for European goods, but little else. Attempts were made by sympathetic Moravian missionaries to establish schools but there was little response from the tribespeople, and they remained without missionary influence throughout the eighteenth century. Their policy of neutrality extended to political and cultural independence: '[they] wanted neither close political involvement nor educational or religious influences from the Europeans' (Spicer: 1969, p.20).

At the height of their power in the 1770s, the Creek council meetings numbered in excess of 10 000 people drawn from numerous settlements, and as a confederacy they could muster some 6 000 warriors for war. There was no paramount chief or king as in, say, certain African societies. Having no-one with absolute authority, agreement was reached by consensus, with each settlement making its own autonomous contribution, and each having its own war-leaders. As was common among pre-literate societies, there was no codified system of law or regulations, but there was an underlying unity which was effectively disguised by the frequent independent actions of individual tribes. In the 1780s, when the French were no longer serious contenders for power in the south-eastern area of the embryonic United States, the Creeks found it difficult to maintain their policy of non-involvement, especially in the face of increasing white incursions and the raids of rival tribes, especially the Cherokees and the Choctaws. With the threat of disintegration, they had little choice but to put themselves under the protection of the new United States government, even though their confidence was eventually to be betrayed.

The confederacy, as a system of organization, had largely come about as a response to the European invasions. It was one way in which the Indians could hope to defend themselves against the now dominant culture. The trouble was that there were just too many 'incidents' such as those perpetrated by 'white savages', notorious frontiersmen who needed little excuse to murder Indians when they had the chance, humiliating them first, and sometimes decapitating them afterwards. Eventually, the Creeks rebelled, and their attacks on the settlers called forth the most violent denunciations from the white politicians. Andrew Jackson offered to lead Tennesseans against 'those deceitful [and] unrelenting barbarians' (quoted by Sheehan: 1973, p.206). The writer, Joseph Doddridge, who took an extreme ethnicist view, spoke of the 'ghastly wounds of the tomahawk and the scalping knife of the savage ... the shrieks of the victims of the Indian torture by fire ... the yells ... of savage warriors rioting at all the luxuriance of vengeance ...' (ibid., p.236). He expressed his horror at how the Indians killed at random, with women and children all suffering the same fate. Foetuses were even torn from the bodies of murdered women and stuck on poles as trophies of victory. A moderate and knowledgeable observer of Indian life, James Adair, who defended the natives against the more scurrilous accusations of the whites, suggested that Indians could not really solve their own disputes without war, and that they cultivated torture as an art. He asserted that once a contest began, Indians had no sense of where to stop: 'their thirst for the blood of their reputed enemies is not [easily] quenched' (ibid., p.195).

Thomas Jefferson, who can hardly be classified as a redneck, became disillusioned by the civilizing process, such as it was, and in the face of Indian violence, maintained the the Creeks ought to be driven beyond the Mississippi, adding that their barbarities really merited extermination. After the Creeks were defeated (Creek war 1812–14), there was considerable pressure on the Indians to conform to government policies. But the tribespeople were still restive. In 1825 they murdered a chief for ceding land, even though it appears that he was only acting as an intermediary in a treaty that – admittedly – was in the interests of the whites. In his tour of the conquered territories in 1826–7, the head of the Indian office in the War Department, Thomas McKenney, a moderate, also endorsed the need to remove the Creeks to new lands in the west. He found them dispirited and hungry, 'habitually drunk [with a] total abandonment to vice' (ibid., p.252) and he pleaded their cause on the grounds that they were more degraded than any other tribes. McKenney felt that only their removal would facilitate the civilizing process. For him, re-settlement was tantamount to a philanthropic programme, but for the majority of settlers it was the only sure way of appropriating the Indian lands. The settlers were supported by the government who maintained the fiction that by purchasing the Indians' traditional homelands, the natives were participating in a mutually advantageous deal. It was rather reminiscent of Engels' observation that in social democracies the people are persuaded to cut their own throats.

Another confederacy, that contrasts interestingly with the Creeks, was that of the Iroquois. Whereas the Creeks tried to adopt a neutral stance *vis-à-vis* the whites, the Iroquois in the north-east were noted – and feared – because of their belligerence. The Iroquois' confederacy, sometimes known as the League or Five Nations (later six) may also have developed because of the disruption brought about by the coming of the Europeans. Being in the area of some of the earliest contacts, the Iroquois were in conflict with the colonists almost from the beginning. Their hostility was a byword, and the Europeans came to respect their warrior prowess, and the apprehension they inspired among many of the surrounding tribes.

The Iroquois comprised about 30 000 people consisting of the core organizers of the League, the Onondagas, plus the Mohawks and their satellite, the Oneidas, and the largest nation, the Senecas, together with their lesser partners, the Cayugas; these were joined to make Six Nations by the Tuscororas in 1722. They reached the peak of their power and influence between about 1640 and 1700. During that time they succeeded in subduing all other tribes from New England to Illinois, including a related, rival tribe, the Hurons. Indeed, it is estimated (Spicer: 1969, p.26) that in the period 1650 to 1750 they probably massacred more of their fellow Indians than the British and the French combined. Their militancy brought them into conflict with the French, who themselves were in an on-off war with the British – which was really an extension of their European war. The Iroquois controlled New York and areas to the west and south, while the French held the Saint Lawrence area and the British the Atlantic seaboard. Iroquois dominance was such that the French tried for forty years to conquer them, and then failed to draw them into an alliance. The British, who treated them as a foreign power, then managed to enlist their help against the French in their struggle to control the north-east, particularly in the French and Indian War (1756–63).

The Confederacy was much more formally organized than that of the Creeks, and was therefore that much more capable of unified military action. Each clan was represented and the entire system, which was run on strictly hierarchical lines, was unique among the contending Indian tribes. The Onondagas, the 'fire keepers' of the League called the yearly councils at which the laws were rehearsed and differences resolved. The council included fifty chiefs, and when one died he was replaced by another chosen by the senior women of the respective matrilineal clan. Unlike the Creeks, who tended to absorb conquered tribes, the Iroquois kept them in a state of subjection and designated them 'women' with no voice in the affairs of the League. Warfare was not primarily about territory although, again with the arrival of the Europeans, the economics of the fur trade became increasingly important. The frequent inter-tribal engagements were more about personal prestige, the taking of scalps, and the capture of prisoners for torture. Women and children were often slain on the spot, but male prisoners were either adopted into the tribe, possibly to take the place of someone who had been killed, or they were tortured, sometimes for several days, after which death came as a welcome release. Stoicism, the brave endurance of pain, was one of the highest virtues. It is known that prisoners were often taken back to the villages for public torture which might include the pulling out of fingernails, tearing the flesh off victims' fingers, then perhaps amputating them to wear as necklaces, and so on. One recorded incident of the mid-seventeenth century was of an Iroquois taken prisoner by the Hurons who was meticulously tortured by fire during which time he spoke and sang to his captors. Mercifully, he died after only twelve hours (Taylor and Sturtevant: 1991, p.236). True, the increase in inter-tribal rivalry may well have been occasioned by the activity of the whites, but the *method* of warfare and the treatment of captives, partly for the entertainment of the home village, appears to pre-date the arrival of the Europeans, and seems to have been part of a well-established tradition.

Atrocities were committed against the Indians by the Europeans, and the practice of scalping, for example, became characteristic of war in America – perhaps as a substitute for taking heads. Both whites and Indians took scalps, and colonial authorities encouraged it by paying bounties for these trophies. The flexibility of frontier life allowed the white man to maintain forms of civilized life and at the same time to act like a savage. When the tribes proved intractable, the whites sometimes employed devastating force, particularly in the face of Indian atrocities. In retaliation for the Indian massacres in Virginia, for instance, in 1622 and 1644, the settlers actually instituted a policy of extermination. The New Englanders reacted similarly against the Pequot Indians who were eventually brought to near extinction by the French.

Such incidents were common at the time (Sheehan: 1973, pp.203–10), and were all part of a concerted effort, primarily by the settlers to encroach upon Indian lands, a process that continued well into the nineteenth century. The official response to this was, on the most generous interpretation, ambiguous. The authorities often displayed what appears to have been a genuinely sympathetic attitude towards the plight of the Indians but, at the same time, professed a kind of impotence to override the local regulations. To take one example, by the 1830s we find the Creek Indians complaining of hundreds of unauthorized whites pouring into their territory and marking out plots for habitation: 'we are weak and our words and oaths count for nothing, justice we don't expect ... [but] we expect murders to be more frequent .... They daily rob us of our property; they bring white officers among us, and take our property from us for debts that were never contracted .... We are made subject to laws we do not understand; we never know when we are doing right' (contemporary document quoted by Foreman: 1972a, pp.107–8). Poorer Indians were destitute and starving, but the government said it was unable – or was it unwilling? – to countermand the wishes of the state (of Alabama) authorities. Even when the Indians appealed for the President to keep his solemn promises to protect them from the incursions of the whites, political and economic expediency obviously proved too strong, and the government repeated these specious promises, and actually did nothing. Delegations got nowhere, and one local military officer was even reprimanded for acting on those promises and trying to get the intruders off the Indian lands. When yet another treaty was signed and the government promised 100 000 dollars in compensation, white traders descended on the Creeks only too willing to exploit their weakness for whiskey and sundry gimcrack articles. All the government seemed to be able to do to soothe the justifiable grievances of the Creeks was to assure them that, if they gave up their lands, there would be homes 'in the West'. Meanwhile, the Indians were being hopelessly defrauded. A contemporary wrote, '[the] Indians [are] seized and put in gaol, and compelled to surrender all they have, either their land claims or their property ... certain men [are] fleecing the Indians [and] have obtained bonds for all the valuable lands ... and one half the Indians are not aware that it is for their lands ...' (quoted by Foreman: 1972a, p.117). Perhaps the speculators needn't have bothered. Ultimately, the vast majority of the Indians were forcibly removed from their lands after the Creek war in 1836 and settled in Indian territory (Oklahoma).

A very similar fate befell an offshoot tribal grouping of the Creeks who had migrated southwards to Florida. These people, the Seminoles, were extremely difficult to deal with because they inhabited dangerous swamplands that were really only penetrable with the help of experienced guides. Many expeditions had tried, but with very limited success. The authorities did their best to set up meetings on their own ground to which delegations of Seminole chiefs were invited. But nothing succeeded. The military even argued on practical, economic grounds that as the tribespeople had settled in territory that could not be exploited for agricultural purposes by whites, the Indians should be left where they were. The government was half-hearted about this, and wanted to rationalize their predetermined policy of removing the bulk of the Indian population to the west. The Seminoles were promised new homelands, but all to no avail. They wanted to stay, regardless of the inhospitable nature of their environment – something the authorities found difficult to understand.

Eventually, the military commander in charge resorted to treachery and made the fatal mistake of violating the flag of truce under which a delegation had approached him. Instead of negotiating with the Indians, he had them arrested. The Seminole war which followed lasted six years, cost the whites some 1 500 lives and cost the authorities around twenty million dollars. Needless to say, it caused untold suffering to the Indians who, although defeated, could still not be persuaded to leave their homeland. They refused all sorts of financial inducements from the government, and it wasn't until some twenty years later when whiskey and disease had done their worst that more Seminoles left the Everglades to join their brother Creeks in the areas designated for them.

We can see now that the white administration in America, first under the colonial powers, in this case the British and French in particular, and then that of the United States, which was essentially no different, was vitiated by the problems of *perception* and then of *policy*. How the Indians were 'seen' by the Europeans helped to determine policy, but this, in turn, was modified by practical exigencies in specific circumstances. Indians were perceived to be in a state of 'savagery' or 'barbarism'. For some, they were like animals, with unrestrained animal passions; for others, they were more like nature's children who, as yet, were not amenable to reason, while to other observers Indians were just uncivilized and uncultured. Opinion, therefore, differed as to whether or not they were ultimately redeemable. Some felt that their practices – especially their often undisciplined brutality – clearly testified to their inherent degeneracy. Religious conversion was probably out of the question according to some missionaries, especially those of an extreme Calvinist persuasion. Indians were therefore regarded as a kind of devil's brood who had been delivered into the hands of the whites for judgement. On the other hand, others held that even these savages were not beyond redemption and that it was not 'the nature of men, but the education of men which makes them barbarous and and uncivil .... Change the education ... and you will see their nature ... greatly rectified and corrected' (quoted by Axtell: 1981, pp.44–5).

Indians were admired for their physique: 'straight bodied, strongly composed ... merry countenanced ... broad shouldered ... well thighed ... handsome grown legs ... and small feet'. They were also envied for their relative freedom from disease, that is until they were introduced to smallpox, measles and so on. Indeed, the descriptions of some Indian women – especially the young and nubile, 'plump and round ... and soft and smooth as mole-skin' (quoted by Axtell: ibid., p.154) – betray more than a passing interest in their sexual possibilities. Infringements did occur but, to be fair to the colonists, their penalty for rape of an Indian woman by a white man was death, although this was sometimes commuted to a whipping and expulsion from the colony. And if a white woman enticed an Indian man, she too might be flogged and forced to wear a 'badge of sin' on her sleeve.

However, there is little doubt that, justified or otherwise, one of the most critical issues was that of the Indians' almost exquisite capacity for torture – both their own and that of others. Disgust at such practices was so intense that, at times, governments actually offered bounties for Indian scalps. Even such a well-known Puritan as Cotton Mather, who had preached that the Europeans had 'very much injured the Indians' by teaching them European vices, also insisted that the Indians of Maine should be punished because they had 'horribly murdered some scores of our dear countrymen whose blood cries in [our] ears ...' and appealed for 'vengeance upon our murderers' (quoted by Axtell: ibid., p.312). From time to time, these early settlers seriously contemplated genocide and in certain cases – as with the Pequots – it was actually carried into practice. Exasperation was such that in Virginia in 1711, £20 000 was voted for the extirpation of all Indians, whether friends or enemies, but this was not implemented with any consistency. Sweeping as such policies were, the actual practices were mercifully localized and spasmodic. Enforced migration, which entailed considerable suffering, became the only organized programme.

There were obvious failures on both sides. Even the noble efforts of the Quakers to establish amicable relations with the Indians in Pennsylvania did not succeed in the long term. They were neutralized by the influx of non-Quakers into the territory, and ultimately the pacifistic Quaker policies – little understood by the Indians – failed to protect the settlers from tribal raids. The real issue was not addressed: why were the Europeans there at all? They occupied the land as though it was theirs by right because the indigenes were not worthy to possess it. Such actions invited reprisals.

Some very early explorers in the sixteenth century, including Columbus himself, had written about the Indians' way of life, and had been aghast at many of their practices. Their nakedness and 'lewdness' (they were accused of incest and of prostitution with the Europeans), and particularly cannibalism, aroused indignation and incomprehension. Europeans noted their ferocity and generally uncivilized behaviour, and agreed on their marked differences from people in the Old World. As we have seen, the Indians were variously described as 'savages', 'infidels' and 'barbarians' which terms were regarded as synonymous with 'heathens': 'creatures who had their eyes of their understanding as yet blinded .... Their priests ... no other but such as our own English witches are .... They serve the devil for fear, after a most base manner, sacrificing sometimes ... their own children to him ...' (quoted by Berkhofer: 1978, p.19). There was a marked tendency to see all Indians as alike, and to judge them – quite understandably – in terms of their failure (or even incapacity) to measure up to European ideals.

With time, some of these views became modified, and whites began to see certain positive virtues in Indian culture, and came to judge the natives more generously and not simply in terms of their deficiencies. This came with an increasing sympathy with the notion of cultural pluralism and – more dubiously – the growing intellectual climate of moral relativism. But the old prejudices died hard. Were settlers of a more puritan persuasion projecting their own sins or secret vices upon the Indians to justify their extermination, as some writers suggest (for example, Berkhofer: ibid., p.27)? This is an extremely debatable idea. Perhaps the most remarkable thing about these negative perceptions of the Indian was not their 'invention', but their persistence and perpetuation over such a long period of settlement.

Our second issue, that of policy or – more accurately – the conflicts of policy, arose partly out of the problem of perception, and partly for reasonably transparent political and economic reasons. The governments in question were naturally anxious to pacify the occupied territories in one way or another. We have seen that they tried various measures: force, bribery, often worthless treaties and a general assortment of chicanery, all with modest degrees of success. On the credit side, they and certain of their agents were genuinely sympathetic to the natives, and really had their welfare – as well as their own – at heart. There could have been a general policy of extermination, but although there were massacres in particular tribes there was *no concerted programme* of genocide to make room for white colonization. Really, there didn't have to be. White technology and development was such that they had to win in the end. Their superiority was immediately recognized by the natives who naturally wanted the best of both worlds, European artefacts *and* the retention of their own cultures. But again, it couldn't work. The ways of the Europeans, who were better housed, better fed, better educated, and better medicated, had their own appeal. Everywhere that has been touched by civilization, as we know it, has responded; with all its drawbacks and disadvantages, no significant indigenous culture has remained unaffected (see Gellner: 1963).

The War of Independence brought the colonial phase to a close, but disputes over territory continued under the newly constituted United States. The particularly shameful aspect of this was that the land allocations that were agreed virtually ignored the claims – or indeed needs – of the native population. By and large, the Indians were treated with cynical indifference even by the new democracy. Promises were made, and treaties signed, often with well-intentioned solemnity. But when white interests demanded it, the authorities inexorably turned the screw so that the Indians were left with practically nothing. For the survivors there was little to do but to assimilate. The Department of Indian Affairs which was set up in 1824 spent millions of dollars on alleviative and educational programmes, but to little effect. The traditional economy was destroyed, and Indian culture survived only in run-down reservations and pathetic demonstrations for tourists (Carlton: 1992).

CHAPTER FIVE

Elitism by Moral Right: Europeans and Early Colonial Contacts

The study of the cultures of tribal society – the assumed province of social anthropology – has been, perhaps unjustly, accused of naïve realism, a charge that might well be levelled at history generally. Some theorists have called for a dissolution of the linear narrative, a break with the repressive ideology of story-telling (Jameson: 1987), a distrust of so-called 'facts'. The suggestion is that the recounting of events by missionaries, travellers, administrators and the like may be little more than dangerous illusions, mere texts charged with self-interested ideologies. Such writings are held to lack objectivity – if, indeed, objectivity can ever exist. They are said to be replete with ambiguities and inconsistencies, notoriously so in the case of white interpreters of black culture.

The plea for a more theoretical orientation is not without some cogency. But does this mean, as other authorities have argued, that we must deny 'the possibility of any kind of social science?'. And, by extension, does this imply that we are moving towards 'a world in which all life, all history, all society is really ... [just] ... a text? In which all representation is arbitrary?' (Comaroff and Comaroff: 1991, p.14). The *reductio ad absurdum* of this position is that there is no material reality behind the cultural world; all we have are 'texts' that are open to an infinity of different readings. Anything may turn out to be anything – or nothing at all. Of course, all social action is open to a variety of interpretation, but does this mean – as some postmodernist critiques of social science appear to do – that all theoretical orientations are simply strategies 'embedded in institutions [which themselves are] implicated in and productive of particular configurations of power and knowledge?' (Hebdige: 1988, p.186).

Any discussion of colonialism demands that we give due consideration to the indeterminacies of meaning and action, and especially that we see 'power as a many-sided, often elusive and diffuse force which is always implicated in culture, consciousness and representation' (Comaroff and Comaroff: 1991, p.17). But to suggest that this is all historical texts are about is either to become consumed by a kind of hubristic heuristicism which is convinced that we alone hold the keys to understanding or, failing that, it is to become imprisoned in an epistemological hall-ofmirrors in which nothing is true but illusion. History – agreed, with serious qualifications – must be taken at something like face value. Without it we have nothing. We just have to begin with the assumption that we are dealing with at least *some* facts, and that the meanings given to these incidents, statements, interpretations and so on, especially if they are considered and perhaps contemporary, have *some* approximation to 'truth', and must therefore be given due credence (as in the previously cited *History of the Peloponnesian War* by Thucydides).

The underlying problem here is one of intellectual and moral relativism. Must cross-cultural value-judgements always be misjudgements? Or are such value-judgements legitimate and unavoidable? And is the problem one of understanding or merely one of language? (Jarvie: 1972, pp.40–3) If we maintain that the beliefs of those in ancient and primitive cultures are false, we are necessarily indulging in a form of intellectual and moral élitism. And yet when we are faced with the seeming irrationalities of witchcraft, primitive medicine, rudimentary cosmology and the like, are we not justified in thinking that metaphors, analogies and political correctness apart, Western ideas may not be infallible, but they are certainly nearer the 'truth' – whatever that may be?

Narratives and interpretations of colonialism in specific areas must take account of colonialism generally. And this, in turn, raises the issue of the pervasiveness and potency of Western culture as a whole. Some writers (such as Gellner: 1963, Parsons: 1977, Roberts: 1986) strongly suggest that the whole process of change that has taken (and is taking) place in what we term the Third World has a kind of exponential inevitability. The adoption of Western cultural forms is seen as irrevocable, a process which generates its own momentum. Its suitability and directionality are not seriously questioned. Such developments are regarded as 'progress', advances which need no validation. This is something which has been contested by some non-Western theorists (for example, Edward Said, who teaches in the West). These developments are seen as self-evidently 'good' in that people everywhere want to be better educated, better medicated, better housed and so on, and industrialization and the recognition of the supremacy of Western cultural and political forms alone will bring these benefits.

This general process, usually (and somewhat euphemistically) called convergence, has actually been more of a takeover than a merger. In the eighteenth and nineteenth centuries particularly, it was largely a matter of exporting ideas, especially moral ideas, and of obtaining supplies of much-needed resources and more ready markets for cheaply produced European goods. Of course, in the 'scramble for Africa' and elsewhere there was also an obvious status dimension; any state that was anything in Europe had to possess a colony or two. In the present century, it has been taken for granted that Third World states will follow the Western model and they have developed bureaucracies, money/market systems of exchange, the requisite technology, and embryonic industrial procedures on broadly based meritocratic principles. There is often also what passes as a democratic or quasi-democratic political order, the implication being that the non-democratic will eventually become democratic because there is an incipient egalitarianism everywhere, and that consensus will out.

That this is now happening – to a greater or lesser extent – in one-time colonial territories is not seriously in doubt. There is a notable growth in the idealization of science, and this extension of technical knowledge has led to a greater variety and division of labour. This, in turn, has had a knock-on effect on gender and family relations. The breakdown of extended families has, so it is said, 'produced' family structures that are more conducive to modern technological societies. In the economic sphere, we are also witnessing greater capital accumulation and a wider variety of investment and commercial applications. As in the West, there is a general value-consensus that what is happening is good *in itself*, and the pursuit of common goals of production and consumption have become fundamentals of the new ideology of these reborn societies. The implicit assumptions are those of:

- *commonality*, a basically similar pattern underlying the whole industrializing process,
- *practicality*, in that Western forms of rational action are seen as the only mode of economic behaviour – a mode that has been empirically (and successfully) validated, and
- *moral worth*, in that the adoption (or imposition?) of these forms – despite certain manifest disadvantages – is, on balance, something that is universally beneficial for mankind.

There have been a number of cogent objections to these assumptions. Are Third World societies *really* aping the West? Are the similarities merely superficial? Japan, for example, has many of the trappings of American materialism grafted on to an age-old culture. So how 'Western' is Japan? We note that Japanese kinship structures are slow to follow the West and the traditional values of mutual family support and loyalty to elders still exist. But for how long? Will these too decrease with time? (But note the rapid changes in Hawaii, South Korea and Taiwan.) Both East and West are now largely dominated by technological and economic imperatives. Galbraith (1972) points out how even occupational structures, especially service sectors and white-collar professionalism, have altered with changing economic conditions. Perhaps what lies behind many of these objections and reservations is the perennial problem of determinism, the fear that individual freedom is now threatened by material forces that can no longer be averted.

How has this all come about? What antecedent factors in the colonial past contributed to the present dilemma? Perhaps we can trace some of these if we look broadly at colonialism, concentrating on one or two areas to see how moral as well as economic ideas have changed the faces of continents. Let us take Africa first of all: the 're-discovery' of Africa dates from the Portuguese expeditions in the fifteenth century, although Arabs were trading in certain coastal areas, partly for slaves, at least 400 years before this. By the sixteenth century, the Portuguese were presumably anxious to emulate the profitable example of their Spanish neighbours in the New World. These were followed by the Dutch and the English, with the English assuming from the Portuguese the dubious distinction of being a major carrier in the slave trade. The English established a series of chartered companies to exploit the new found possibilities of the 'dark continent', and soon other European states wanted a share of the action: the Danes (from the seventeenth century) who later sold out to the English, and the French, who settled mainly in the west. The competitive rush to secure African colonies, eventually formalized by the Berlin Conference (1884–5), did not really get under way until the nineteenth century when the Spanish, Germans and Belgians also began hustling for the territorial leftovers. It was from this time that the colonizers, not content with their toeholds in the coastal regions, began to venture into the largely unknown interior. At first, a consul and a couple of assistants might well constitute the government of a Protectorate, but as these administrations were enlarged, troops were moved in to consolidate the gains. Inevitably, this resulted in disputes with the neighbouring territories ruled by rival European states. The British and French differences in the 1880s concerning the Upper Nile, for instance, led to Lord Kitchener's reconquest of the Sudan which resulted in the death in battle of some 20 000 Sudanese. In some ways, however, the most serious conflict was that between the British and the Boers in South Africa and Matabeleland/Mashonaland (present day Zimbabwe) which dragged on through the 1890s, and was not finally resolved until the surrender of the Boers in 1902.

By the outbreak of the First World War in 1914 all these powers, except the Dutch who were settled but not yet dominant in South Africa, had effectively carved up the whole continent into their respective spheres of influence: '... all Africa was gripped in the vice of a false stability which is the earmark of every successful colony. Boundaries were established, chiefs were appointed, and "responsible" leadership was ensconced in foreign-dominated political systems' (Bohannan: 1966, p.118).

The ideal colony was one that was economically self-supporting. The less its administration cost the taxpayer at home, the better: 'Whether it produced much or little, whether its people progressed fast or slowly, whether its economic development was undertaken by the people themselves ..., the colonial government, or by European settlers or mining companies, all these things mattered little in comparison with how nearly the budget could be balanced ...' (Oliver and Fage: 1969, p.196). White officials were often given niggardly sums with which to run their affairs. Colonies were meant to be profitable, but often they turned out be an acute financial drain on the conqueror's exchequer. The Italian colonies in North and East Africa are a case in point, although in this instance there were all kinds of anomalies. The north, Libya (Tripolitania and Cyrenaica), was treated much better than the east (Eritrea, Somaliland and, after 1935, Abyssinia), and extreme cruelty was mixed with a genuine caring paternalism (Mack Smith: 1979). Generally, no matter which colonial power we are speaking about, the only thing that brought reinforcement of troops and increased grant aid was a military crisis of some kind. Once colonies were firmly established and, in some cases, viable entities, that aid began to diminish. Left to their own economic devices, some rulers were not particular how the monies were found. Taxes had to be raised, but not everyone was like Leopold of Belgium, whose personal rule in the Congo led to such incompetent administration and loss of revenues that he employed a treacherous and ill-disciplined force of native soldiery to enforce arbitrary levels of tax collection. The appalling atrocities which ensued were such that international opinion was outraged, and he was compelled to hand over his private empire to the Belgian Government in 1908.

Exploration of the African interior can be conveniently dated to the epic journeys of Mungo Park in the Sudan (1795–7) and René Caillié from the Gambia through the Sahara to Morocco (1827–8). But these men and many that followed were not consciously acting as pathfinders for later colonists. Their ambitions seem to have had little or nothing to do with conquest or even of commerce. Rather they seem to have been motivated by curiosity, philanthropy and – as with H.M. Stanley – an understandable desire for fame. Imperialism, at least at first, was not on their immediate agenda.

Foreign occupation was hardly welcomed by the indigenous populations but, resented as this was, it has to be set against the inquisitiveness and, to some extent, the admiration that many natives evinced regarding the newcomers. It is just here that we see the differences in the orientations of the colonizers and the colonized. The colonizers were there to take territory and materials, in short, to exploit their advantages; yet some were also there as a kind of moral enterprise. They had come to open the eyes of the intellectually blind, to bring knowledge and enlightenment. It was a mission as much as anything else. The interests of the indigenes, on the other hand, were quite different, especially in the initial phases of colonization. They were often not greatly smitten with Western ideology, but they were fascinated by Western novelties, particularly military hardware. Their concerns were not primarily cerebral or spiritual, but economic and material. It was not unusual in the early days of exploration for native dignitaries such as tribal chiefs to keep European 'visitors' waiting for several days before seeing them and when, at last, they condescended to do so, spent as much time with the explorers' guns as with the explorers themselves.

The question of the interpenetration of cultures is one of the most interesting aspects of colonization studies. New values meant new demands. The introduction of just a few aspects or practices of Western culture often had enormous repercussions on the natives' way of life. For instance, the gradual switch from traditional agricultural procedures to the growing of cash crops and the development of new industries such as mining, meant wholesale changes in the division and utilization of labour necessitated by the demands of large-scale – later international – markets. And this, in turn, led indirectly to modifications to the family and kinship structures in many societies. The role of religious ideas was also important. Missionaries from the 'West' founded schools and medical stations, and so in many ways had a profound influence on the lives of ordinary Africans.

The abiding, and perhaps irresolvable problem – what the anthropologist, Paul Bohannan, calls the 'ultimately destructive paradox of colonialism' (Bohannan: 1966, p.38) – was how to maintain control of these territories. Should they allow the Africans to run their own states? This policy minimized the distinctions between colonizers and the colonized, and was a risky though sometimes profitable expedient. Or should they adopt a more authoritarian stance which could have dangerous, counterproductive results? Although different colonizing states varied in their practices, their motivations were much the same. The French, for instance, were seemingly more haphazard in their patterns of conquest, especially in Africa, and were probably rather less rationally exploitative than the British. They gave local entrepreneurs among the settlers more opportunity to make their own way, although this may have been less to do with magnanimity than with the fact that

French bankers were reluctant to invest in an uncertain market (Davidson: 1974, p.260).

Colonization did not always come about through outright conquest. Often it was (as in the case of North America) a matter of effective infiltration, a process of settlement and treaty – though hardly to the territorial advantage of the indigenes. In 1898 in German-occupied Cameroons, the German-run South Cameroons Company, which was mainly capitalized by Belgians, received 20 million acres where it could collect rubber free in perpetuity; while the North-West Cameroons Company was given a fifth of the entire territory – and both concessions were often brutally exploited. Where wars were not fought to *obtain* the land, they were often fought to *secure* it. This is well illustrated by the experience of the British in Nigeria in the late nineteenth century. In the north of the country there were several emirates ruled by the Muslim Fulanis whom the British wanted to 'use' (as they did many Indian princes) to control the country for them, but this was not done without a struggle.

The French, who in some ways took quite an enlightened view of colonization, could be particularly unfeeling towards native workers when the situation 'demanded' it. A well known case is that of the building of the Congo–Ocean railway: 127 250 men were recruited for work on the line between 1921 and 1932 of which, according to official figures, some 14 000 died, although the actual death toll may have been considerably higher than this. Perhaps most notorious of all were the actions of the Germans in South-West Africa and East Africa between 1893 and 1907. Well documented accounts of German imperial rule show that whole tribes in both areas were decimated on the assumption that they understood nothing but force. In the South-West especially, some tribes, notably the Herero and the Nama, were reduced to a fraction of their original size. This is all now freely admitted, yet even such inexcusable behaviour should be set against the overall picture. As one authority has remarked, '... the process of imperial enclosure was more often coercive than not, and [was often] violently destructive ... [but that] should not be allowed to obscure the humanitarian and civilizing efforts of many excellent men and women, nor sully the reputation of many colonial officials and soldiers whose principal sins were no worse than Victorian smugness, ignorance, and insensitivity to the claims of pre-industrial peoples. Nor should they, perhaps above all, form any sort of reason for modern Africans to "blame their condition" only on the failings or excesses of colonialism' (Davidson: 1974, pp.270–3).

Colonialism was an attempt to implement radical changes on an often unwilling and frequently uncomprehending population. Colonial rule, in its fully developed phase, presents us with unrivalled examples of planned social change and control, the imposition of one way of life on another of a very different kind. It was often motivated by a *sense of mission*, the extension of one vision of culture to an alien people. It was expansionist and proselytizing, and even in its most well-intentioned forms manifested an ethos of what might be termed paternal guardianship. It involved a believed duty to transform a subject people, who were deemed to be inferior, to a higher type of civilization, insofar as this was thought to be possible. This, as we have seen, might be achieved either by coercion or persuasion, or (as the following will show) by heightening the curiosity of the natives about a technologically superior culture. In Africa, paramount chiefs were unlikely to be impressed by a few bedraggled white strangers who turned up at a central kraal, whereas in the Americas and in the island societies of the Pacific, the natives were vastly intrigued by what to them were great ships, 'floating islands', and they were initially inclined to treat the newcomers as gods.

Encounters with alien cultures are necessarily fraught with problems. Perception, understanding and representation are all obliged to use stereotypes. This is unavoidable; the members of one culture are bound to see others in terms of their own preconceptions. The danger, of course, lies not in their use, but in supposing that these preconceptions are adequate. Thus even contemporary accounts of such encounters by travellers, explorers, missionaries and early traders are all subject to some possible misrepresentation because their value-systems differed so widely. For example, on the Gold Coast colonialists could not readily understand why they could only *use* land but not own it. The people insisted that it all belonged to the Ashanti king who held it in trust from the gods; therefore it was not theirs to sell. The otherness of aliens was sometimes explained by insisting that they were either sub-humans, something between higher animals and imperfect human types, or simple people without civilized arts, technology or acceptable social conventions. They might be demonized as barbarians practising cannibalism and incest, or (as in the Pacific island context) admired as 'noble savages', living in a shaming simplicity which we would all do well to emulate in one way or another. Very commonly, members of alien cultures were designated as 'pagans', a term which, unlike 'primitive', had – and still has – pejorative ideological implications. It is really tantamount to 'unbeliever' and suggests, rightly or wrongly, that the religious orientations and practices of the colonialists were superior to those of the indigenes, although in some cases, notably that of the Spanish in Peru, the invaders were surprised at the many similarities in European and Inca religious rituals.

Some theorists have related such attitudes to xenophobia, the fear and distrust of 'outsiders'. In the ancient world this often took the form of apprehension about the unknown. Writers such as Herodotus repeated travellers' tales about monstrous creatures that inhabited the little known parts of the globe. In relatively modern times, such views were still with us. 'Xenophobia [was] widespread and intense, directed against stereotypes of the bloodthirsty Turk, the usurious ... Jew, and the devil-worshipping witch ... [this] helps to explain why over three-quarters of victims in the great European witch-hunt were female' (Richie Robinson in Bitterli: 1989, pp.10–11). The writer may have a point here, but when he goes on to state that 'Judeo-Christian tradition represented women as prone to sensuality and malice, and as a potential source of social disorder' he is perpetuating yet another myth. The tradition he criticizes is no *one* tradition, and was not particularly noteworthy for such sentiments. Actually, expressed distrust – or, more specifically, ambivalence – regarding the female sex is very ancient indeed, and can be found in the literature (presumably the product of men) of Classical Greece and early Egypt.

The first encounters of European explorers often set the scene, and could be indicative of things to come. Natives were sometimes greeted with gratuitous hostility, as if to let them know who was in charge. So the eminent explorer, Fernando Magellan, tended to adopt a policy of shoot first and ask questions afterwards. Similarly with the Spaniard, Luis de Torres, in New Guinea, and the seventeenth century sailor, Captain John Smith, in his investigations of the Virginia coast. Admittedly, the natives could sometimes be equally hostile, but then they had the presence of mind to doubt the good intentions of the men in the tall ships. Wherever they went, the Europeans, even when well-disposed as they often were, never forgot that their numbers were small and that they were always vulnerable to attack, so they tried to stamp their authority on the situation right from the beginning, if not by a show of force then by some form of ritual display that was calculated to overawe the natives. This compares interestingly with early contacts between Europeans and the rulers of developed civilizations such as those in India, China and Japan, where the Europeans were quite astounded by the magnificent palaces and their courts. In these situations it was the non-European rulers who were putting on a show for those they regarded as *their* cultural inferiors.

It is also well-attested that in the initial encounters with undeveloped peoples the newcomers were often regarded as gods. Travel narratives testify to the incredulous amazement of the natives in their first contacts with Europeans, whose appearance and superior artefacts seemed to indicate that they must be supernatural beings. Understandably, and a little unscrupulously, the visitors were sometimes ready to exploit these misconceptions. When the conquistadores under their leader Hernando Cortés arrived in Mexico, the Aztecs thought at first that it was the anticipated return of the gods, an interpretation that seemed to be confirmed by omens and prophecies. Then, when their deeds seemed to belie such an assumption, it was thought that they must therefore be evil spirits and the Aztecs fatalistically awaited their next moves. In other circumstances, there was native suspicion and distrust from the outset: there was no fearful resignation, but hostility. European forts in the Americas were attacked and their garrisons murdered. In these cases where retaliation often followed, contact was transformed into collision (Bitterli: 1989, pp.29–34). Such incidents merely reinforced the European impressions (prejudices?) of the general perfidy and savagery of the natives.

Disease, or perhaps one should say the exchange of diseases, was another and particularly devastating result of these contacts. Epidemics were recorded, for instance, in Mexico and Peru before the arrival of the Europeans, but the newcomers did bring with them diseases against which native populations had no defences. Because the ratios favoured the whites (small numbers of explorers and settlers in relation to large numbers of indigenes) the mortality figures for the indigenes were particularly frightening. It should be added that Europeans also died in appreciable – though not comparable – numbers of illnesses that were foreign to them, for example, malaria, yellow fever and so on, in West Africa. This 'intrusion' of disease generated a variety of responses: indigenes often saw it as a judgement of the gods which some extremist Europeans endorsed on the assumption that the native peoples were being divinely destroyed to make way for the new inheritors of the land.

Religion was a critical factor in colonization. Among the earliest settlers were usually missionaries, some of whom had a genuinely sympathetic attitude towards these 'simpler' peoples, though others regarded them as some sort of 'devil's brood' who were a very long way from redemption. Because missionaries usually took the trouble to learn the languages and to set up schools and medical facilities they were therefore frequently more successful in cultivating the indigenes than administrators or traders. In retrospect, this approach strikes us as more enlightened, but at the time the teaching they gave tended to alienate their converts from their native cultures and gave them an uncertain identity *vis-à-vis* their communities. The overall impact of missionary activity on the native cultures varied. Broadly speaking, where cultures were relatively undeveloped (as in non-Muslim Africa, much of South and North America and in the Pacific islands), missionaries were relatively effective despite the fact that many of the institutional values of the indigenes (such as polygamy) were often proscribed by their new teachers. But in societies of 'high culture' such as China and Japan, they often had only limited success until modern times. In general, however, although traditional ethnic patterns were retained in many areas of social life and behaviour, the process of acculturation continued. The élite dominant culture, with all its many undesirable features, had so many advantages that its manners and practices, and especially its technology and scientific learning ultimately proved to be irresistibly attractive to native populations (Adas: 1989, pp.32ff.). As for the Europeans, there is little doubt that their interaction with native cultures increased their own sense of material and ideological superiority.

There are probably few better examples than that of the European contacts and eventual settlements in Polynesia. What began as an attempt to find the hypothesized, but chimerical, 'southern continent' ended with the discovery of a whole series of islands which were then introduced to European culture, with questionable results. In the Society Islands, for example, perhaps the best documented of all the eighteenth century cases, the first European visitors were won over by the apparently idyllic existence of the inhabitants. On the island of Tahiti, the natives lived in a near-perfect climate (the annual range is 20°–29°C) with rich soil and good fresh water. They were relatively untroubled by disease (one particularly unpleasant skin disease was not uncommon), had plentiful and easily attained supplies of food, mainly fish and fruit, and seemed to live reasonably and harmoniously with each other. For sailors who had been cooped up on board for months on end subsisting on meagre rations of weevil-ridden biscuits and without any sexual consolations, the place seemed like paradise. The island was beautiful, the women were beautiful – and available – indeed, everything was beautiful. The diarists speak of both the men and the women as having well-proportioned bodies, light smooth skins and perfect teeth. What is more, it could all be had on the cheap. In the very early contact days, the women could be most accommodating for the price of a few ship's nails. But then this was not exactly out of keeping with Tahitian sexual norms, although Tahitians, who were monogamous, had strict rules about copulation between classes. Captain Cook, who made four visits to the island in the late eighteenth century, notes, '[they have] a very indecent dance ... [sing] the most indecent songs and [use] most indecent actions in the practice of which they are brought up from the earliest childhood' (quoted by Moorehead: 1987, p.46). What we might regard as promiscuity was almost *de rigueur* among certain classes of natives, and what was more disconcerting to the Europeans, it was done in public. As Cook records on another occasion, 'The day closed with an odd scene ... where a young fellow above six feet high lay with a little girl about ten or twelve years of age, publicly before several of our people and a number of natives. What makes me mention this is because it appeared to be done more from custom than lewdness, for there were several women present ... and these were so far from showing the least disapprobation that they instructed the girl how she should act her part, who, young as she was, did not seem to want it' (Moorehead: 1987, p.49).

Tahitians lived in extended family groups, and kinship rights and duties were organized on a patrilineal basis. Primogeniture was paramount, and families were proud of being able to trace their descent over numerous generations. There were two main tribal groups, and each was hierarchically organized. The total population at the time of contact is not known, but it is interesting that in such a relatively small and unsophisticated society, social ranking was extremely important, and embodied economic, political and religious powers. The three-class system comprised the chiefs and the leading lineages (*Arioi*), the heads of lesser lineages and their families (*Ra'atira*) and the remainder of the population (*Manahune*). The chiefs were held to possess a sacred power (*mana*) because relationally they were closer to the ancestral gods. Special gifts and privileges were given by those of lesser rank to those of greater rank, and contact between those of lesser power and those with greater power was subject to certain prohibitions (*tabu*).

The idea of *tabu* extended to various kinship categories. People of different classes did not eat together and men, who were believed to have greater sanctity, did not eat with women and children. In some instances, chiefs were thought to possess such *mana* that all their needs were supplied by attendants. As in so many relatively undifferentiated pre-industrial societies, it is virtually impossible to say where secular concerns ended and religion began. Certainly, religious imperatives were very important to the people and influenced their familial, economic and political arrangements. The Tahitians had high gods and numerous nature spirits besides the divine ancestors. They had no temples, as such, but they did have simple structures (*marae*) which functioned as focal points for some cultic activities. Ethical requirements were not enjoined by a religious system whose main features were prayer and propitiation. To the early missionaries sent to convert the islanders 'most of the native religion seemed particularly heathenish, amoral and barbarous, and [they] set about to change it as quickly as possible' (Service: 1978, p.276). *Marae* were destroyed, much of the dancing and music was banned, courtship and marriage rituals were changed, and women were induced to wear dresses. But as compensation, Tahiti was saved initially by strict Protestant missionaries from many of the depredations inflicted on some of the other islands by increasing numbers of rowdy and ill-disciplined sailors.

There was no market exchange among the people; the redistribution of the produce given to the chiefs was the only kind of exchange in operation. Likewise there could be no accumulation of wealth, mainly because most goods could not be stored, and also because living arrangements did not lend themselves to privacy or secrecy of any kind. By and large, people were underemployed, spending what time was necessary repairing nets, making canoes and fishing, and generally beautifying themselves.

After their first introduction to island life, visitors found that Tahitian society was not quite as idyllic as was first supposed. Cook discovered that a previous ship had been attacked by some 500 canoes; the islanders, like their Polynesian kin in Hawaii, could be quite aggressive, not only when the occasion called for it, but even when there seemed to be no discernible cause at all, as in the case of Cook's murder by Hawaiians as he went ashore in 1779. Shortly before Cook's arrival in Tahiti there had been a civil war between Greater Tahiti and Little Tahiti (parts of the same island) which had cost many lives including those of women and children, and caused great distress generally. It was quite common to sacrifice some prisoners of war, although Tahitians, unlike some of their Polynesian brethren on other islands were opposed to the consumption of the victims. Cannibalism may have been out, but infanticide was in – at least, among the *arioi*. The offspring of the 'royals' in Tahitian society were deemed to be children of the gods; apparently the chiefs then abdicated and became regents to the children. The rest of the *arioi*, although numerous, were childless even though they were quite promiscuous within their own ranks. This was because they strangled their own children at birth, perhaps as one means of limiting the population of what was, after all, quite a small island, though possibly also as a way of maintaining the exclusivity of their class. It is interesting that this took place among the 'aristocracy', and was not required of the more menial members of the society. Perhaps – but only perhaps – this was also a form of sacrifice or self-denial somewhat akin to the practices of the Carthaginians who believed that the 'dedication' of infants of the aristocracy was more pleasing to the gods and was more likely to elicit their favour.

It would be a mistake to think of European intentions as being entirely rapacious. In fact the instructions to Cook before he embarked were quite explicit: 'endeavour by all proper means to cultivate a friendship with the inhabitants, if you shall find any, presenting them with such trifles as they may value, and showing them all possible civility and respect' (quoted by Bitterli: 1989, p.165). The exhortations from the learned societies who financed such expeditions almost always included some injunction to treat the members of alien societies tolerantly, and as 'human creatures ... the natural ... legal possessors of the several regions they inhabit. No European nation has a right to occupy any part of their country, or settle among them without their voluntary consent' (the President of the Royal Society quoted by Bitterli: ibid.). Such instructions were both humanitarian and practical, in that the islands were so distant and dispersed, and – as far as was known – devoid of any valuable natural resources, that their exploitable value was limited. Furthermore, in the wake of the near contemporary American débâcle and the loss of the colony, it may have been considered unwise to make the same mistake again; although this did not prevent the 'scramble for Africa' in the next century.

Despite the good intentions, there was the downside. Before colonialization, the islanders had only a mild intoxicant (which Europeans said tasted like soapy water) but once stronger alcohol was introduced, as in the Americas, it wrought its potent, consolatory but destructive effects. The Polynesians were spared the massacres (some might even suggest the genocide) that attended the entry of the Europeans into some other foreign territories such as the Americas. Such depredations can be incidental, even accidental, as well as intentional. The Polynesians suffered terribly from the diseases, especially venereal diseases, that were introduced by the whites from the time of their initial contacts. Their whole economy was disrupted; though, significantly, the islands (unlike so many other colonies) were not necessarily expected to 'pay' their new overlords. But their traditional culture was destroyed for ever. As in other colonial situations, the élite culture had its benefits. It inhibited inter-tribal warfare, broke down the old – some might say undesirable – class divisions, displaced entrenched élites (for example among the Maori in New Zealand), dispelled certain kinds of ignorance (but is it better to be an unhappy Sokrates than a happy pig?), established new social and religious conventions, and gradually acquainted the Polynesians with a literate science-orientated world that they could not ultimately resist.

CHAPTER SIX

Elitism by Special Election: The Millenarian Phenomenon

The notion of a special elect, a chosen people, race or group, has a considerable antiquity, and its many manifestations – not least in its millenarian forms – have been well documented and are well known in our own times. The millennium or 'thousand year rule', is an hypothesized (or anticipated) time when current evils will be banished, and a new order of society established. This may be conceived as a supernatural or a natural order, and may be ushered in either by a cataclysmic divine act or by some form of socio-political upheaval.

Millenarian movements have appeared at different periods of history in widely different cultures. They were common in Judaism from at least the second century BC, and modern manifestations of millenarianism have been popularized by such writers as Peter Worsley, in his studies of twentieth-century Melanesian 'cargo-cults' (Worsley: 1957). The millennium may be conceived of as an *event*, a sudden – perhaps imminent – happening, or as something that develops progressively. It may be 'achieved' violently or pacifically. It may be a feature of the belief-system of some small cult or sect, or it may be something which is held to affect an entire society. Indeed, it may be envisaged as world-wide in extent, as in such very different conceptions as the *Parousia* of some religious eschatology (literally, a doctrine or theory of the 'last things') or the 'Thousand-year Reich' of Nazi ideology. It can also be particulary bizarre – and tragic – in its manifestations. In the last century in South Africa, groups of Bantu destroyed their crops and stock in anticipation of the millennium. In the 1850s, after sixty years of disastrous wars and 'negotiations' that had cost them much of their ancestral land, the Xhosa people gave way to what proved to be a strange and dangerous form of millenarian teaching. Their prophets declared that if they destroyed all their stocks, on a certain day in the near future, they would be supernaturally more than compensated for everything they had lost, and the white men would be expelled from their lands. Needless to say, the day came and went, and thousands of Xhosa starved to death. In the present century, groups of Esquimaux consumed their scarce stores and stopped hunting for similar reasons. And in some societies, massacre and suicide have been thought necessary as precursors of the millennium. In Guyana, some 400 Indians sacrificed themselves as a condition of the promise of the millennium and in the hope that they would return as whites.

Is millenarianism, therefore, mainly a religious phenomenon, or a political phenomenon, or is it a combination of both? Millenarian beliefs have always had a great appeal for the oppressed and the disinherited because they promise salvation and/or compensation for known or assumed injustices and grievances. Their function varies in different types of society: such beliefs may provide a unifying ideology for those who wish to protest against the dominant order, or they may help to transvalue the experiences of those who feel that they have no place in that order. Though their beliefs and values often represent an 'intrusion' into conventional society, believers, in attempting to promote them, may work within a known tradition. This gives their message the kind of authenticity which has an attraction for possible converts. Here we should make an important distinction between sub-cultural and counter-cultural movements. A *sub-cultural movement* works within accepted religious and political frameworks. The wish is to bring attention to some known or assumed injustice, or perhaps try to promote some particular cause. *Counter-cultural movements* are revolutionary in type. They work outside the normal religious and political frameworks. Ostensibly, they may be promoting a cause, but their intention is to remove the current system and radically restructure society. In millenarian forms, a movement may not actively try to advance any cause but its own. Some millenarian cults, for instance, take a strict retreatist stance – their élitism is bound up with their exclusivity.

Perhaps, above all, millenarian movements tend to be *utopian* in emphasis, holding out the promise of a radiant – if illusory – future in place of an unsatisfying and transitory present. Since classical times, people have been obsessed with ideas about 'golden age' pasts and utopian futures. We find this in well-known literary traditions: in Plato, for example, who initiated the myth of Atlantis (which he said originally came from Egyptian priests) and the blueprint of the ideal society in the *Republic*. In modern times, we have the work of Aldous Huxley (*Brave New World*) and George Orwell (*1984*), although these might be better described as *dys*topias rather than *u*topias. In religious traditions, so much depends on whether a movement is seeking this-worldly or other-worldly fulfilment, though it should be noted that in certain movements, for example the Watchtower Society, these may be combined in the setting-up of a future spiritual community on earth.

The millenarian mentality is characterized by certain fundamental ideas which, one way or another, apply no matter what kind of special electionism we are considering:

1. *The asumption of exclusivity*: this connotes separatist attitudes which carry with them implications of distinctiveness and superiority. This is found particularly in certain religious sects with their notions of divine favour, and esoteric cults that emphasize their own 'inner gnosis' or special knowledge which is only granted to the initiated. Not infrequently these are sectarian movements which arise within the general compass of traditional religious systems.

2. *The assumption of feasibility*: it is often believed that the past is somehow recoverable ('golden age' nostalgia) and/or that the future is therefore realizable (the utopian aspiration). These two can, of course, go together: one can assume the other. On this point, it is interesting to see how traditional Marxist and conservative philosophies of history are reconcilable, how, in fact, extremes meet. Both see the ideal in terms of some lost past; therefore the future – with suitable qualifications – is seen in terms of the past. In millenarian terms, the promise of a glorious and *attainable* future is reserved for an elect, a spiritual or political élite.

3. *The assumption of volitionality*: this does not apply in all cases, and is much more likely to be a feature of social/political movements than religious movements. It implies a certain view of human nature, and a particular interpretation of human freedom. Some movements take the view that if the will is there, there is always the prospect of success. Disillusionment must not mean disengagement. This would apply to socio-economic experiments such as Bruderhofs and the early Israeli kibbutzim, organizations that are probably better suited to transitional situations than to developed societies.

4. *The assumption of desirability*: underlying any utopian endeavour must be the assumption that what is anticipated or created is altogether better than the present situation. This may present believers with an intractable (and even ominous) means/ends problem in that the goal may be regarded as *so* desirable that extreme measures will be taken to achieve it. In the political sphere, we find the Nazi dream of the perfect (for them) political order involved the implementation of their genocidal policies. The most atrocious means were employed to rid society of its undesirable elements, especially the Jews who were regarded as the enemies of humanity. This was so generally endorsed that well-respected German firms vied with each other for the privilege – and profit – of supplying the equipment for the mechanized slaughter in the death camps. Among some religious movements we find analogous ideas. The Fifth-Monarchy men who flourished during the English Civil

War period took an essentially chiliastic view of the anticipated new order, and were prepared to butcher their enemies – the 'unbelievers' – in order to make way for a better and more desirable spiritually-orientated society. It hardly needs to be stressed that, in general terms, those systems and organizations that purported to be religiously-inspired have not been demonstrably more moral or humane than politically-inspired systems and organizations. But it must always be borne in mind that all too often the political has masqueraded under a religious guise

5. *The assumption of inevitability*: again, the political–religious divide is important. Both involve the notion of determinism, so it is necessary to distinguish the inevitable from the conditional. Traditional Marxism, for instance, insisted that capitalism must die in order to make way for socialism. Capitalism is going to die, but Marxists were (are?) divided on the issue of whether capitalism must be destroyed (revolution) or whether it should be left to choke on its own contradictions (evolution). Conditional determinists, whether of a political or religious persuasion, take a qualified view of inevitability. They accept that there is a compelling and possibly unstoppable movement taking place, but it is incumbent on humans to aid, abet and generally facilitate this movement to bring that movement to fruition.

Millenarianism in its this-worldly form constitutes a kind of realized eschatology insofar as it is either an attempt to create a heaven on earth, or to hasten the inevitable advent of the divine order with special benefits for the spiritual élite. Not unusually, the this-worldly and other-worldly aspects of millenarianism become fused. In 1706, three prophets from south-eastern France came to London bringing with them a prophetic tradition that had taken root among French Protestants during their persecution by Louis XIV. They gained a sympathetic hearing from some English audiences who saw that the message was consonant with their own culturally distinct brand of millenarian teaching. But this led to all manner of social tensions, and soon the mission of the French Prophets – as they came to be known – lost its essential vitality and coherence. Millenarianism can therefore be *cohesive* in that it may collectively mobilize resources, harness energies, and personally infuse believers with ambition and give them a sense of hope and purpose. Or it can be *divisive* in that it is based on the premiss that the elect/élite know better than others, and will therefore be the rightful legatees of the privileges that others cannot share.

6. *The assumption of infallibility*: this is a central ingredient in certain
    kinds of millenarian movement, especially those with a strong
    religious orientation. This is often given special significance and
    potency by the presence and authority of the 'charismatic leader', an
    almost invariable feature of such movements (the term 'charisma'
    popularized by Max Weber needs to be treated with some caution.
    Does it refer to someone's personal qualities, to his consistent
    success, to his followers' perception, or to some combination of
    these?). In Lower Burma in 1931, the colonial police encountered a
    band of some 700 peasants armed with knives, spears and a few old
    firearms. They were warned to disperse by a British officer in charge
    of a unit of Indian and Burmese military personnel. The leaders of
    the rebels chanted incantations and rang gongs, presumably to
    mollify the opposition, but also – so it would appear – to render the
    colonial forces militarily impotent. As added insurance, the
    insurgents carried talismans and had sacred symbols tattooed on
    their arms and chests in order to make them invulnerable to their
    enemies. They believed that victory was certain because they were
    marching under the banner of Saya San, the prophet who claimed to
    be the latter-day emissary of Buddha (the Enlightened One). He
    promised to oust the colonialist infidels and restore the monarchy
    and Buddhist religion as a preliminary to a new age of prosperity.
    Convinced of their invincibility the rebels continued their advance,
    and in desperation the troops opened fire, killing and wounding
    several hundred peasants (Adas: 1979, p.xvii). Stories of
    revitalization movements of this and similar kinds can tragically be
    numbered by the score, especially in colonial or enemy occupation
    situations.

Anthropological literature is replete with accounts of millenarian
cults, especially those found in undeveloped and underdeveloped
societies, together with the now mandatory attempts to try and explain
them. Fascinating as these are, movements such as the 'cargo cults' have
been extensively documented (for example, Worsley: 1957), appraised
(as Jarvie: 1964), and re-appraised (see Hill: 1973, Nelson: 1987 and
others). Perhaps, therefore, it would be a little more novel to look briefly
at three types of movement that we might broadly term fatalistic,
nationalistic and futuristic, but which do not fall into the well-attested,
easily recognized categories.

The first type is akin to what one theorist terms a *crisis cult*. This
expression is used both for its brevity and indecisiveness, and implies a
problem or crisis which is unresolved by ordinary secular means
(Barkun: 1974). The Ghost Dance of the North American Indians,

especially the Sioux (again well documented), would be a case in point. In the 1870s, the tribes responded to the depredations of the Europeans by developing a ritual known as the Ghost Dance which may have originated in Mexico. It was belived that this would lead to the destruction of the white man, possibly by flood or earthquakes, or possibly with the help of dead warriors (ghosts). Then the land would once again belong to the people of the Plains. Some even held that the 'Dance', which sometimes involved self-torture and falling into trance-like states, would render them invulnerable to the white man's bullets (Burridge: 1969). It was a ritual of desperation, an alternative to warfare which the tribes were finding increasingly ineffective (the defeat of Custer at the Little Big Horn in 1876 was an isolated and ultimately fruitless victory which only brought further problems culminating in the massacre of defenceless Indians at Wounded Knee Creek in 1890). A lesser known ritual but one that was essentially similar in principle was the Snake Dance of the Hopi Indians of Arizona. This is believed to stem from an early central American religious tradition which, though intended to secure supernatural help and deliverance, was implicitly fatalistic with respect to the gods. The ritual may have originated with the Aztecs who, according to some myths, migrated from Arizona and settled in the valley of Mexico some two hundred years before the Conquest and established their own high civilization possibly under the cultural influence of the Toltecs and the even earlier Maya.

One of the principal gods of the Aztecs was Quetzalcoatl, the plumed serpent, a deity-cum-culture hero who – again according to their myths – had come and gone but who was one day expected to return. (Remarkably, Quetzalcoatl's return was prophesied for about the same time as the arrival of the Spanish in 1519 – something their leader, Hernando Cortés, was able, initially, to exploit to his advantage.) The snake was an important symbol to the Aztecs; the ruler carried a snake sceptre, and his vice-regent was called the 'snake woman' presumably in honour of some chthonic cult goddess (Vaillant: 1962). The Aztecs believed that the cosmos operated on 52-year cycles, and that the end of each cycle threatened impending disaster which could only be averted by the appropriate rituals. These included a vast system of human sacrifice, usually – though by no means exclusively – of prisoners of war. The Aztec ruler at the time of the Conquest, Moctezuma II, is reported to have had as many as 12 000 prisoners killed at one festival and their hearts offered for the 'replenishment' of the god of war. No wonder that it has been persuasively hypothesized that the need for ritual fodder was the main reason for extensive Aztec militarism, although they also certainly profited economically from the capture of neighbouring city-states. Their considerable wealth enabled them to develop a culture that confounded the Spaniards who were amazed that a society that practised such inhuman acts, especially in the name of religion, could also lay out magnificent plazas studded with palaces and temples which, in their own way, compared with the architectural achievements of the 'civilized' world from which they had come. Behind this splendid façade was a culture that was frightening both in its cruelty and in its sterility and pessimism. The Aztec's entire existence was hedged about with taboos and punishments, and a foreboding concerning the arbitrariness of the gods and the hazards of human life (Hultkrantz: 1980). It was a culture marked by the kind of negativism which played not so much to win as not to lose. The Aztec system of human sacrifice, perhaps the most extensive in history was a measure of their religious devotion – and desperation.

The Hopi Snake Dance which to all intents and purposes was a ritual designed to bring rain to a barren land is almost certainly related to the Aztec ceremonies. The Dance was preceded by chanting and purification rites, and prayers were then offered to the Plumed Serpent to ensure the growth of the corn, beans, peaches and so on. As part of the ritual, grotesquely painted Indians defied death by dancing with venomous rattlesnakes and diamond-backs clutched in their mouths. The snakes were regarded as couriers who would carry messages to the deities. After the ceremony the snakes were taken far out into the desert and released; Hopi myths taught that unkindness and cruelty to snakes would bring drought and disaster. The Snake Dance was held at the beginning of the rainy season; if and when the rains came they were regarded as a blessing from the gods (Forrest: 1969). The ceremony can therefore be interpreted in positive terms as a request *for* something, in this case rain. Or it can be seen as being really a plea to *avoid* something, namely, drought and consequent starvation. There was no sacrifice, as such, although snake-handling of this kind is so dangerous (fatalities are known to have occurred in snake-orientated cults), that one might see such a practice as a willingness to make a personal sacrifice, again one feature of Aztec ritual. Such beliefs can be regarded as, at least, quasi-millennial insofar as they are concerned with supernatural intervention and an assurance of special favour if the rituals appeared to be efficacious. As far, then, as one can ascertain, Hopi rituals and the ideas they enshrine are economic and religious, that is unless we prefer to interpret them in socio-psychological terms and see them as forms of group strengthening and sources of social solidarity *à la* Durkheim. But then almost anything can be seen to serve such amorphous ends.

We can compare Hopi fatalism with a type of millenarianism that might be categorized as *nationalistic*, the Ras Tafari movement in Jamaica. Black millenarianism has been almost exclusively an urban phenomenon. The ghettos of the United States have bred a number of cults which look for political, even revolutionary, forms of deliverance. Some of these have decidedly religious undertones especially those that repudiate the term Negro, and prefer to associate themselves with Islam, 'the religion of the Asiatics'. In this respect, it is interesting to compare the militancy of the Black Power movement of the self-styled Elijah Muhammed, the more moderate movement of Noble Drew Ali, and the avowedly pacifistic Human Rights movement of the late Martin Luther King. It may also be significant that a number of key figures on the Black 'Liberation' scene have, or have had, strong connections with the West Indies where millenarian stirrings were known from the late eighteenth century (Barkun: 1974, p.175).

The Ras Tafari movement began in 1930 and was an offshoot of the Universal Negro Improvement Association founded by Marcus Garvey in 1914, which was organized on a back-to-Africa platform. This potent idea that Negro people needed – indeed, deserved – a country of their own if they were to find freedom and respect, influenced the new Ras Tafarians who saw the fulfilment of their destiny in (of all places) Ethiopia, which in the early 1930s was perhaps the worst centre of slavery in Africa. Adherents believed that their 'emancipation' would come not as Garvey suggested through economic betterment but by the miraculous intervention of the Emperor of Ethiopia, Haile Selassie, who was regarded as a living god. Its principal doctrines were that black people were the reincarnations of ancient Israelites exiled to Jamaica, that they are superior to white men, and that one day after their repatriation they would exercise that superiority and the whites would then constitute the underclass. It is thus a this-worldly rather than an other-worldly movement though much of its rhetoric is couched in pseudo-religious terms.

Since that time, deep divisions have appeared among Ras Tafarian groups: some adherents allied themselves with the 'Ethiopian World Federation', some, though certainly not all, have adopted eccentric modes of dress, and sport the characteristic dreadlocks. Ganja (marijuana) has also become *de rigueur* with some, but it is not indulged in universally. There are cleavages too between young and old, between urban and rural 'members', and perhaps most of all there are differences between those who still look for a supernatural solution to their problems and those who think that these can only be remedied by some form of radical social action. So they share the same goals, but differ over the means for their realization.

For Ras Tafarians, then, Africa is a promised land, and they have become resentful when told by African officials that as largely unskilled persons they are not welcome in African states where there is already enough unemployment. Some adherents decided to lower their sights a little and in 1960 applied to the Jamaican Minister of Home Affairs for a special allotment of land where they could govern themselves. Needless to say, this was refused as the government had no intention of establishing a state within a state (Simpson, 'The Ras Tafari Movement in Jamaica' in Thrupp: 1962, pp.161–2). Prior to this in 1959, one of the movement's leaders, the Revd. Claudius Henry, had persuaded many of his sympathizers to sell their possessions and join him in order to sail to Ethiopia. It is still not absolutely certain why the ship never turned up. Soon afterwards, members of the same group were charged with the possession of explosives and weapons, and later sent to prison for treason, including Henry himself. In the same year, there was another abortive *coup* in which members of the security forces were killed, and some Ras Tafarians were subsequently executed for murder. Some of those convicted were actually US citizens, and there was clear evidence of fairly widespread plans for insurrectionary activity. In this case, it would seem that a reversal had taken place, and some US blacks had come to see Jamaica rather than Africa as the focus of their millennial dreams; perhaps yet another expression of relative deprivation.

It is perhaps readily understandable that millennial hopes should centre on a location, and it is not unusual to find that the place in question is revered both for its antiquity and for its fabled associations with the predecessors of the group or community. For the Jews and Palestinians it is Israel, especially Jerusalem; for the Arabs, Mecca; for the Khmer, Angkor Wat. For others the scene of their millennial aspirations is more highly generalized, and involves the entire planet. This is particularly so of those whose millenarianism can be designated *futuristic*, namely those who indulge in what one writer terms 'Exo-Theology: the religion of Outer Space' (Story: 1980, pp.127ff.).

One of the best known devotees of exo-theological speculation is the popular but now much criticized writer Erich von Daniken. In his book 'Gold of the Gods', one of many in the genre covering the same theme, he outlines his general thesis:

● In the unknown past a battle took place in the depths of the galaxy between intelligences similar to those of human beings (this idea of a 'war in heaven' is not uncommon in mythology, especially that of the Greeks). The losers escaped in a spacecraft and settled on the planet Earth even though it was not ideally suited to their needs. They gradually adapted to the less than ideal conditions, and by living under the earth hoped to escape detection by their victorious pursuers.

- In order to deceive their enemies, they set up transmitters on what was then the fifth planet in the solar system (in the 'unnatural' gap between Mars and Jupiter). Their pursuers, picking up the signals, destroyed this planet, and the remnants now constitute the planetorial belt that now exists there. Thinking they had been successful, the pursuers returned to their own star systems.

- The explosion of the fifth planet temporarily upset the balance within the solar system with the result that the Earth's axis moved out of position, hence widespread flooding (again common in myths in widely dispersed cultures).

- After the deluge(s), people emerged from the underground habitations and began to develop civilization as we know it, and increased their numbers either by molecular biological techniques or by cohabiting with indigenous primitives who saw them as 'gods'.

- These biological experiments made slow and not always acceptable progress, and the newcomers had no hesitation in eradicating the failures and starting again and again. Successfully-created humans learned slowly, and still went in fear of the 'gods'.

- The ancient astronauts left but are still communicating with us through visions and apparitions that are often mistaken for religious experiences, and one day they will return. Those who claim to have had contact with beings from outer space (see Orfeo Angelucci, *The Secret of the Saucers*; and Howard Menger, *From Outer Space to You*) claim that space-beings are actually directing cosmic ideas to Earth via chosen contactees who experience these ideas either as intuitions or as revelations, and that these are validated by the many 'sightings' of UFOs from time immemorial.

Fascinating and colourful as these speculations are, the details and 'proofs' that are offered to support them are hardly convincing. Where people become disenchanted with organized religion and fearful of future uncertainties, they begin to seek help and inspiration elsewhere. Instead of looking for conventional solutions in social renewal or political change, some look to the skies and see their salvation in terms of extraterrestrial intervention. When help fails to materialize for soteriological Saucer devotees, it does not necessarily lead to disenchantment but to cognitive dissonance and a reinterpretation of the event as a test of their faith (Festinger: 1956).

It is easy to dismiss all such stories as the product of opportunistic charlatanism, as surely many of them are; or – more excusably – as somewhat naïve wishful-thinking. But it is always as well to remember that the wish does not invalidate the idea, only the way the idea is interpreted – and perhaps promoted. Arthur C. Clarke points out that a 'small proportion of UFOs have never been satisfactorily explained, and the theory that they are visitors from outer space is a perfectly reasonable one; I would be the last to condemn it, since I have spent most of my life expounding the possibility .... What I am condemning is the credulous naïveté of those who have accepted this theory and made almost a religion of it' (Clarke: 1967, p.169). This is a view endorsed by many – perhaps most – critics. Looking at the complex problem of possible extraterrestrial intelligence compels thinking at a meta-level, of theories about theories involving so many subject areas, especially religion. It likewise raises profound questions. Is there such a thing as revealed knowledge? How can we discern this? Does the claim to possess it constitute a kind of élitism? And does it matter if it does? The whole intriguing issue is still ongoing, and has yet to be convincingly resolved (see Randles: 1981 and Good: 1987 and 1991).

We can conclude this section of the discussion by summarizing some of the theories that have been advanced to account for the millenarian phenomenon.

1. *The social change thesis*: This argues that millenarian groups form when there is a breakdown in the current social order, especially when social change is rapid and seemingly ungovernable. This is particularly evidenced by the religio-political responses to the impact of industrialization and urbanization on relatively simple and underdeveloped societies. In these instances, millenarian ideologies often provide liberating and unifying themes. The upheaval produces revitalization movements, and in their own way may give incentive and opportunities to construct a more satisfying future. This is most noticeably true of *activist* millenarian groups, but is not necessarily the case with *quietist* groups such as the Indian Ghost Dance devotees who attempted to re-establish native values by rehearsing the traditions of the culture by ritual acts.

2. *The social protest thesis*: Lantenari (1965) has stressed that millenarian ideologies are ways of articulating discontent. We have found this among the deprived and unprivileged. The Ras Tafarians are an example of a movement – if, indeed, it is one discrete movement – that constitutes a form of unorganized and uncoordinated millenarianism. Their social protest is often expressed in terms of sub-cultural practices, such as dreadlocks, reggae, ganja, and so on, to the despair of left-wing activitists who cannot mobilize them into a state of energetic political consciousness.

3. *The psychological approach*: This is endorsed particularly by Norman Cohn who argues that millenarian ideologies are outlets for extreme anxiety, delusion and despair. They are forms of paranoid fantasy born of *ir*rational fears and fantastic expectations. Believers have an apparent inability to accept life as it is, and this gives way to an hysterical emotionality symptomatic of mental illness. Cohn cites various kinds of Jewish millenarianism (for example, under the leadership of Sabbatai Zvi) especially during the medieval period when there was extensive persecution of the Jews in European cities, including the atrocities in York and Seville.

4. *The pre-political movement hypothesis*: Psychological explanations are rejected by writers such as Peter Worsley and Eric Hobsbawm. They insist that millenarian movements are not irrational, but rather *non*-rational attempts to cope with political powerlessness. Such ideologies may harness new energies and actually mobilize those who were previously pacifistic, but not unusually these energies are given religious expression because political protest – and certainly political activism – is effectively denied them. It is also contended that millenarian movements often provide new recruiting grounds for ambitious, would-be leaders who were previously unknown and unrecognized, such as Jim Jones who led his members of the Temple Cult to Guyana where, under investigation from the authorities, they were persuaded to commit mass suicide. It should, however, be stressed that not all movements that *could* become political do so; some millenarians are content to express themselves in purely religious terms, as with certain modern Western Adventist groups.

CHAPTER SEVEN

Elitism by Conquest:
The Tragedy of Cambodia

Relative to its size (about the same as England and Wales) and population, Cambodia (Kampuchea) must be the most devastated state in modern history. Not that it had ever been the 'smiling, gentle land that foreigners liked to see' (Shawcross: 1980, p.37). Formerly it was divided, the southern state being known to the Chinese – from whom we derive our early records – as Funan, and the northern Khmer state as Chenla. A third century BC Chinese envoy testified to its prosperity, and reported that the people 'lived in walled cities, palaces and houses ... [devoted] themselves to agriculture ....' and paid their taxes 'in gold, silver, pearls and perfumes' and that they had 'books and depositions of archives' (quoted by Ablin and Hood: 1987, p.xvii). It was occupied by a number of tribal groups, and especially influenced by Indian culture from the second century onwards. After some conflict, the north took over the south, and this uncertain amalgamation became roughly what we know as Cambodia. There were countless disputes and civil wars, and it wasn't until the eighth century AD that anything like unity was achieved in the remarkable – and in some ways quite unique – civilization of Angkor which was not re-discovered until the second half of the nineteenth century (Pym: 1968).

The religious ideology of Angkor, which until the twelfth century was strongly Hindu, later became a subtle amalgam of Hinduism and Buddhism (which is really a refined offshoot of Hinduism). This supplied the philosophical underpinning for a state system based on divine-kingship. In its pre-Buddhist phase, the autocracy was near enough absolute, and the kings were able to mobilize enormous numbers of their subjects (whether as slaves or by corvée, is not absolutely certain) to work on their architectural projects. As with other notable divine-king systems such as ancient Egypt and Inca Peru, power was largely maintained by control of the water supplies. This was done by the construction of a vast complex of dams and resevoirs that was all part of an intricate pattern of irrigation canals by which the state was able to produce three harvests a year. The state was rich and expansionistic, and expended much of its considerable wealth on creating temple and palace structures which once housed thousands of officials and servants.

Although now largely in ruins, they still excite the attention of historians and archaeologists.

Angkor was not able to sustain the momentum, and as its power declined, so there were encroachments from Siam (Thailand) which eventually resulted in the complete breakdown of Khmer society. The Siamese sacked the capital in 1431, stripped the temples and palaces of their riches, deported huge numbers of Khmers as slaves, and destroyed the canal system. Subsequently, the Khmers unsuccessfully attempted to re-establish their one-time supremacy, and in the sixteenth century, the Siamese set up a puppet government under a compliant Khmer prince. Thus began the humiliating practice of having rulers enthroned by foreign powers.

With the passing of the centuries, Cambodia remained a vassal of Siam with whom she shared very similar cultural and religious values. A certain degree of integration took place, especially when both states found themselves facing a new enemy from the north, the Chinese-orientated Vietnamese. This combination was almost ruinous to the Khmers. There were more and more factional disputes, sometimes with the Siamese but increasingly with the Vietnamese – to whom the Khmers paid tribute – in which some thousands were killed. This intense hatred continued well into the nineteenth century, when the French intervened. They took over the territory and made it a French Protectorate in 1864. In 1884, the French tried to take full control of the country, and thus incited a rebellion which resulted in some grudging concessions being made to the Cambodians, but the country continued, sadly, to suffer from under-investment.

This uneasy state of affairs continued into the present century. In 1941, the French installed the eighteen-year-old Prince Sihanouk who has been variously described as 'head of the main political movement, jazz band leader, magazine editor, film director and gambling concessionaire' as ruler (Shawcross: 1980, p.46). He was said to be inordinately vain – how many rulers aren't? – petulant, a showman and something of a womanizer. On the other hand, he was obviously far from stupid, and showed a certain amount of political skill in trying to play one enemy off against another. Soon after his accession, the Japanese conquered much of South-East Asia, but left Sihanouk in place in a country that they obviously considered something of a backwater and which was, in any case, still under collaborationist Vichy administration. Towards the end of the war, early in 1945, when the Allies were quite definitely in the ascendant and France had been emancipated from German control, the Japanese, as part of their belated policy of trying to win friends by encouraging aspiring nationalist movements in the occupied territories, forced Sihanouk to declare independence from the now discredited Vichy regime. Once hostilities ceased, France again took control, but of a country that was plagued by guerrillas, many of a Communist persuasion, who were firmly set on a nationalist course.

The Indochina Communist Party (ICP) had been founded in Hong Kong in 1930, coincidentally the same year that the Buddhist Institute was established in Cambodia's capital, Phnom Penh. This ostensibly religious organization was, like the ICP, to become a main centre of anti-colonial activity. The ICP leader was Ho Chi Minh, later to become better known as the foremost figure in North Vietnamese politics. Its Cambodian cell was devoid of any influence until the 1940s and did not become a real force in Cambodian affairs until the 1970s, by which time it was a completely independent body, the Khmer People's Revolutionary Party (KPRP). A breakaway Khmer independence group staged a number of anti-colonial demonstrations, and by the early 1950s controlled large areas of the Cambodian countryside. Its power was undermined when France, precipitately or presciently, decided to grant independence to Cambodia. The whole anti-colonial movement was neutralized, and its organizations were denied representation at the 1954 Geneva Conference on Indochina.

The moves towards independence were supported by Sihanouk. He ruled only a small country, and his position was at best precarious. So he tried to steer a neutral course as far as the Great Powers were concerned, especially the French who had been severely worsted in their débacle in Vietnam. As one authority commented, 'In his foreign policy, Sihanouk courted all, but took vows with none' (Ablin and Hood: 1987, p.xxi). The USA, however, declined to sign an agreement, mainly a concerted effort of the then Eastern bloc, and instead pressured Cambodia to join the anti-communist South East Asia Treaty Organization (SEATO) by granting liberal amounts of military and economic aid. Sihanouk refused and his subsequent resentment at the retaliatory attempts to destabilize his regime by the US led him directly into the communist camp.

For constitutional reasons Sihanouk abdicated in 1955 in favour of his father, and formed the Popular Socialist Community which dominated Cambodian politics until 1970. In 1960, his father died, and Sihanouk returned to power, though not technically as monarch, but as Head of State. He renounced all US aid in 1963, roughly equivalent to 16 per cent of Cambodia's GNP, and actually severed diplomatic relations two years later. The effect was economically disastrous. His nationalization plans were ineffective; foreign investment took an ominous dive, exports were in limited demand, corruption was rife and opposition was rigorously suppressed. All in all, the country was in serious financial trouble. Politically things weren't looking too good either. The USA was becoming embroiled in Vietnam's civil war, and was making surreptitious attacks on the supply route that went from China, North Vietnam's economic ally, through Cambodia – a situation which polarized political opinion in the state. It was unsurprising, therefore, that when Sihanouk decided to mix business with pleasure, and took a vacation which was also an aid-seeking itinerary in Europe in 1970, the opposition, led by a general, Lon Nol, staged a *coup d'état* with the help of the army, and possibly also, the CIA.

Sihanouk was forbidden to return to Cambodia, but nothing daunted he made his way to China, presumably to solicit sympathy for his situation. He obviously wanted to regain his former position, so self-interest was a dominant motive, but it is probably also correct to assume that he genuinely wanted the best for his country. Cambodia had been overrun so many times in the past, and he had a fear of history repeating itself. 'Above all, he once told me, he dreaded that his serene land and apparently placid people would someday become extinct as a nation, remembered only by the mute magnificence of the temples of Angkor' (Karnow: 1983, p.56).

The Chinese, however, were nothing if not pragmatists. They offered to back the party in power, but Lon Nol was wary of becoming more involved in the Vietnamese conflict and would not co-operate. His new government refused Chinese patronage and thought they could go it alone. They were not going to allow the passage of arms through Cambodian territory. Not only did they prohibit this traffic, they also demanded that all Vietnamese troops must vacate the area. Needless to say, it was all so much beating the air. The Chinese had other plans to help the North Vietnamese and their allies, the Vietcong (the South Vietnamese guerrilla army), and at the same time to embarrass the Americans. They undoubtedly saw Cambodia as another potential satellite, so they 'introduced' Sihanouk to the Khmer Rouge, a tiny subversive organization with big political ambitions led by a one-time peasant-cum-failed electronics student, Pol Pot. Together, they formed the National United Front of Kampuchea (NUFK) with Sihanouk and his supporters posing as the legitimate government-in-exile.

Since 1950, the Americans had helped the French to maintain their hold on Indochina, primarily to block Chinese Communist expansion. They assumed, mistakenly, that the revolutionary leaders in both Vietnam and Cambodia were nothing more than pawns in a larger Chinese game of keeping up with the Soviets, and creating a Far Eastern empire of their own to counter-balance Soviet claims to be *the* leading communist power. But the revolutionaries had ideas of their own, and these didn't include China, except as a short-term facilitator of their long-term political aims. Similarly, the Americans felt that by checking

North Vietnamese incursions, they could 'contain' China whereas, with hindsight, it is now felt that they should have tried to exploit the traditional hostility that existed between them (Karnow: 1983, pp.55–6). The CIA appear to have been behind a number of plots to further US interests in the Far East. In 1963, they helped to engineer a *coup* in South Vietnam which involved the assassination of a dictator, and they may even have been party to the sacking of the embassy of the Provisional Revolutionary Government in South Vietnam in 1970. In the same year, South Vietnamese forces invaded Cambodia, and within days were joined by American troops.

If the main purpose of the invasion was to thwart communist encroachment, the secondary purpose was to save the South Vietnamese Government in Saigon, and the tertiary purpose was to prop up its Cambodian 'agents', the Lon Nol regime. Something had to be done. The Lon Nol Government had incited a great deal of anti-Vietnamese feeling among the people, and some hundreds of Vietnamese who had been living in Cambodia were killed by mobs, and others had been forced to flee for safety. Whether the Government meant things to go as far as this is difficult to know, but they were undoubtedly incensed that thousands of Vietnamese Communist troops were encamped in Cambodia's Eastern provinces. The situation had reached the stage where the people could hardly call the country their own. But this meant taking on the North Vietnamese, a confrontation that they didn't want and for which they were ill-prepared; hence US assistance which may – or may not – have been requested.

The whole area was now affected by the war which was singularly devastating for the innocent and the defenceless. After their defeat of the French in 1954, the North Vietnamese were determined to continue the 'armed struggle' by infiltrating cadres into the South in support of the Vietcong. This began in 1960, and in reply the USA sent 'advisers' to help the South Vietnamese Government. At first, hostilities were rather sporadic, but by 1962 all were engaged in a sizeable shooting war which escalated still further when the USA started bombing operations in the North in 1964. By 1970, the Americans were employing a considerable array of advanced technology. Casualties mounted on all sides, and it was in order to break the deadlock that both sides extended the fighting to Cambodia, each trying to secure an advantage. In fact it is arguable that the North would have been beaten in 1970 if the USA had also invaded Laos and cut the Ho Chi Minh trail by means of which the North Vietnamese were bringing troops and supplies to the South.

The combined presence of the South Vietnamese and US forces in Cambodia destroyed any semblance of Cambodian neutrality. The South Vietnamese, in particular, antagonized the people by a 'frenzy of raping and looting' in the villages (Ablin and Hood: 1987, p.xxv). The unsavoury reputation of the South Vietnamese and the unwelcome appearance of Western troops hardened Cambodian attitudes, and certainly facilitated the recruiting drive of the Khmer Rouge. In early 1970, the Khmers probably had less than a thousand men under arms, but by the end of the year the numbers had reached 12 000 and this was more than trebled by 1973 when the war between the North and South Vietnamese came to an inglorious end.

The USA did not, ideally, want to become involved in Cambodia, and their troops left the country after only two months, and allowed the local contestants, the newly formed Khmer Republic and the Khmer Rouge, backed by their respective allies, the South and North Vietnamese, to sort out matters for themselves. The then US President, Richard Nixon, and the US Senate were anxious to extricate themselves from yet another untenable situation. They were prepared to give friendly nations all manner of support providing it didn't extend to some kind of military commitment. Armed intervention often helped to create a 'bottomless well' situation; no one knew exactly what resources it would eventually require, or even when it would all come to an end. In Cambodia where they were relying on US military assistance, this led to inevitable disillusionment, as ultimately it also did in South Vietnam when the Americans decided to withdraw.

It has often been remarked that there is no war as brutal as a civil war. This may be somewhat exaggerated, but in its execution, and certainly in its aftermath, the Cambodian civil war was arguably worse than most. Although the Republic was able to build up its forces roughly on a par with those ranged against it, the whole course of the war can be seen as a slow and wearing process of destruction with the honours going to the Khmer Rouge. As the Government became more and more desperate, so oppression and corruption became more widespread, even to the point where wages were being paid to officers for troops that did not exist, while those doing the actual fighting were not being paid at all. The economy was in tatters, and many of its principal institutions, especially education, were barely functioning.

By 1973, things looked very bad for the Government, and the Americans, concerned that the defeat of the Republic would mean the end of their Far Eastern anti-communist strategy, decided again to intervene. But there were restrictions: the War Powers Resolution, despite Nixon's veto, imposed restraints on the President in committing US forces overseas. This time, intervention was not with ground troops; this would have been contrary to the spirit of the Senate's ruling, and would have enraged a large percentage of the American public. Instead, they sent in a huge bomber force to try to destroy the Khmer Rouge. The tonnage of high explosive used actually exceeded that used against the Japanese in the Second World War, but to little effect. Pol Pot's troops, who had been trained in North Vietnam, were fighting a guerrilla campaign mainly in rural areas where indefinable targets were hardly affected by the American bombing initiative which ruined much of the countryside and did little for the cities, yet left much of the Khmer Rouge intact. If anything, it further alienated the people, and this radicalization of the peasantry played directly into the hands of the Khmer Rouge.

The Watergate scandal in the USA effectively destroyed Nixon, who resigned in 1974. His successor, Gerald Ford, did nothing – perhaps could do nothing – to improve the situation, and things went from bad to worse in South-East Asia as far as the USA was concerned. The Vietnamese counterpart of the Khmer Rouge, the Vietcong, were similarly irrepressible, and by 1975, the USA decided to withdraw altogether, and left Vietnam to the not-so-tender mercies of the Communists. The US war effort was certainly undermined by the stridency of anti-war factions at home. It was a war the Americans *could* have won if they had pulled out all the stops, but it was a war they chose not to win, as the profits of such a policy were grossly outweighed by the losses. The USA spent some seven billion dollars on the bombing programme, and then helped to save the people by airlifts of supplies (US humanitarian aid in the Far East actually ran to over 500 billion dollars). Such are the ironies – one might almost say the idiocies – of war.

At almost the same time, the Lon Nol Government, now bereft of support, surrendered to the Khmer Rouge and their unlikely ally, Prince Sihanouk. The Khmer Rouge had already dismissed its Vietnamese 'advisers' (the Vietnamese being still considered as the long-term enemy) and executed a number of Vietnamese communists. Now they even turned against their pro-Sihanouk confederates, some of whom were actually killed. They then commenced a programme of ruralization which was to bring unimaginable suffering to the Cambodian people. Many thousands had fled from the American bombing; probably as many were now to flee from the Khmer Rouge who, in their turn, probably alienated the people more than the Americans.

The atrocities began only days after the victors entered the capital, Phnom Penh. They were carried out – as atrocities usually are – by the rank-and-file, in this case mostly teenagers, but planned in some detail by the *Angha Loeu* (Higher Organization) a group of middle-class ideologues – chiliastic dreamers – who intended to obliterate the past, and create an entirely new society. The plan, already known to the US State Department, seems to have been to telescope into one concentrated operation what it had taken the Chinese some twenty-five years to accomplish. It is interesting to note that this 'Democratic Revolution' was formulated and orchestrated by an élite of twenty intellectuals led by an élite-within-an-élite of eight people: five teachers, an economist, a university professor and a bureaucrat, who were all educated in France in the 1950s, and were all indoctrinated with the views of the radical left. 'What they did illustrated the ultimate heartlessness of ideas. In any other age or place, the plans of these savage pedants would have remained in their fevered imaginations. In Cambodia in 1975 it was possible to put them into practice' (Johnson: 1983, pp.654–5). Ultimately, this utopian blueprint was to claim the lives of about a quarter of the Cambodian people.

Pol Pot, who headed what came to be called the Communist Party of Kampuchea, probably came to power by organizing the assassination of its previous secretary-general in 1962. The minuscule Party at this time had to endure a certain amount of Government harassment, and Pol Pot spent several years in self-imposed exile in the inaccessible north of the country. The Party was faction-ridden in these formative years, but Pol Pot's victory over the forces of the Khmer Republic really established his position as leader of the Party. Military victory was the precursor to the intended revolution. Pol Pot's policy, and that of his Party élite, was nothing less than total social transformation. Some three million people were herded into the countryside from Phnom Penh ostensibly to avoid a famine which was said to threaten the city. There everyone was forced to work on the land; in keeping with Mao Tse-tung's teaching, the revolution had to begin with the peasants.

What happened in Phnom Penh was then repeated elsewhere. Class, occupation and status no longer counted for anything. The process of *social transformation* meant the complete dismantling of the state and its institutions. This first of all meant an attack on all so-called 'intellectuals'. Not that the Khmer Rouge were totally against learning; as we have seen, their own élite were intellectuals of a sort. What they opposed were intellectuals of the wrong kind, especially potential critics of the regime. This automatically led to the wholesale slaughter of teachers, students, civil servants and the like, indeed anyone who posed a threat to the new Government. With this, needless to say, went the closure of all 'anti-democratic' institutions and the destruction of books, together with all papers and records, always anathema to repressive ideologically-motivated regimes. Traditional religion was disparaged, and Buddhist priests were unfrocked and made to join the rest of the labourers. Hospitals were closed down, and in a number of cases, patients – especially the incurably ill – were murdered in their beds. Doctors and nurses too, together with the sick and wounded, were all compelled to join the exodus to the countryside. Any refusal or hesitation was met with brutality and – not uncommonly – death.

Indeed, it is thought that only fifty or so doctors out of 500 survived the purges. Some officials of the deposed Republic are known to have been tortured and mutilated before being killed, and many ex-members of the armed forces, who were also seen as 'traitors', were forced on to minefields, and others shot out of hand. Anyone who owned a luxury such as a car was in danger, and undesirables such as prostitutes and beggars were killed *en masse*. A company of 500 ballet dancers – hardly a menace to the state – was virtually destroyed one way or another (Pilger: 1989, p.386). And, most poignant of all, many of the children of the executed in all categories were dispatched, often by girl soldiers, on the 'justification' that they might take revenge for their parents sometime in the future.

Those that were 'fortunate' enough not to be killed immediately, but who were organized into collectives and worked on the land, also fared badly. All previous social categories were ignored. People were 'rated' according to their economic class and their political attitudes. It does not appear that the Khmer Rouge ever had the works of Marx, Lenin or Mao translated for the benefit of the people, yet government policies rested on a peculiar – and eclectic – interpretation of their teachings (Chandler: 1976). The peasant-orientation of the Khmer Rouge did not extend to those who, for whatever reason, had migrated to the towns; these were regarded as suspect, having been 'contaminated' by the insidious values of urban life, and were subjected to 'life-style' meetings which were designed to effect the *psychological transformation* of the individual. Participants were instructed how to change their whole manner of thinking. They were taught the proper ways of talking, walking and working. Any slackness was punished, sexual intercourse was forbidden, and adultery and fornication might actually merit the death penalty. Even married couples were not allowed prolonged conversations. Any disobedience to the rules could bring summary execution or mutilation involving entire families. On some occasions the emphasis seems to have been on humiliation. Pupils, for example, might be made to participate in the deaths of their own teachers (Johnson: 1983, p.656).

It is not known exactly how many died from some combination of starvation, disease and exhaustion in addition to those who were executed. In all, the death toll was somewhere in the region of one-and-a-half to two million people, although some authorities give slightly higher figures (for example, Pilger: 1989). The situation provoked attempted *coups* and uprisings in 1977–8, but these were put down with customary brutality and the leaders executed. The Khmer Rouge took little heed of world opinion; the only real friends they had were the Chinese who continued to help them in their ongoing struggle against the

Vietnamese. Yet ironic as it may seem, they were given recognition in the West, largely because this was regarded as one way of encouraging divisions within the communist camp. The country was understandably seething with discontentment, and ultimately the Vietnamese launched a full-scale attack in December 1978, and within just a few weeks had taken control, and inaugurated the People's Republic of Kampuchea. The Khmer Rouge regime collapsed and its forces divided, some joining the Vietnamese, others led by Pol Pot retreating to the mountainous areas near the borders of Thailand, where they carried on a developing guerrilla campaign against the new Republic.

Despite all this, the Cambodian agony was not over. The Chinese, incensed at the treatment of their allies, embarked on a four week punitive invasion of North Vietnam in 1979. It was not that effective, although some 50 000 are thought to have died as a result of this rather pointless exercise. At much the same time, the Thais now thought fit to expel the huge number of Cambodian refugees that had escaped from the Khmer Rouge. Several thousands are believed to have died from starvation and from the direct actions of the Thai troops. By 1980, both Cambodia (Kampuchea) and Laos were effectively part of the North Vietnamese 'empire' which had, excepting Cuba, the largest army, per capita, in the world. It has been argued that the Vietnamese merely replaced one despotism with another in Cambodia. For example, William Shawcross (Shawcross: 1980), having written critically about the US role in Cambodia (laying much of the blame on the inner governmental élite, especially Nixon and his adviser, Henry Kissinger) went on to accuse the Vietnamese of similar genocidal intentions to the Khmer Rouge. Massive aid has poured into Cambodia since the Pol Pot regime lost control. About a billion dollars has come from non-socialist governments, and about 250 million dollars from Vietnam and the one-time Soviet Union. In addition, there has been generous giving from the public in several countries including Britain. But Shawcross has accused the Vietnamese of misappropriating a good 50 per cent of this aid – an allegation which has done little for the cause of Cambodia in general. John Pilger has contested these charges (Pilger: 1989, pp.416–20) insisting that Shawcross is out of date with his information which, anyway, comes from suspect sources. He maintains that such allegations are without evidential support, and were probably made to justify the accepted American view of the North Vietnamese.

Pol Pot, who still hopes to regain power, saw himself – like Mao – as someone with a mission to 'purify all élites, subversives and revisionists and to create a totally self-reliant state ... sealed off from the "virus" of the world' (Pilger: 1989, p.388). His new society was never realized – perhaps never could be realized. When the Vietnamese entered Phnom

Penh in January 1979, they found it much as the Khmer Rouge had left it years before, virtually deserted, shops and offices abandoned, and services at a standstill. 'Year Zero' had come and gone, and nothing had changed. What is now particularly remarkable is that a hesitant recognition has been given to the resuscitated Khmer Rouge still led by Pol Pot and the hopeful opportunist, Sihanouk. The Khmer Rouge still hold many thousands of Cambodians in the camps in Thailand which have been visited by various dignitaries, including America's Dan Quayle and Britain's Margaret Thatcher, who looked upon the Khmers as 'reasonable people'. But there are other camps which no celebrities visit, which have a high death rate because of ill-treatment and because they are denied international relief. The Khmer Rouge are threatening to make a comeback, yet the West still sees them as part of the anti-North Vietnamese resistance, and accords them the kind of quasi-legitimacy that they desire. They have a representative at the UN, and from 1982 became the dominant partner in the US/China-inspired Coalition of the Government of Democratic Kampuchea. Support from the West has been largely covert. Indeed, there is a strong suspicion that a small team of British SAS personnel has secretly trained special sabotage units of Cambodian guerrillas. And there is also some evidence that between 1980 and 1986, the USA funded Pol Pot to the tune of 85 million dollars. The regime's respectability can be seen in its public face, Khieu Samphan, who was a key figure during the massacres and who, 'in pinstriped suit has smiled his way around the world at "peace" conferences ...' (Pilger: 1992, p.178).

It is disputable whether anyone will ever pay for these crimes. Even the UN Human Rights Sub-Commission, which was once prepared to condemn the atrocities in Cambodia that 'reached the level of genocide', has now (1991) advised that member Governments – perhaps out of a wish to appease the Chinese – should no longer seek to 'detect, arrest, extradite or bring to trial those who have been responsible for crimes against humanity in Cambodia' (Pilger: ibid., p.196). The murderers now have effective immunity from prosecution, and enjoy equal status with those they have persecuted. Apparently no Western government has even officially condemned the Khmer Rouge government-in-exile for its pretence to represent the interests of the Cambodian people. It is now a definite prospect that they will be reinstated in their new guise as 'liberals'. If they ever do come back to power, they may still not be moved by the wasteland they have helped to create, but they may pause briefly at the rack upon rack of neatly stacked skulls with open, unbelieving mouths – mute memorials of their last, lethal visitation.

CHAPTER EIGHT

Elitism and Ecclesiastical Authority: The Church and Medieval Heresy

Many years ago, the writer James Westfall Thompson ably summarized the contradictory elements in the medieval Catholic Church, saying that it was 'democratic, yet aristocratic; charitable, yet exploitative; generous, yet mercenary; humanitarian, yet cruel; indulgent, yet severely repressive [about] some things; progressive, yet reactionary; radical, yet conservative' (Thompson: 1928, p.684). In the so-called Age of Faith it was an organization that was, in many ways, more powerful than any of its contemporary Western states, and was consequently loathe to relinquish any of its authority. And in order to maintain this authority it had a whole armoury of sanctions at its disposal, its own armed forces (in Italy) and the forces of sympathetic states, its considerable wealth, and not least the power to impose excommunication, 'a singularly potent weapon ... which no believing ruler could safely ignore' (Lenski: 1966, p.266).

Throughout the Middle Ages, there were repeated attempts to reform the Church, to eradicate abuses, and to give credibility and coherence to its teachings. In the tenth century the state of anarchy that existed in European politics was to some extent reflected in the Church. Moral leadership and spiritual zeal were largely lacking, especially among many of the higher clergy who lived more like feudal lords. Some monasteries, however, still tried to maintain the early traditions, especially those of the Benedictine Order which enjoined the virtues of chastity, piety and learning. It was just at this time that the Papacy was challenged by the new reforming movement stemming from the monastery of Cluny in Burgundy where the Abbot and a growing number of priests began to call for a renewal of faith and practice. The Cluniacs appealed for stricter discipline and higher standards of morality if the Church was going to have any influence on the people. They taught that the Papacy must free itself from the influence of German kings and Italian nobles, and dissociate itself, as far as possible, from the abuses of the feudal system.

The Cluniacs also argued that lay rulers must be reduced to subordinate positions and that the Church must be independent, owing allegiance to no earthly monarch – a conception that was to have ominous implications for both Church and state. By the middle of the eleventh century these ideas were being put into practice by the then pope, Leo IX, who chose his own bishops and would allow no lay people to interfere with his decisions. In practice, this meant that bishops and abbots could retain their lands over which local lords had no longer any control. In 1073, when Gregory VII was elected pope, the reforms were taken a stage further. Popes were to be recognized as inviolable Bishops of Rome, as political leaders in their own right in central Italy (popes were rulers of the Papal States until the nineteenth century), and as spiritual heads of the entire Church. As far as one can tell, Gregory was not personally ambitious, but he was a passionate idealist, and deeply convinced of his own righteousness. He maintained that divine mercy had created the power of bishops, and that popes were 'masters of emperors' even to the extent that they could depose them if they wished (Weech: 1946, p.425). In effect, the Papacy was to be above all human jurisdiction, and this meant not only control over all human agencies but also all other thought or belief systems. The Papacy would determine what was acceptable or not. It would decide what constituted 'true doctrine'. Thus the path was now open for the Church élite to decide what was to be branded as 'heresy' and subversion.

Where there was acquiescence to Papal authority by the secular powers or some kind of symbolic relationship between the two, it often conferred very real advantages (a problem satisfactorily solved by a number of ancient societies where the ruler was also the Chief Priest). Rule by naked force is always liable to be counter-productive, so to rule with the blessing of the Church often brought definite benefits to the political élite, especially in terms of religious validations. (Wasn't it Polybius who said that he thought of Roman religion simply as an instrument of government?) Complementarily, the political élite could often be of real service to the Church. Sometimes it was felt that a little none-too-subtle coercion was necessary to aid the task of evangelization, and the secular arm could be particularly useful in suppressing what the Church regarded as dissent.

It should be stressed, however, that although it is clear that standards within the medieval Church often fell far short of its ideals, and also that it contributed to the perpetuation and legitimization of some very doubtful regimes, it – or some of its clergy – often opposed despotism and supported the case of the weak. For example, as early as the twelfth century, the Church raised its voice against slavery, and in the next century argued for some mitigation in the position of serfs. Furthermore it established charitable and educational institutions. Sometimes the influence of the Church was indirect and not at all the result of official ecclesiastical policy. Religious traditions often provided the *ideological basis* for social reform, as in the late fourteenth century when the Peasants' Revolt was led by a priest, John Ball. Not uncommonly, sectarian agitation was generated in opposition to Church practices, as with the Lollard movement in England and the Hussite movement in what, until recently, was Czechoslovakia.

The actions of the Church were not always determined by the whims of the Pontiff or by theological necessity but often by the demands of political expediency. Not least they were conditioned by the context in which such actions took place, and this put automatic limits on what was done. Situations set boundaries on ecclesiastical power. Even in the Papacy, office never conferred absolute *carte blanche*: the popes and the higher clergy had specified functions which involved specified procedures and force of tradition demanded that they could not easily exceed their designated powers. Normally authority of office was circumscribed by rules and convention. But exceptions were always likely. Much depended on the nature of the personalities concerned and the necessity of having to deal with unique or atypical circumstances such as the emergence of a particularly 'virulent' heresy.

In the medieval Papacy, there was a characteristic conservatism; experimentation and change were generally regarded as hazardous. As with any other large-scale organization, there were time-tested procedures, and these made for much-needed stability, especially when schism was rife, and the nobility, as ever, were restless. In these circumstances, any proposed modification to the status quo was regarded as a potential threat. Popes were elected on a 'damage-limitation' basis. Cardinals tended to favour candidates who lacked personal initiative and who were not prone to radical innovation, even if they did indulge in a little self-aggrandizement on the side. But when the Church began to find its authority and teachings seriously challenged from the twelfth century onwards, it required, and generally got, popes that were equal to the task.

Dissension came from outside the ranks of the clergy in the form of dissatisfaction on the part of the nobility (papal dues were never that popular), and from social unrest among the people. More subtle, even insidious, from the Church's point of view, was the enemy within. Peter Abelard, better known for his romantic – but fateful – escapade with the niece of an abbot, was a theologian of the first rank who asked questions that the Church was disinclined to answer. A contemporary of Abelard, Arnold of Brescia, followed in a similar tradition, and also wanted to see restrictions on the wealth of the higher clergy. Needless to say, he was given short shrift. He was actually deemed dangerous enough to be deprived of his benefice and banished from Italy. But he returned to Rome in 1143 following the death of Innocent II, and was then unwise enough to translate his opinions into political activism and join an insurrection against papal government. After a long struggle, he was taken and handed over to the civil authority for punishment. He was then executed by Frederick Barbarossa, who was crowned by Pope Adrian IV for his services to the Church.

The twelfth century saw something of a renaissance of learning with the establishment of the universities of Oxford and Cambridge in which the works of Plato were studied alongside those of Augustine – something that was hardly calculated to still the questioning mind. At much the same time, there was an outbreak of heresies on a scale larger than the Church had experienced for a very long time (Revill: 1962, pp.206–7). These heresies differed in a number of quite significant ways, but they did have two particular features in common: a genuine antipathy to ecclesiastical wealth, especially the life-styles of many of the higher clergy, and a critical approach to certain aspects of Church doctrine. Some were more radical than others, some even going so far as to reject altogether the authority of the Church and the State. The sects that were considered most subversive were those which could not accept a number of key elements of orthodox theology, and were ruthlessly persecuted for their convictions.

These sects' common orientation was Manichaean, deriving from the teaching of a third-century itinerant preacher and writer from Ctesiphon (modern Iraq) named Manichaeus (or Manes). Obviously perplexed by the apparent inconsistencies between the Old and New Testaments concerning the divine nature (as had also been the millennialist Montanus, a century earlier) and also presumably unable to reconcile the ideas of divine benevolence and the existence of pain and death, Manichaeus argued that there must be two principles at work, one Good and the other Evil. These forces of Light and Darkness (a conception found pre-eminently in the much earlier doctrines of Persian Zoroastrianism) were held to be in perpetual contention. The creation was seen as inherently evil, 'a casualty of the eternal struggle between the Good Mind and the Spirit that Denies' (Bowle: 1979, p.231) and it was argued that teachers and prophets appeared in history in order to liberate mortal humans from the thrall of evil and to direct them towards the eternal Realm of Light. Manichaeans were divided into two 'classes', the élite, the Righteous Elect, who lived like monks and nuns apart from the world and were pledged to vegetarianism and to refrain completely from sex; and the Hearers, who lived in the world but who promised to avoid any form of killing (as had also the Montanists who were forbidden to watch the customary butchery of the Roman Games) as well as idolatry, sorcery and fornication.

The Manichaeans were fiercely persecuted by both the emperors of Constaninople (Istanbul) and the popes of Rome. Manichaeus himself was executed and flayed by the then King of Persia as a heretic, and all his books are now lost – possibly destroyed. But, one way and another, remnants of the sect survived until the tenth century and became the inspiration for a number of later dissident groups, notably in the Balkans. These included the Paulicans, founded in the seventh century by one Constantine of Mananalis in Syria, who was executed in 687. The Paulicans followed very much the same dualist doctrinal line, and also condemned Mariolatry, the Sacraments and the professional priesthood. They too were proscribed, and in 752 many of them were deported to Bulgaria where they gave birth to another sect, the Bogomils who held similar though – if anything – stricter views of both religious practice and social morality. Basileius, a Byzantine physician, was the sect's first martyr being burned alive in 1119, as was customary for heresy. The Emperor and the Patriarch of Constantinople did their best to extirpate the heresy and its adherents, and by the fifteenth century some had turned to Islam for respite from the persecution of the Church. Others survived and lingered on in Europe to influence those sects at the centre of our discussion, the Albigenses and the Cathars. The scene was now set for an unequal contest between one élite, the Church which held that it had an unassailable universal mandate, and sectarian communities that were convinced not only of the rightness but also the superiority of their cause.

By the late twelfth century, these dissident views had spread to Bosnia, northern Italy and especially southern France. The Albigenses, who flourished in the neighbourhood of Albi in southern France, are still something of an unknown quantity. Their doctrines are not clear in detail largely because what accounts we have are based upon the writings of their bitterest enemies. They certainly rejected the political claims of the Church, and were hostile to many Church practices. There is little doubt that they shared the Manichaeism of their sectarian forebears because they could not believe that the Divine mind could conceive anything so appalling as the Creation. They also adhered to very disciplined ideas concerning sex and marriage, something they had in common with the Cathars with whom they were often identified. Not that they abjured sex; they *may* have advocated and even practised fairly unrestrained sex (Bowle: 1979, p.231) providing no children were conceived. It was an evil world, and humans had no right to make it worse by propagating the species. But, again, this may be a distortion of the teaching and practices perpetuated by their persecutors. We are also not sure just how the teachings were applied. The Cathars (*Cathari*) or Purified Ones were an ascetic élite, and certainly made exacting demands on their members; though not, apparently, on the more numerous lower grade Believers, who did not have to comply with the moral impositions that the Purified made upon themselves. As far as we can assess, the Cathar élite actually abstained from sex and marriage, fasted three days a week and adopted a vegan approach to food. They also vowed never to lie or swear a legal oath or to kill either man or beast. In effect, members were to put themselves entirely at the disposal of the sectarian community and its rulers, and not to encourage social ties outside that community – an insularity that was bound to excite suspicion in others.

They were thus a world-renouncing sect, implacable in their hostility to the Church which they regarded as a counterfeit church which existed to delude people with false hopes of salvation (note the similarity with extreme Protestants today and their attitudes to 'Romanism'). In this sense, it was markedly different from the contemporary sect known as the Waldensians. Founded by a rich merchant of Lyons, Waldo (or Valdes), the Waldensians tried to return to a life of apostolic poverty and evangelical preaching. They were rigorously investigated by the Church and exonerated because they did not repudiate any main points of Catholic doctrine, and therefore aroused little popular animosity. But Catharism was different. It constituted a radical alternative and, therefore, a dangerous challenge to the orthodox Church, an alternative that the Church could not allow to exist.

Initially, the Cathar movement tended to recruit people from the lower classes, those who would have a natural antipathy to the wealth of the higher clergy. But, with time, more prosperous and high-ranking individuals were drawn into its ranks. The earliest recorded case of persons of rank being brought to trial was in 1022 when some church notables in Orléans were arraigned before their fellow clergy in the presence of Robert (the Pious), King of France. It was discovered that one of the accused had actually been the Queen's confessor, and the king 'reacted to these revelations in much the same spirit as an American President might do if he found a Senate Committee packed with members of the Mafia' (Hamilton: 1981, p.24). He ordered that if they would not recant they should be unfrocked and burnt at the stake. Apparently, this established an ominous precedent as it was the first occasion when heresy was treated as a capital offence in Western Europe in the Middle Ages.

It should be noted that the initiative did not always rest with either the clergy or the monarchy; it was often the people who were so affronted by heresy, which for many was tantamount to witchcraft, that they took matters into their own hands and killed the unrelenting sect members. This happened in Milan in 1028, and in Soissons in 1114 and Cologne in 1143, after the clergy had done their best to persuade the offenders to change their minds. It would seem that in these instances, the burnings had taken place against the advice of the clergy, but how much the officials actually did to prevent the 'executions' is not really known.

Until this series of outbreaks of heresy, the Church had enjoyed a welcome period of relatively trouble-free tranquillity. In what might be broadly termed the early Middle Ages, such heresies as it encountered proved to be little more than a mild irritant. But with the revival of scholarship and the increasing – some might also add, oppressive – demands of the Church, doubt and dissension became more widespread, and are still a normal feature of the Western religious tradition to this day.

The rise of Catharism was something different. Not only was it a more serious challenge to orthodoxy, it also polarized opinion within the Church as to exactly what should be done about heretical ideas. Could the Church possibly entertain some of the more moderate forms of heterodoxy? Did these sects raise issues which were worthy of some consideration? What should be done about the sects themselves? Should attempts be made to reform them or at least modify their attitudes? Or should they be stamped out, eradicated altogether? This whole issue was exacerbated by rumour and misunderstanding, and by the fact that reactions to the sects varied from place to place and – perhaps more importantly – that secular and ecclesiastical authorities were not always at one on the matter. Initially, it was state officials who wanted action, especially when they met with resistance from sect members who adopted a pacifist position. At first, it was social pressure rather than public morality that presented problems for the Cathars, but with time Catholic apologists supplied the necessary theological and ecclesiological justifications for a concerted campaign against the sects. Had Catharism been confined to the quite small numbers of 'purified' elect, perhaps the Church authorities would not have been too concerned; but the majority of *Cathari* were still technically members of the Church, and it was incumbent on members that they recognize it was only the Church that could ensure that they remained in a state of grace.

Tolerance of religious belief and practice, as we understand it, is very much a modern phenomenon. Extremism, of course, still exists, and cannot live alongside those with different views even within its own faith (for example, Shi'a within Islam) for very long. But, in general, society is more relaxed about – perhaps just indifferent to – religious issues. It is thus difficult to understand the consternation that such matters aroused in the Middle Ages. Moderns look back and wonder what all the fuss was about. But then many today are not so preoccupied about the nature of eternity and the possible fate of man's immortal soul. The medieval Church, for all its theological misapprehensions, ritual flummery and institutional abuses, was certainly concerned about these matters. So when nothing else worked, it was prepared to resort to repression to eliminate error and bring people back to the truth as it saw it.

As trouble increased, Church lawyers scoured the texts in order to find the necessary precedents for the treatment of heresy. A study of canon and civil law revealed that in earlier times – notably in the reign of Justinian in the sixth century – heresy had been classified as a form of treason, and punished accordingly. The Church was deemed correct in turning over unrepentant heretics to the civil authorities, which meant that they would certainly forfeit their property and even their lives. The alarm over heresy was such that these ideas became incorporated into canon law in 1199 shortly after the accession of one of the most powerful of the medieval popes, Innocent III – himself a lawyer – who exhorted local rulers to bring heretics to trial. The Church still persisted with its attempts at reform, and even decreed that those whose lands had been confiscated could have them returned if they later repented.

This whole initiative came to an abrupt halt when a papal representative was assassinated in 1208 with the complicity – so it was said – of Raymond, Count of Toulouse, partly out of sympathy for the *Cathari* and partly to assert his independence from the king. This time it was determined to extirpate the heresy root and branch, and so was inaugurated one of the least known, yet most atrocious of the Crusades – if such it can be called – against the Cathars in the south of France. It is an episode which the Church would rather forget, and which history rarely mentions (even the otherwise excellent Richard Southern, a noted authority on the Middle Ages, only devotes a few lines to it). Yet, in its own way, it had serious repercussions, and really paved the way for later Protestantism, which was again ruthlessly persecuted in France in the seventeenth century after the revocation of the Edict of Nantes.

Rarely has there been such a campaign of royal and ecclesiastical terrorism as the Albigensian Crusade, as it has come to be known. The disillusionment with institutional religion was well understood, even by the Papacy; Innocent himself admitted that simony was rife, and that some clergy were prepared to sell justice, damning the poor and giving absolution to the rich. The Cathars, by contrast, had impressed many people with their piety and lack of ostentation. They were admired for their forthright condemnation of clerical abuses and their repudiation of repeated ritual formulae as a substitute for an evangelical religious faith. The Cathars confronted Rome with a crucial theological problem – what to do about heterodoxy. But even more they presented the Papacy with the problem of ecclesiastical order and authority, and the secular powers with the critical issue of social control. What happened was that onto papal politics were grafted the ambitions of certain barons and the Paris monarchy – a fatal combination for the dissidents.

The situation was further complicated by the fact that the State and the Church were not opposed by merely a few wretched peasants, but by a burgeoning religious movement supported – for whatever reasons – by a nobleman who was not only the Count of Toulouse but also the Marquis of South-West Provence; and as cousin of the king, and brother-in-law to the kings of both England and of Aragon, was one of the most powerful princes in Western Europe. An already tense situation ignited when the Papal Legate was killed by one of the count's officers; the murder of the pope's own ambassador was a capital crime. Yet the normal sanctions of the Church were ecclesiastical – and by implication spiritual – in nature: excommunication or interdiction (the prohibition of participation in religious observances), the threat of which was usually enough to deter any kind of contravention. Only a few years before, the French had been put under interdiction for several months as the result of the illegal divorce of the king who was eventually forced to submit to the will of Rome. But when the pope pronounced actual excommunication on Toulouse it was ineffectual; the people had already effectively severed their links from Rome. Four years before the Crusade began, the pope had written to the King of France that it was his responsibility to make things difficult for Raymond of Toulouse and to remove the heretics and transfer control of territory to those who were sympathetic to the Church; but all to no avail. Even the Archbishop of Narbonne, within the Count's jurisdiction, was obdurate and refused to be intimidated by the papal envoys. The Legate that was murdered, Peter of Castelnau, had actually tried to get some of the Count's signeurs to rebel against their liege lord, again to little effect. Exasperated and frustrated, the Legate had pronounced excommunication and Raymond had ostensibly made his submission, but it was too late to save the unpopular Legate from the assassin's sword, or Raymond – whose personal life was far from being unimpeachable – from the wrath of the Papacy. Plans were already being formulated to deal with the recalcitrant sects and with the man whom the Church saw as a 'limb of Satan' and whom Innocent himself pronounced an 'impious, cruel tyrant' (Oldenbourg: 1961, p.14).

The 'chosen instrument', the agency of this 'cleansing' operation, was a force of Crusaders drawn mainly from other provinces in France. Crusaders were recruited on a voluntary basis, but many of them were little more than professional mercenaries; fighting was what they did, and almost any excuse, honourable or otherwise, would have brought them to the colours. Yet it would probably be a mistake to assume that they were without any vestiges of nobility. The evidence suggests that, in their own way, they were quite sincere. What seems so incongruous is that they could believe that in a religious cause any means were justifiable. One has only to read about earlier Crusades in the Holy Land (Israel/Palestine) to see how this operated against infidel Islam; and this too was done with the Church's *imprimatur*. Innocent's injunctions to Philip of France to choose the right leaders for this 'army of the Faithful' are somewhat reminiscent of Himmler's speeches to his higher SS officers concerning operations against the Jews; SS personnel were to be assured that although what they had to do was distasteful and distressing, it was their sacred duty as good National Socialists.

Among the army which embarked upon the enterprise in 1209 were several barons and other members of the nobility, a number of untrained pilgrims who were ardent supporters of the cause and – appropriately – not a few bishops and even archbishops acting in a quasi-military capacity to leaven the crusading host. But to everyone's surprise, the Count, after his public Act of Submission in which he had to promise never to protect heretics, never to entrust Jews with public office and to relinquish all rights to the religious institutions in his province, asked to join the Crusade. This was an astute, if devious, move, for by associating himself with the cause, his property became immune from seizure. Regardless of his patent duplicity, it may be that with all his faults and weaknesses, he remained 'human to the end – especially when contrasted with adversaries whom bigotry, fanaticism, ambition or plain ignorance had robbed of all humane qualities' (Oldenbourg: 1961, p.17).

The man that was entrusted with the leadership of this campaign, Simon de Montfort, is a somewhat enigmatic figure. He came from aristocratic stock, had proved himself years earlier in the Fourth Crusade, and was now a seasoned warrior in his late forties. Nominally, he was Count of Leicester, but his possessions had been confiscated by the King of England, and he was now a vassal of the King of France. De Montfort has been seen variously as brave, modest, prudent and indefatigable in his pursuit of the Church's interests, *and* as a heartless, ferocious knight who cared nothing for those who were massacred. Certainly, he seems to have been a particularly proficient man-at-arms, well versed in the arts of war, and highly respected by both men and fellow knights who served with him. So much depends on which authority one accepts. That he could be cruel in the extreme is not in serious doubt; the issue is to what extent that cruelty can be seen as being in any sense justified. War is nasty at the best of times, but this war must be regarded as one of the cruellest in the Middle Ages. Both sides were given to unspeakable acts of violence, and, as is so often the case, as the war dragged on and frustration and desperation increased, so did the atrocities.

Nobles of the region under proscription (known generally as the Languedoc) were divided in their allegiances. Some, anxious to be on the 'right' side, joined the Crusade, but others sensing the possibility of losing their possessions were determined to defend their independence. The first victim of the Crusade was the city of Béziers whose viscount was the nephew of Raymond of Toulouse. Before the siege began the viscount – perhaps for the best of reasons – left the city with some Jews and some known heretics to prepare for the defence of his capital, Carcassonne. Béziers was left in the charge of the bishop and his various city burghers who offered to hand over the leading heretics (the list of 222 names still survives) to the invaders providing the city was spared. But the people, both orthodox Catholics and heretics, refused to support their leaders; to their credit, they felt that they could not negotiate on such a basis. The Crusaders set about investing this heavily fortified city, and both sides prepared for a long siege.

What happened next need not have happened at all and must be attributed to the stupidity and impetuosity of some of the inhabitants, although the Crusaders saw it as an act of divine intervention. Against all expectation, some citizens rushed out of one of the city gates to show their contempt for the invaders, and thus gave their enemies the opportunity to get inside the walls. The citizens didn't have a chance. They became the victims of the agreed Crusader policy that communities that would not surrender should be put to the sword. The cry was 'kill them all', and as far as can be ascertained no-one escaped. Every man, woman and child was butchered – perhaps some seven thousand in all. And with the bodies still warm, the Crusaders held a service to express their gratitude that Providence – their particular view of Providence – had delivered the city into their hands. The cathedral and a large part of the city was then burnt to the ground. The Crusaders left, convinced of their own virtue, and cursing the mercenaries who had started the fires and deprived them of the rich plunder they felt was rightfully theirs.

After the officials of Narbonne and various châteaux had made their submission, the army moved on to Carcassonne, a city that was generally regarded as impregnable. However, its outlying suburbs were barely defensible, and were easily taken by the invaders. There was then the usual parleying which got nowhere until the lord of Carcassonne, the Viscount of Trencavel, went personally to the enemy's camp, presumably under a flag of truce. The evidence is confused at this point but it would appear that, contrary to military norms, he was forcibly detained together with his retainers and put in chains (he died three months later, possibly of poison). The city, now deprived of its leader, made a formal surrender, and its inhabitants were allowed to leave unharmed providing they left all their belongings behind. The Crusade, it would seem, was not just about eradicating heresy; accumulating booty was obviously also high on the agenda. It was an almost effortless enterprise which the Abbot of Cîteaux confidently declared another 'miracle'.

It was at this relatively early juncture in the campaign that de Montfort assumed effective command. He consolidated his position by levying monies which he then distributed to supporters, and led the army to accept the surrender of numerous other towns and châteaux. But the army still hadn't done what it came to do. Many of the *Cathari* had gone to ground and heresy was still alive and well, if not quite as visible as it had been. Soon the voluntary service period (normally forty days) of the knights expired, and the army began to lose many of its most important leaders; yet de Montfort still had most of the territory to subdue. That he was able to do this with a much reduced force says something of the ruthlessness of policies and the fierce single-mindedness with which they were pursued. For example, after the capture of Bram which had only resisted for three days, he took the hundred men of the garrison and had their noses and upper lips cut off and their eyes gouged out. Intimidation was the name of his particular game, so he cynically left one with a single eye so that he could lead his comrades to the site of his next intended conquest. This sort of thing was not that unusual: both sides could be equally vicious. Some knights were flayed alive and others – especially mercenaries – had limbs hacked off not just as punishment but as a method of instilling fear and respect. People tend to forget the dead, but they freeze in their tracks at the sight of such brutal mutilations which were deemed necessary *pour décourager les autres*.

The fortunes of the Crusaders fluctuated as they met increasing resistance. De Montfort presided over more mass executions, though not before he had exhorted the accused to make their confessions. He was encouraged to proceed with his proscriptions by the pope who promised him title to the lands wrested from the Church's enemies. Death by burning seems to have been reserved for the *Perfecti*, the élite Cathars, who despite the intense persecution still maintained a pacifist stance. Their heresy was regarded as so abominable that they were given only summary justice, and killed without trial. There were more sieges and more surrenders, and as the campaign gathered momentum it became increasingly immaterial whether the suspects had to be crushed because they represented a defence of heresy and a defiance of the Church. Their offence amounted to treason. So, for instance, when the fortified town of Lavaur was captured in 1211, its seigneur was hanged together with eighty of his knights.

The key test for de Montfort came with the siege of Toulouse, a city in which he had an effective 'fifth column', the White Brotherhood of the fanatical and ambitious Bishop Foulgues. He received reinforcements of more forty-day Crusaders, mainly from Germany. But now there were complicating political factors to contend with; the traditional enemy of France intervened and Toulouse was sent help. A contingent of Basques arrived, courtesy of the King of England, and there were disquieting noises from the King of Aragon, a powerful monarch, who also had interests in the area. The Crusaders broke off the siege and settled for ravaging the countryside instead.

In 1212, after a three year campaign, the pope declared an end to the Crusade. He inconsistently reprimanded de Montfort for pursuing his own interests – something he himself had encouraged – and cancelled the indulgences of those 'pilgrims' who had accompanied the Crusade. Events, however had really overtaken Innocent's rather belated decisions. The King of Aragon had taken it upon himself to raise a huge army to come to the rescue, not of heretics (he had burned plenty of these himself in his own domains) but of the territories themselves. In opposing de Montfort he was really trying to prove who was the greater warrior. As things turned out, he was defeated by a considerably smaller French army and, though displaying conspicuous personal bravery, was cut down in the battle.

The Church hardly gained in credibility with two of its most doughty defenders doing battle with each other. But this was not that unusual; indeed, it was a common medieval phenomenon. All the Church could do was to try to take advantage of the situation whatever the outcome. Not that its representatives spoke with one voice: as de Montfort continued on his triumphant way, he found that some bishops retained their suspicions about his personal ambitions, while others, including the Cardinal-Legate of France, confirmed him in all the lands he had conquered. Furthermore, the Pope's special Legate insisted that the rightful owners of these lands who, by association, were deemed to be implicated either directly or indirectly in the heresy scandal, must offer their submission, do penance, and re-dedicate themselves to the service of the Church. Meanwhile, de Montfort sought to further his dynastic aspirations by marriage alliances, and increase his possessions by finding heresy wherever it was convenient to do so. But he received something of a setback when the Church again changed direction at a special Council in 1215 at which it was decided that he would not actually possess the lands he had taken – including Toulouse which was declared an open city – but instead act as a kind of Papal Lieutenant whose task was to police these territories.

Late in 1215, a great Lateran Council was convened at which anyone who was anyone in the ecclesiastical hierarchy was present. The Council asserted the legal and spiritual superiority of the Church over secular authority. The problem of heresy was paramount as the topic of discussion, and it was re-affirmed that heresy was unconditionally condemned, and that secular authorities had a sacred duty to prosecute wherever they found it. Any who did not comply were liable to excommunication and the dispossession of their rights and lands. The Count of Toulouse was deprived of his lands and these were given to de Montfort despite some prelates' ambivalence and previous hesitations. In effect, the Crusade and its mission were underwritten by the Church even though at the highest levels its clergy were well aware of the barbarities committed by its army. In confirming the campaign, the Papacy was not only condoning these acts, it was also absolving those who had perpetrated them. In all but name, the Inquisition had begun.

The following year, Innocent III died, but the campaign in Languedoc (it was no longer strictly a Crusade) continued, with frightful atrocities on both sides, especially in the still contested possession of Toulouse where the campaign began in earnest in 1217. It was during this prolonged siege when the indigenes were trying to wrest their city from the invaders that de Montfort, fresh from his devotions, was hit by a large missile from a stone-gun which smashed his head in, killing him instantly (June 1218). His son took over, but gradually lost all the territory his father had gained. The new Pope, Honorius III, then inaugurated a second Crusade, this time to be the responsibility of Philip, King of France. Command was given to his son, Prince Louis, who led a formidable army, consisting of knights and archers, and which was suitably sacralized by the presence of twenty bishops. It began with the capture of Marmande where the garrison was spared, possibly for bargaining purposes, but about 5 000 townspeople were horribly massacred and the town burnt. It would appear from the evidence that this was no spontaneous act of revenge by the troops, but coldly premeditated murder as part of a deliberate policy of intimidation. Yet despite this – or because of it – the invaders were still unable to re-take the city of Toulouse itself. From then onwards, the second Crusade too began to falter and at least, in 1223, the two sides agreed terms.

But Honorius was not happy: heresy had still not been eradicated. He pressed Louis, now King of France, to resume the campaign, but Louis' price was too high, including among much else, plenary indulgences for his troops. Negotiations continued, and eventually Louis, who was now technically overlord of the Languedoc, led his troops back to claim his rights in June 1226. Many towns offered their submission including Avignon, but Toulouse was still not taken and the king's army, now suffering from sickness and dissension, discontinued its campaign. Within weeks the king himself had died (only a month after the death of Francis of Assisi – a Catholic who had taken a very different view of the Church's mission).

In the following year, the nobility on both sides were again engaged in contesting the territory. The Church tried to bring some harmony to the situation, but the whole affair was fraught with anomalies. The problem, as ever, was that the objectives of the Church and the secular powers were not the same. They were not totally at variance, as we have seen, but fundamentally the nobles were avaricious for territory, some to get it and others to keep it. The Church, on the other hand, was out to eliminate dissent and – we should not forget – to exert and to test its authority. (One can hardly imagine the modern Papacy having the power to scourge a member of the nobility as Raymond of Toulouse was in 1229.) The crusading nobles saw that the best chance of satisfying their ambitions was to go along with the Church, whether they really believed in its mission or not.

The Church in its campaign against heresy – and against what the Church perhaps regarded as worse, unashamed anti-clericalism – became increasingly content to work through the Inquisition. This was largely promoted by the energies of Dominic (died 1221) and his colleagues who, at first, made strenuous efforts to convert heretics by their preaching. It was confirmed in its office by Pope Gregory IX in 1215 and gradually became an instrument of terror, so much so that by 1234, the same year that the ageing chameleonic Raymond of Toulouse issued his statutes against heretics, two leading Inquisitors were able to condemn 210 people to the stake at Moissac. And although its representatives were often hounded by the public, in 1239 it had 183 Cathars burnt at Marne in the presence of the Count of Champagne. The jurisdiction of the members of the Inquisition was considerable and extended to all those living in the areas in which it operated except only diocesan bishops and their officials. In theory, the Inquisitors were responsible to no-one but the Pope.

Strictly speaking, a person could only be condemned and punished for heresy on the evidence of witnesses 'of good character' – effectively, public denunciation – and a refusal to recant. But there is little doubt that this was sometimes waived, or ignored altogether as in the case of the Cathars of the Languedoc. In practice, evidence was sometimes taken from those already excommunicated, and husbands and wives were allowed to testify against each other. The only people exempt from interrogation were boys under fourteen and girls under twelve. Mass interrogations were not that unusual: in 1245–6, the Inquisition at Toulouse took as many as eight to ten thousand depositions from the population (Hamilton: 1981, p.42). One is left wondering just how many of the people really appreciated the finer points of what was being asked, and how many were tempted to denounce others in order to absolve themselves. Suspects were arraigned before a tribunal, and although technically entitled to a lawyer, found that lawyers were loathe to represent them in case they too were accused of having heretical sympathies. It was not until 1252 that Pope Innocent IV gave permission for the use of torture with obdurate suspects who refused to disclose information. In the end, it was either a matter of confession or conviction.

It was, of course, possible to confess while not recanting. *Cathari* impressed even their accusers: they almost never recanted and received the tribunal's judgement and – so it is reported – even death without fear. Offenders could appeal their sentences from papal courts, but there was no appeal from the verdict of the Inquisition. Contrition might save the heretic from eternal damnation, after possibly a requisite spell in Purgatory, but it did not save his body from earthly justice: for example, even Henry II had earlier had to undergo a flogging by monks for his part in the murder of Thomas Becket. The Church effectively absolved itself from the imposition of capital punishment by handing the guilty over to the secular authorities. Possibly most of the sentences passed by the Inquisition were canonical, thus incurring a penance. But in most states where the Inquisition operated the sentence for heresy was death. Technically, therefore, in surrendering the most recalcitrant to the State, the Church could be seen to have done its best. It was now up to the State to do its worst.

How effective this all was, is a matter of some debate. Certainly among the Cathars, the results are ambiguous. Heretics were hunted down mercilessly, and by 1244 matters had finally come to a head. Some months earlier the siege of Montségur had begun, where the last remnants of the heresy had taken refuge. They were forced to surrrender and were told their past crimes would be pardoned including the murder of some inquisitors. But, as was so often the case in this interminable conflict, things didn't work out as anticipated, and over two hundred survivors were burnt to death. Persecution worked insofar as Catharism had ceased to exist in most of Europe within a hundred years. Yet, in another sense, it didn't work because the vast majority of the Cathars themselves (and especially the *Perfecti*) never recanted, and because heresy – albeit in different forms – was to appear elsewhere, not least as incipient non-conformity.

CHAPTER NINE

Elitism by Sex: The Gender Issue

This discussion will be concerned with radical and reactionary approaches to gender-role and gender-preference, and will take up some of the questions posed by the 'political correctness' debate. The main argument has been summarized by Neil Lyndon (who admits that some would see this as a gross caricature of feminism): 'Consider the intrinsic claims of ... feminist propositions ... that one half of humanity ... held [the other] half in subjection through the use of economic power and brute force ... and [they were therefore] obliged to fight a war of liberation ... to emancipate [themselves] from the oppressions inflicted by men ...' (Lyndon: 1992, p.57).

It is a contention of feminist writers that until relatively recently women's roles have been either underplayed or completely ignored by most (male?) theorists. It is suggested that even within the social sciences – arguably a discipline sympathetic to the feminist cause – the tradition of academic objectivity has often made women 'invisible'. It is further argued that the uncritical use of terms such as 'sex-role', 'female-role' and 'male-role' have often been ill-defined and have obscured differences in power between men and women in that the sex-roles tradition has primarily focused 'on men's worlds and women's places within these patriarchal spheres' (Ollenburger and Moore: 1992, p.11). Indeed, it is emphasized that there is an inherent flaw in using earlier theories about women because they are said to be based on masculine paradigms, although it is conceded that some aspects of other discourses (Marxism, critical theory, psychoanalysis, hermeneutics and the like) are useful in that they contribute ideas to the general debate (Harding: 1987, pp.1–14).

Feminism, as it has come to be known, has been around longer than many people think, but it only received reasonably clear articulation in the last century, and only came to be considered a movement from the 1960s. Initially, it sought equality after what is sometimes termed 'exclusion' by patriarchal attitudes and values. Later, the emphasis shifted to the issue of women's autonomy, that is, to women's right to socio-political and intellectual self-determination. This inevitably meant a re-assessment not only of women's role, but also of previous theories and discourses that purported to examine that role (Gross and Pateman: 1986).

Most of these re-assessments are in the liberal-feminist tradition, but differ in their interpretation of the causes of female 'oppression'. By and large, the liberal feminists maintain that women have not succeeded because they haven't been given the right educational and economic opportunities. The assumption – certainly borne out by recent (1994) secondary education statistics – is that given equal access to compete they will certainly do as well as men. Liberal feminists, however, are criticized for their failure to include other factors in their analysis, especially the ways in which institutional expectations are inculcated so as to reproduce traditional patterns of inequality. What is particularly understressed, so it is argued, are the ways in which women are shackled to domestic tasks including child-rearing which necessarily inhibits their true fulfilment (Eisenstein and Jardine: 1980).

Moving further left, as it were, along the protest spectrum are the Marxist feminists who see their oppression in terms of inequality within an unjust economic order. They regard the class structures of capitalism as the cause of their subordinate position in society. And insofar as women, who are often seen as a source of cheap labour, are also consumers and unpaid housewives, women unwittingly contribute to their own subservience. Marxist feminists see their oppression as a result of structural factors rather than a lack of individual opportunities, and insist that things will only change when society itself undergoes radical change, possibly of a revolutionary character. However, whether the whole question of class and the class-struggle should intrude upon gender issues is the occasion for some debate, even among feminists themselves (for example, Mies, et al.: 1988) as it is really to confuse the issue of stratification with that of differentiation.

Radical feminism in its many guises takes in 'multiple oppressions such as racism, able-bodiedism, heterosexism and classism' and relates these to what it regards as the 'most fundamental of oppressions', the patriarchal social system (Ollenburger and Moore: 1992, p.21). Radical feminists insist that women's oppression is found in all societies, and is therefore a ubiquitous and 'original' phenomenon which provides a model for all other kinds of oppression. It is 'original' in the sense that it is biologically based, and some feminists advocate a movement of liberation from such oppression. One early proponent, Shulamith Firestone (1970), demands a 'biological revolution', but just how this is to be achieved all the time women are tied to child-bearing and largely to child-rearing is difficult to know; though with modern contraceptive techniques, certain options are now available. Some would like to see the eradication of the family, certainly as it is presently structured, and others – not unusually with homosexual orientations – would like to see the demise of all heterosexual norms (for example, Dworkin: 1979,

Cruikshank: 1982). But given the way most of us are sexually constituted, this seems rather an unlikely prospect. True, we are now said to have entered the age of the liberally-minded 'New Man', the 'Man with the Apron' ('I always have the last word in our house – even if it is Yes'). But modified forms of patriarchy are still with us, alive though perhaps not quite so well as they once were – in the West, at least.

There are groups of radical feminists who, instead of stressing the equality and complementarity of the sexes, insist on perpetuating the superior–inferior distinction in favour of women. They are particularly influenced by the incidence of male aggression. This 'sexual terrorism' they say can be either psychological or social in nature in addition to the physical violence which is usually associated with the male sex. Indeed, there are those who see all men as potential bullies, rapists or whatever, with all women as potential victims. Needless to say, this is an allegation that is unproved and unprovable. In its own way, it is another form of sexism. Undoubtedly, men can be – and are – aggressive, and where violence is a feature of male–female relations, men are usually the aggressors. (That this is not always the case is evident from the sex attacks found in women's prisons, and the disturbing – and growing – incidence of violence in girl gangs. Teachers now testify also to the growing phenomenon of playground fights between girls as well as boys.) But the mistake is to confuse acts of aggression of whatever kind with the idea of inherent and ineradicable aggressiveness, as though every man was just waiting for the opportunity to vent his anger or exercise his sexual power with the first available female. We are all capable of violence in given circumstances, but very few of us are roaming the countryside looking for victims, or secretly longing to way-lay some unsuspecting woman to sate our unspeakable lust.

In some ways, the most extreme feminists are those who embrace the teachings of postmodernist culture. They do not recognize the superior–inferior distinction as such; in fact they want to abolish all dichotomizing distinctions and deconstruct the language of sex. They argue that all definitions of women have been formulated by men. So they want to do away with 'these products of patriarchal language', and 'destabilize' the traditional categories of social and sexual identity (Tong: 1989). Such views are subject to the same strictures as all postmodernist thinking. Nothing is assumed to be what it seems; everything has its hidden meanings. Once deconstructed, statements, concepts, and so on, reveal implicit presuppositions which are often interpreted in terms of power relations. (One could presumably deconstruct, say, the nursery rhyme 'Jack and Jill went up the hill' to demonstrate the believed primacy of the male in courting disaster and the good-naturedness of the female on whom he eventually comes to rely.) It all becomes an extremely relativistic, know-nothing word-game which can only be understood and unravelled by the postmodernist *cognoscenti*.

Feminist theory is seen as emancipatory theory, and it is argued that gender issues should be a central concern – indeed, a problem – for society which should be tackled urgently. But whether the challenge should take an activist form or not is something that betrays a division in feminist thinking. More contentiously, gender is also regarded by some as neither natural nor immutable (Chafetz: 1988). Masculinity and femininity are not regarded as givens, and many feminists insist that there should be a clear distinction between a person's sex and their given gender preference. There is an abject fear of 'heterosexism', the superiority of heterosexual behaviour, and of 'heterocentrism', a term which indicates the cultural domination of heterosexual norms. In fact, some theorists (for example, Fontaine: 1982) maintain that heterosexism is the pivotal political and cultural mechanism whereby patriarchy binds women to male-defined norms. Indeed, as we have seen, there are those who would go so far as to argue that all heterosexual relationships are by their very nature oppressive (a little odd for those who tend to query nature's insistent dichotomies), because social and economic power is invariably (?) held by men. This is not to suggest that all feminists are homosexual though, arguably, very many homosexual women tend to be feministic in orientation. Whether the two are causally related is debatable. Certainly, feminism can be a defence for homosexual women who want to exercise their autonomy. (This text abjures the term 'lesbian', which has unproven historical connotations, and the term 'gay', an innocent old word which has been rather frivolously hijacked by the male homosexual community. It should also be pointed out, in case there is any doubt about the etymology of 'homosexual', that it can apply to men *and* women because it is not from the Latin word for 'man', but from the Greek meaning 'of the same kind'.)

Feminist theory, then, is addressed to a society that is held to devalue women, and which largely ignores their capacities and aspirations. Women maintain that they are often treated as commodities. They have *use value*, that is, value for their socially useful activity, and also *exchange value*, which historically implied an exchange of sexual favours and fidelity for economic support and social status, but which today can connote the exchange of one's labour for financial remuneration. Here the debate centres on the ways in which women have been socialized for roles in society that are regarded as inferior to those of men. The traditional roles of housewife and mother define women in relation to some 'other(s)', namely husband and children, and are said to be demeaning in that they divest a woman of any personal identity. It is further argued that even in today's more advanced society, these expectations still persist, and although women now have many greater opportunities in the labour market, they are still underrepresented in the professions and overrepresented in the large corps of low-paid part-time employees.

Again, the matter of sexuality is cited as a key issue. Sexuality, particularly women's sexuality, has been highly commercialized. Prostitution is obviously a prime example, as is also pornography which exploits the male as well as the female form. In both prostitution and pornography humans are treated anonymously and, rather strangely, are said to be 'without control over their own labour' (Ollenburger and Moore: 1992, p.54). It is true that both 'industries' are male-dominated, but it is by no means an exclusive male preserve (note, for instance, the female staff, including editors, in the soft-porn market). Women's sexuality has also generated a whole welter of advice books, novels and new magazines (*Cosmopolitan* and so on). Women are said to enjoy revised media images which no longer portray them as sex objects for men. But do they, perhaps inadvertently, do so for other women? The new autonomous-woman image, the woman who is her 'own person', is seen as a product of the feminist reclamation of sex. 'Clearly women have been deprived, sexually stunted in service to the vaginal and phallocentric sex imposed by men' (Ehrenreich, et al.: 1986, p.71). The same writers contend that, by and large, women have now laid claim to new sexual possibilities that are 'broader, more playful ... more compatible with women's broader erotic ... needs' (ibid., p.193). Women's pleasure in sex has been largely equated with what advocates call the 'sexualization of society'; the untenable implication being that this new 'individual meaning' did not exist until 1970 or thereabouts. However, it is conceded that in recent years the frequency and variety of sexual practices has increased, as has also stated levels of satisfaction (D'Emilio and Freedman: 1988, p.338). Exactly what such 'new possibilities' are beggars the imagination. After all, what can be *really* new about sex except the trimmings? Whatever the preliminary frolics, it all has to come to the same thing in the end: orgasm. Everything else is merely hors-d'œuvres. And how one measures or is in any way able to calculate increased levels of sexual satisfaction other than in terms of orgasmic frequency – admittedly a crude indicator – is beyond the social investigator.

The sexuality issue has also been understandably related to reproduction and motherhood. But once these are divorced from sex *per se*, they become disconnected from marriage and the family generally. Motherhood is regarded by many feminists as something which oppressed women. The whole mystique of reproduction and motherhood is seen as part of the inescapable ideology of all societies, even in the so-called liberated West (Hoffnung: 1989). Reproduction cannot be discussed without reference to the question of contraception, abortion and sterilization, all part of feminism's extensive armoury. We are reminded that 'the early history of birth control and abortion [*sic*: strictly speaking, birth control *is* abortion, so presumably the authors mean conception control] is an oral history of inventions, not by scientists or physicians, but by women' (Ollenburger and Moore: 1992, p.50). This 'technology', we are told, was handed down from generation to generation until the development of gynaecology, 'a surgical-medical speciality dominated by men'. We are not informed, however, of the specific methods that were used; presumably anything from Japanese vaginal balls to vinegar-soaked rags, most of which were singularly unsuccessful.

It is sophisticated contraceptive devices that have greatly reduced the high birth-rates in the West in modern times. And it is salutary to remember that world population has doubled in the last 30 years or so, and by the year 2000 will probably stand at about 6.5 billion, some 90 per cent of births being in the developing world. To insist, as some feminist writers do (for example, Hartman: 1987), that overpopulation arguments are simply specious attempts by male-dominated governments to conceal their own lack of investment, must be more than a little suspect. Have these governments actually got the resources to change things? It is estimated that if a developing country wanted to equip just *one* hospital to Western standards it might take 40 per cent of their entire health budget. It is also advanced gynaecological techniques that have considerably reduced the hazards of childbirth in the West where only 11 per thousand children die at birth compared with an average infant mortality of 1:13 in the developing world. Admittedly, high birth rates in the Third World are partly a function of patriarchal norms, but feminists should also bear in mind that the average maternal death rate in Africa without these male-dominated facilities is 1:21 (source: Population Concern).

This is not to argue that women do not have the right to control their own reproductive capacities, but in view of the general world population problem, which is probably the most urgent problem facing humanity and from which so many other social issues follow in both the developing and the developed world, it is a matter that everyone must face responsibly. Conception control must not be regarded as part of some deeply-laid 'white plot' to enfeeble the Third World. And though we may applaud the technological ingenuity of the West for the development of conception control techniques, we cannot ignore the abuses of that ingenuity by economic exploitation, such as the dumping of banned contraceptives in Third World countries where there is a lack of regulation. It does little for the feminist cause for devotees to call for an end to aggressive family planning programmes in the Third World where they are said to be linked to the intersection of capitalism, patriarchy and colonization, while other 'sisters' in the West are simultaneously clamouring for pro-abortion rights.

To remonstrate about the devaluation and marginalization of women in the West today is surely somewhat antiquated. Surely very few men would contend that there should not be equal pay for equal work, or that women are not capable of almost all the kinds of work done by men (perhaps we should exclude the most strenuous forms of manual labour), especially in the professions. Indeed, the general ethos of modern society might be said to favour women. The media, in particular, have done much to cultivate the female section of the market – not least for their exploitable potential. The tobacco industry now has more success with females than males, if current statistics are to be believed. The brewers too are doing their best to extend their welcome to women drinkers, by portraying beers/ales/lagers, traditionally men's fare, as being equally delectable to the female palate. Notable too is the way in which much modern television, including advertising, has swung in favour of women. This is sometimes taken to the point of trivializing and even ridiculing the male as either incompetent or inconsequential. This is often a feature of popular sit-coms where the marginalization of the male is evidenced by the almost mandatory pricking of masculine pomposity and the scarring of the macho-image. This can be seen in programmes ranging from domestic comedy series to dramas about the fortunes of female football managers, female lawyers, female detectives and so on until we reach the hard-eyed female serial killer – the ultimate anti-heroine who, inevitably it transpires, has been betrayed, raped, sexually assaulted, endured alien abduction, or been otherwise ill-used in her youth.

Pythagoras once suggested that all things are composed of contraries. Feminism, too, in its many forms, is premissed either on the assumption that the human propensity for dichotomous distinctions is misguided, especially as far as masculine/feminine is concerned, or – in extreme cases – on the assumption that the distinction is valid, and that it is women who have the superior edge. It is claimed by some (such as C. Lévi-Strauss) that dichotomous categorizations are at the very foundation of social structure. This kind of conceptualization is said to be 'economical, rewarding [and] seductive' (Epstein: 1988, pp.12–14) but only serves to reinforce current prejudice. This is especially so when such polarities are held to have qualitative connotations such as good/bad, inferior/superior and the like, in which case they may become ideological weapons with which to confront or confuse the opposition. But whether these distinctions are best explained as 'social constructions rooted in hierarchy' (ibid., p.15) as opposed to alternative theories of socialization propounded by sociologists and psychologists is a moot point. And whether there is 'overwhelming evidence' for such an assertion might also occasion some debate. To suggest that the division of the world by sex is an ideal construct, hints at a male conspiracy. But to deny this, as feminist writers in their anti-sociobiology fervour tend to do, is to supervene or distort what many would regard as the ruling of nature, difficult as this is to define or even recognize. This is not to assert male dominance à la sociobiologists (for example, Wilson: 1975) but simply to reaffirm the complementarity of the sexes.

Having exhausted the uncertainties of the biological arguments, it is not unusual for the protagonists of both sexes to resort to the less tangible discipline of psychology. This immediately conjures up such amorphous things as emotions, intellectual abilities, proclivities and so forth – in short, personality traits. Are men and women really different? There has been extensive research into this question – again, with no very clear conclusions. Specialists are generally agreed that human development occurs through some combination of biological inheritance and social experience – nature and nurture – but are not at all sure how much relative importance to give to each. Some, however, are prepared to argue that men and women *are* differently 'wired'; not that one or the other is innately inferior or superior, just that they each tend to approach certain issues from different perspectives. The problem is similar to – though not the same as – that of why individuals of the *same* sex differ in ability, outlook and rates of development. Undoubtedly, men and women tend to excel at different things. Women, by and large, appear to have greater verbal facility whereas men may have higher analytic ability; women display considerable manual dexterity, while men seem to possess better judgement about such things as speed and distance which contribute to their skill at various sports. But these various abilities are by no means mutually exclusive, as most of us know from experience. There is considerable overlapping, and it is still impossible to say what is biological endowment and what is culturally acquired.

The study (beloved of many professionals) of personality traits, such as dependency, sociability, vulnerability, being impressionable, temperamental, and the like, can barely disentangle them in respect of any particular individual, let alone the sexes; and this despite the penchant so many psychologists have for personality testing. These batteries of ostensibly searching questions which may be dismissed as commonsensical or fatuous depending on the high or low patience threshold of the subject, may give insights into the nature of the personality, but are seen by many as having only a doubtful scientific validity. Furthermore, to assume that personalities are 'set' and unchanging, or to take the view that they all pass through pre-determined stages may be equally in error. There are just too many exceptions to the accepted stereotypes. It is fairly obvious from research and from experience that men and women *are* different (which many would endorse with *'vive la différence'*) but as far as intellectual and emotional capacities are concerned, these seem to be reasonably evenly distributed throughout humanity regardless of sex, nationality or race.

The issue of personality difference is not that far removed from that of status difference and questions of power and influence. It is argued, in neo-Marxist fashion, that the relatively low economic status of women traditionally, and 'male domination' generally, derive from pre-history when men exercised their ability to control women's labour (Charles: 1993). Certainly, in very simple tribal societies there was a more egalitarian approach to work, though even here foraging was largely the work of women while men did the hunting. In what are classified as matrilineal societies, inheritance was marked by ambiguity. Women had the right to own, but men had the right to *use* that which women owned. In complex pre-industrial societies this certainly changed, with men more concerned with production and women preoccupied with reproduction. But these changes took place for reasons that were not exclusively economic, far from it. Much had to do with military recruitment and the need to protect relatively small autonomous communities. Those who did the fighting felt that they were entitled to make the decisions. But even in what are acknowledged as highly patriarchal societies (for example, Classical Greece) there were huge variations in the status of women (compare Athens and Sparta). And even then women had a very real and vitally important domestic role even if they were without direct political power (Finley: 1973). Similarly, in Rome, an upper-class woman's indirect influence on affairs could be considerable (Finley: 1972).

Where some feminists must be in error is in their unfounded assertion that there is a *qualitative* difference between men and women; an issue raised especially in connection with violence. Even such a high-powered female lobbyist (and lawyer) as Helena Kennedy, QC has argued that the murder of women by men is in a different dimension from the murder of men by women. Yet it is interesting to note that, in the United Kingdom at least, most murders are committed by women – against their infant children. The death rate by violence for children under one year is much higher than for any other social category including teenagers. Of course, it is not called murder, it is in a special category of infanticide. The women concerned are thus accorded sympathetic treatment by the courts, usually on the grounds of post-natal depression. But whatever it is called, by any standards these are acts of violence against innocent and helpless victims (see Lyndon: 1992, pp.36–8).

Has feminism really brought about the changes that have taken place in modern society regarding the position of women? Feminist writers and broadcasters have undoubtedly heightened awareness of women's issues, but arguably the changes that have come about have been largely the result of medical and institutional factors. Medical, because the extensive use of the birth pill and safe legal abortion made it possible for women for the first time in history to control their own fertility. These near-infallible techniques were a true source of liberation for women from the 1960s onwards. Institutional, because, as Michael Oakeshott might have argued, what was already *de facto* became *de jure*. Divorce was becoming a matter of routine (figures doubled, for example, from 1971 to 1981), and the number of women in higher education increased fivefold after the Robbins Report of 1963. These and other changes came about not by appeals to combat 'patriarchy' but by legislation that had negligible opposition. In other words, the climate was right for change. The public was already conditioned to accept what were perhaps overdue innovations.

In fact, the synchronizing of historical events is particularly interesting here. It is surely no coincidence that a number of Marriage Acts all became statutes during the mid-nineteenth century when women were increasingly wanted for work in a burgeoning economy that was beginning to produce articles that women wished to buy. It was also the period when reliable contraceptives were being introduced, though, admittedly, not on a very large scale. The extensions of women's suffrage continued throughout the rest of the century, and into the present century, culminating in a realization of women's economic potential during the First World War. After something of a quiescent phase this continued with the upturn in the British economy prior to the Second World War, when again there was a need for female labour during the years of hostilities. After this war the lull was shorter: within just a few years, women's rights had been further extended, not as the result of agitation or sloganeering but because of the conducive nature of social attitudes.

So we must ask if the whole idea of 'female emancipation', 'women's rights', whatever we like to call it, has now gone over the top? Are the claims exaggerated? Are some even based on false premises? The logical – or illogical – conclusion of some feminist writing is that in the near future males will be redundant. For example, Jane McLoughlin has made statements to this effect which are tantamount to predictions, although, implicitly, they sound more like aspirations. She writes that one of the anthropological pleasures of the 1990s will be watching how men cope with their new role: that of the redundant male. The assumption is that new technology will eradicate their traditional skills, and that industry will favour other skills based on dexterity rather than strength. With new marriage forms and new bases of the sexual relationship, the father will become marginalized within the family, and may not any longer be the main breadwinner. Artificial insemination will rule out unwanted coitus as unnecessary, and the male reproductive function, at least in its traditional mode, will be lost (McLoughlin: 1991) – a view seriously questioned by some feminists (for example, Curthoys: 1988). Mercifully, there seems to be very little enthusiasm for such a scenario. The prospect of an asexual or female homosexual society based on the superiority of the much-vaunted clitoral orgasm seems, according to present indications, to be just about nil. One feels that the 'sisters' are just not likely to win on this one.

The gender issue, among others, has spawned the current controversy over 'political correctness' (PC). This has permeated all walks of life, especially Higher Education in its various forms. Here, we understand, some of the venerable subject areas such as Medieval History (Stuart Wavell, 'A dark age of ignorance is upon us', *Sunday Times*, 14 August 1994) have given way to modish courses in Social Science and Humanities Departments where gender options have become almost *de rigueur* for students. There is little doubt that the vociferousness and extremism of some advocates of PC has brought this movement into disrepute. In an attempt to rectify what they believe to be a cardinal injustice, the faithful have frequently overplayed their hand and incurred the ridicule of many who might initially have been sympathetic to the cause. In a somewhat confusing attempt to make some sense of it all, a recent collection of essays for and against PC has been produced (Dunant: 1994). But one suspects that for all this, the converted will remain converted.

One subject area that is particularly affected is English Literature. The English Department of the University of London, for instance, now endorses 'strategies of inclusion', that is to say, courses are designed to ensure that texts are ordered (excluded? doctored?) so that no one will feel excluded by virtue of gender, colour or culture. This automatically rules out all sorts of texts – certainly classical texts – that did not treat these subjects in too kindly a fashion. As one critic puts it, 'are we to reshuffle Austen to the bottom of the pack for her snobbery? Shall we relegate Spenser for rejoicing in the massacre of Irish rebels?' (Zöe Heller, 'The way we talk now', *Independent*, 29 October 1994). Must we really reconstruct our heritage because it disgusts, offends or otherwise fails to concur with a particular – and rather singular – perspective? Are academics to be hounded out of the universities, theoretically the havens

of liberal thought and free speech, simply because they offer a viewpoint
or express themselves in arbitrarily unacceptable terms, as has happened
both here and in North America?

These attitudes, while germinating and flourishing in academia, can
now be found in a number of other professional areas, especially what
may be broadly called social work. A case reported in the British press
recently highlights the problem. A Women's Action Group tried to bring
a case against a local Women's Refuge for not employing a black woman
to work with sexually abused clients. The charge of discrimination was
dismissed by the tribunal on the grounds that the woman in question,
who objected to 'personal questions', had not had enough experience of
this kind of work. Inevitably this led to further allegations of racism.
According to *Observer* journalist, Melanie Phillips, this took the form of
a rather hysterical outburst of unsubstantiated allegations by the
Women's Action Group of 'unspecified horrors' perpetrated by the
Refuge workers on the women in their care. The conclusion of the
investigation, as can happen in PC cases, was that genuinely distressed
women had fallen foul of zealots who had done their cause no good by
rather mindless behaviour. Another reputable woman journalist,
Katharine Whitehorn, has also castigated the feminist Left for missing
the point. She says that it's all very well to make a song and dance about
the niceties of much PC language; many such idiocies have been
extensively rehearsed in the popular press, and have become little more
than a joke among ordinary people. Instead, she argues that PC people
ought to look more carefully at the *real* problems of society and see the
ways in which language is used to fudge the issues by what have become
known as 'unconscious codings' (Katharine Whitehorn, 'Rule of the
politically sacred', *Observer*, 9 January 1994).

Of all the needless conflicts in history, none is more needless than the
so-called 'battle of the sexes'. The traditional roles of men and women
have not come about because of some nefarious male conspiracy. There
is no *concerted* plot although there may be plots or alleged plots such as
the charge (*Sunday Times*, 11 September 1994) that the male-dominated
medical colleges in Britain have resisted the recruitment of women into
their ranks (only about 16 per cent of consultants are women, and only
2 per cent of surgeons). What we *do* have is a great deal of self-interest
on the part of both sexes. All people are egocentric; fortunately some a
little less than others. All seek their own advantage where possible. This
is not to imply that we are all thoroughgoing hedonists. Altruism does
exist. But, by and large, we all – where possible – try to further our own
interests, women no less than men. The traditional roles were, at least,
functional. It is a matter of debate to what extent the current predilection
for a unisexist *duplication of roles* is really that necessary. Of course,

there should be equal opportunity for all even though there can never be equality for all – biological inheritance, whether between sexes or within sexes, rules that out. Rationality demands complementarity and functionality. Sokrates said as much; we should all know our place and not usurp another's. The trick, of course, is to know exactly what that place is.

CHAPTER TEN

Elitism by Party: National Socialism in Germany 1920–45

A political party may be broadly defined as 'an organization oriented towards achieving legitimate control of government through an electoral process' (Giddens: 1989, p.312). In earlier societies, for example ancient Rome, the terms party and faction were virtually synonymous, but since the time of the English Restoration in the seventeenth century, the terms have become distinct, and the word party has developed its modern connotation. Strong monarchies and autocratic systems which were predicated on traditional principles had little need for parties, although they did generate factions, cabals and cliques of various kinds. Party in its present sense, therefore may be loosely associated with popular suffrage and parliamentary prerogatives.

But would such ideas apply to National Socialism whose suspect methods included deceit and propaganda and whose medium sometimes involved agitation and physical coercion? Perhaps we should therefore define the term 'party' in ways that does not inevitably imply a democratic process: say, a group that seeks to acquire power in order to benefit its adherents and realize its objective aims. The advantage of a one-party system is that it helps to form or, as in the case of Nazi Germany, to confirm a sense of national identity. This not only enhances a feeling of oneness, but also has practical implications for the rapid development of the economy.

A party is defined by its *platform*, its general statement of principles, policies and issues, and the programme which it promises to enact once in office. It has certain unifying themes, although in its manifestos these may be couched in such generalized – even ambiguous – terms, that the 'message' will have a wider appeal. Its pledges may be carefully hedged about with the kinds of qualifications which give the platform an 'open-ended' look, and which will be defended in terms of flexibility and feasibility. Once in power, everything is likely to be different. Intention is one thing, actual legislation is another.

In looking at National Socialism (something of a misnomer, considering that in Germany it did not confine itself to a purely national dimension, nor was it socialism as the term is usually conceived), we are thinking of a party with totalitarian objectives. And totalitarianism in its National Socialist guise may be defined as an élite system where

unrestrained political power is used by a centralized leadership to effect
a total social revolution based on an all-pervasive ideology. What is
particularly significant is that here we have an interesting variant of
Michels' theory of élites. Michels argued that obligarchies are inevitable,
and that the rank and file of a political party are manipulated and often
betrayed by their leaders who are drawn from higher social strata but do
not share their common interests and values. It is further argued that
those few from the ranks of the proletariat who may be allowed to join
the élite are soon absorbed into the ways of the higher culture.

So far so good. But in the case of Nazi Germany, we find that we have
a proletarian leadership; the inner circle of the Nazi élite were all from
the lower echelons of German society, and all – with the exception of
Goebbels, the Minister of Propaganda – were men of modest educational
attainment. True, they adopted the manners and conceits of their social
'betters', though it is said that Hitler always remained ill-at-ease in polite
society. However, they were able to attract people of considerable talent
into the hierarchy, albeit at the secondary level. How this was done, and
what exactly was the nature of the appeal, especially to the young
intelligentsia, are questions worthy of a good deal of research.

German National Socialism was essentially a revolutionary movement
based largely on the charismatic qualities of the leader. As such, it
presents us with the age-old problem of explanation versus description.
To classify Nazism in this way is merely to identify a particular kind of
social phenomenon. It does not explain why certain personal qualities
are attractive to so many, nor does it help us to understand how it was
that the movement's practices and policies met with such a massive
popular response. In short, to categorize a movement is not to explain
the reasons for its success. A revolutionary movement never appeals to
all sections of the community, and it attracts different sections for
different reasons. Therefore we can only begin to understand the
revolutionary transformation that took place by taking into account the
specific historical antecedents in question. *Pre*revolutionary situations
often have much in common; political instability, economic depression,
an impoverished and consequently disgruntled middle-class, and in the
case of Germany, defeat in war and the imposition of a crippling
reparations debt, the promised abolition of which was a main plank in
the Nazi platform.

The *conception* of the National Socialist movement grew out of the
acute disillusionment in Germany following the First World War. For the
extremists of the Right, the loss of the war was more than a defeat, it was
a national humiliation that demanded redress, even revenge. The
movement began as the German Workers' Party, one of many small
parties that had sprung up in the aftermath of the war, which covered

the whole range of the protest spectrum from the revolutionary Left to the radical Right. In the ferment of anger and resentment, Nazism had its modest and inauspicious beginnings (Hitler, who discovered the Party almost by accident, was in fact only its seventh member). Its orientations were intensely nationalistic at a time when one might have supposed that people would have been rather tired – and fearful – of the conflicts which attended the clash of intense nationalisms. After all, that's what the war had been largely all about. The German people had been led to expect victory in 1918, and, indeed the war was very nearly won. But then came unexpected defeat, and the temptation to find scapegoats was irresistible.

Someone was responsible, and on the assumption that it couldn't be the invincible German Army, many found consolation in the myth of the 'November criminals', traitors, Marxists, civilian slackers, nervous politicians – and, of course, Jewish capitalists. These were all deemed to have 'stabbed the Army in the back' when, in fact, it had been the generals who had initiated the peace moves. Besides the reparations commitment (set a the staggering figure of $32 000 000 000) and the obligation to reduce her forces to token strength, the Versailles Treaty had stripped Germany of her colonies and had dispossessed her of Alsace-Lorraine, the Saar and Upper Silesia, as well as Danzig and the Polish corridor which incomprehensively separated Germany from Prussia; in all about one-eighth of her European territory. All these things had been agreed by the post-war Government of what was known as the Weimar Republic, and it was this socialist-orientated Government that became the main focus of extremist animosity. As both communists and nationalists vied for public attention, the Government found itself losing the confidence of the military, on whom it had to rely to retain law and order, and of the courts, which were expected to implement its policies. The clamour mounted: everything played into the hands of the extremists. Perhaps worst of all was the economic crisis. By 1920, Germany was in the grip of hyper-inflation aggravated by mass unemployment and acute poverty was felt, not only by the lower classes but also by those of the middle-classes who had lost both their savings and their livelihoods; and it was largely from this stratum, the *petit-bourgeoisie* of small farmers, shop-keepers, artisans, managers and the like, that much of Hitler's support was to come.

The German Workers' Party, with just a handful of members, soon became the National Socialist Workers' Party (from which we derive the term 'Nazi') which in just one year raised its membership to 3 000. By 1923, with a vastly increased membership of over 50 000 it had an undisputed Leader (from 1921), its own paid officials, its special symbol, the swastika, its own newspaper, and – more ominously – its own band of uniformed 'strong-men', the Stormtroopers (SA). In the same year, Hitler made his first disastrous bid for power when he took over a

Munich meeting hall and tried to bluff Bavarian officials in session there that a successful revolution was underway. It didn't work; and to compound the folly, next day, 9 November, he led his Party officers and Stormtroopers in an attempt to take over the city, but they were quickly dispersed by police gunfire. Hitler was arrested, tried for treason early in 1924, and given an extraordinarily light sentence considering the gravity of the offence. Perhaps the authorities just could not take him that seriously, a mistake that others were to make later on. Hitler spent only ten months in prison assiduously composing his personal apologia and outlining his plans for Germany's future, later published as *Mein Kampf* ('my struggle').

After the Munich fiasco and his sobering spell in gaol, Hitler decided to adopt other methods. In future, he and the Party would favour the ballot rather than the bullet. It would be slower, of course, but it would be surer and would give the Party the legitimacy that it required. Yet despite the adoption of a somewhat milder *modus operandi*, the public was not persuaded. What is more, the economy was picking up – largely with the help of borrowed money – a situation that hardly favoured a revolutionary movement. The revitalized and more confident Republic decided to outlaw Nazism, and 1925 witnessed the nadir of the Party's fortunes. Ironically, it was because the government now saw the party as an unlikely threat, that it later relaxed its policies, and the Party's membership stabilized and began to increase as the first signs of a reversal in the economic situation became evident. With the Depression came a remarkable improvement in Party support, and in just two years from 1927 to 1929, the membership rose sevenfold to an impressive 178 000. The bankruptcies, factory closures and consequent unemployment and hardship generally, all played into the hands of the Nazis. The people wanted a solution, a remedy, so why not try something different? Before the Depression, the Party had polled less than a million votes which gave them only 12 seats in the state legislature, but even before the Depression had really begun to bite by September 1930 these numbers had rocketed to six and a half million which made them the second largest party with 107 seats.

There was now a short pause, but in 1932 the National Socialist vote doubled which gave them over a third of the seats in the Reichstag. The President and revered ex-military leader, Paul von Hindenburg, offered the Nazis a share in a coalition government. Astutely, they refused: Hitler was going to have real power or nothing. He confidently assumed – perhaps rightly – that he could win the next time round anyway. After several unsuccessful attempts to solve the impasse over the Chancellorship the aged President decided (or was persuaded) to relent and reluctantly offer the post to the 'upstart corporal' (Hitler's wartime rank). For the old Field-Marshal, it must have been like offering an executive directorship to a van-driver. Hitler took power with due solemnity on 30 January 1933, surely the most fateful day in Germany's history.

It has been argued that the development of the Nazi Party is characteristic of totalitarian systems generally, and that the typical sequence is Ideology → Movement → Party → Government (Friedrich and Brzezinski: 1965). The first stage, that of realizing the ideology, is critically important and often involves serious controversies and clashes between members and factions within the Party. This happened during the 'Terror' of the French Revolution when violent arguments about the correct interpretation of the ideology ironically brought all the principals of the Revolution under the knife eventually. It was also certainly true of the formative phases of the Russian revolution, and continued well into the early years of Soviet government, indeed until Stalin consolidated his position in the late 1920s. But, except for the critical conflict between the Government and the SA a year after coming to power, it was not the experience of the Nazis. In adapting the ideology to situational needs both Hitler and his 'ice-cold reasoning' and Stalin, employing what was termed 'the mercilessness of the dialectics', adopted a pseudo-scientific approach to support the Parties' claims and, of course, to justify their own rule. In such circumstances it is always interesting to ask to what extent these were largely personal power struggles overlaid with ideological justifications. The rationale had to appear to be eminently reasonable, so with Hitler the 'racial superiority' myth was perpetuated, together with the idea of Germany's 'providential mission'. Various controls were then instituted such as censorship, re-education programmes and the like to ensure that the ideology was not 'corrupted'. Under the Nazis research departments were set up, mainly by the SS (security police) to trace Aryan/Nordic origins and 'relics', and to investigate folklore in order to validate aspects of the ideology. Efforts were actually made to try to establish connections with the Teutonic Knights. Runes were studied, and later after the invasion of Russia in 1941, an infamous 'commissar order' was issued whereby these officials were to be executed and some of the skulls sent back to Berlin for examination as further 'proof' of Slavic inferiority. Unquestionably, myths have their uses.

It is further maintained by Friedrich and Brzezinski that it is only when the inner contradictions of the system become evident and the ideology is questioned, that violence has to be deployed in order to maintain compliance. But is this really so? How many seriously questioned the regime? A few did openly object – often in their own interests – particularly towards the end of the war when it was obvious that

Germany was defeated, and most of these were duly silenced. Others were prepared to doubt quietly – and survive (see Snyder: 1991).

The development of the Party was, in a sense, the implementation of the ideology. In the early days, as we have seen, the Party fought for recognition in a hostile world, and a sense of purpose and comradeship united the members. However, with success and elevation to government, the movement became increasingly formalized. Despite this, Hitler actually remained 'true' to many of his 'old guard' in later years (even Hermann Goering, the head of the *Luftwaffe*, who became a rather useless appendage to the regime from 1943 onwards), unlike Stalin who had virtually all his old supporters eliminated.

The Nazis had been elected to power on a minority vote, and there is some evidence of ballot-rigging and intimidation even to secure the number of votes they did. Quite soon afterwards, further elections were held which gave them yet more seats though not the majority they required. But by a series of political machinations and the requisite pressure on their political opponents, they were able to persuade the Reichstag to capitulate and pass an Enabling Act which effectively gave Hitler dictatorial powers. This was the real 'seizure of power' which needless to say, was exploited to the full. It gave the Nazis an exclusive claim to legality. There was no longer any pretence of parliamentary government. Other parties were banned, the trades unions closed down (the right to strike was withdrawn, and the unions were replaced by a national organization, the Labour Front), Communism proscribed, the rights of Jews severely restricted, and rivals and undesirables duly dealt with.

By the summer of 1934, Hitler felt strong enough to settle accounts with the leaders of the SA who were looking for a more radical revolution which would have adversely affected both the Army and the industrialists, and generally disturbed the growing stability of the state. There is no certain evidence that the SA planned an actual *coup* but its leadership was ruthlessly purged on the 'Night of the Long Knives' (30 June 1934) by the SS with the undoubted acquiescence, perhaps even connivance, of the military. The charge was treason, that old standby of despotic regimes, underpinned by reasonably well-founded accusations of homosexuality. Together these were plausible enough to convince the electorate that the state had been saved from further upheaval by the percipient and precipitate action of the Führer.

Thus began the full 'nazification' of the state machinery. Party officials were appointed to state positions, certain state functions were transferred to the Party bureaucracies, unwanted personnel were dismissed, educational procedures (curricula and so on) were transformed, and – very importantly – the judiciary was no longer independent of the state. Civil and criminal law became Nazi law (a particularly notorious illustration of this was the farcicality of the trials conducted by the Nazi judge, Roland Freisler, in the aftermath of the failed bomb-plot to kill Hitler in July 1944. He merely screamed at the defendants who were allowed no defence. Later – and appropriately – Freisler was killed in his own court in an Allied air-raid). 'Justice' was served by the rapid development of the state security services – SS, SD and especially the Gestapo – which became instruments of terror. All dissenting elements were suppressed by elimination or (what almost amounted to the same thing) consignment to special camps.

Every agency of government now came under Party control, and the whole economy was centralized to serve the long-term aims of the Führer. The total planning of the economy was well underway by 1936; rearmament had begun in earnest and unemployment was almost a thing of the past now that the German economy was virtually on a war-time footing.

There was, of course, still the problem of how to come to terms with the other major social institutions such as the Church, the aristocracy, the Army (*Wehrmacht*) as well as industry itself. And it was just here that the Party encouraged – at least in the short term – *rapprochement* as an instrument of policy. Coming to an understanding with opposing interests was both necessary and politically astute for this aspiring totalitarianism. It was important to give the people the impression that this Party was *their* party; that their interests were also the Party's interests. In the Soviet Union, this 'coincidence' of interests with a submissive proletariat had been achieved by repudiating the extreme Right: the Church and the aristocracy. But in Germany it was done by repudiating the extreme Left, the Communists, as had also happened in fascist Italy. Mussolini had done the necessary 'deals' with the Church and with industry; Hitler did likewise except that he had much stronger reservations about religion, and (according to his 'table talk' during the war) intended to neutralize the influence of the Church when the time came. He also came to an uneasy understanding with the Army whose generals vainly thought they were using him when, in fact, it was quite the reverse. Interestingly, Hitler had nothing like the same problems with the German Navy whose officers were much more acquiescent, nor with the Air Force (*Luftwaffe*) which was virtually a creation of the regime.

These 'arrangements' ensured that resistant or entrenched elements in the traditional order were accommodated and thus rendered virtually powerless. Whatever Hitler did, he did by the book. All his critical moves – at this stage, at least – were technically correct. He was meticulous in providing legal grounds for everything he did. 'The new, stronger laws on public order, on political offences, on economic crimes, all had impeccable constitutional origins' (Chapman: 1970, p.71). Every aspect of the state became imbued with the new philosophy. The Leader of the Party was the embodiment of the people. Together they constituted a mystical community: 'ein Volk, ein Reich, ein Führer'.

If any were inclined to demur at the margins, there was the always the presence of the security services to ensure compliance. Under 'emergency law', anything was possible. In 1935 it was decreed that local administration courts were 'not competent to examine the orders and affairs of the Secret Police'; it was not politic – or indeed safe – to enquire too closely into the affairs of those taken into 'protective custody'. Furthermore, a law passed in February 1936 made it incumbent on local police forces to co-operate fully with the security services as the ostensible instrument of the Party. It laid down that the Gestapo was to 'investigate and suppress all anti-state tendencies ... to assemble and evaluate the results of any unrest [and] to keep the state informed' (quoted by Chapman: 1970, pp.6–7). In June the same year this was further refined and reinforced with the thorough reorganization of the police and security services which increased still further the latter's power and gave them responsibility for surveillance, concentration camps and counter-espionage. But it wasn't until the outbreak of hostilities in September 1939 that they really came into their own and were able to extend their authority over the occupied territories, in which they instituted a campaign of terror and extermination.

In just a few years these combined services had effectively become a state within a state, a law unto themselves. They were para-military forces that took over the established police, whose activities were now largely dictated by political requirements. They intimidated other state institutions by limiting their freedom, they confirmed the powers of the judiciary, and interiorized the civil service in order to further their interests. Eventually they expanded the scope of their activities to the military by the formation of a parallel organization, the *Waffen* SS, which even challenged the monopoly of the traditional military hierarchy.

Only a minority of Germans actually belonged to the Party. At its highest, membership was about 10 per cent of the total population, or about 25 per cent of all German adults. What attracts one person (and repels another) to any idea or movement is notoriously difficult to say, although it can be reasonably hypothesized that the original motivating factors here were socio-psychological in nature. As time went on however, and the Party grew in popularity, there was undoubtedly a bandwagon effect, especially for those who had an eye to the main chance. Those who allied themselves to such a totalitarian cause were accepting a very specific view of social reality; in effect, they were embracing a particular kind of political myth. Broadly speaking, political myths are devices that are used 'to explain and give emotional meaning to social experience' in order to justify or rationalize certain political goals (Orlov: 1971, p.3). Such myths are often totalizing in that they purport to explain all social life. A new value system is proclaimed. The ambiguities of moral experience are resolved. The adherent now 'knows' what is right and what is wrong; who is a friend and who is an enemy. He doesn't have to worry about these things any more. The Party has told him, and the Party is right.

The Party was thus a kind of synthetic society in that it was motivated by an ideology of blood and race which was at variance with the world of empirical reality. Yet, through its propaganda agencies and its organizational apparatus, it was able to operationalize the myth for state purposes despite its fundamental irrationality (if anyone doubts this, try to answer the question 'Why did Hitler kill the Jews?' and make it sound at all reasonable). The conversion and indoctrination of the individual to this perverted kind of thinking has been described as 'creeping rape' (quoted by Orlov: ibid., p.4), a violation of the intellect. This view has a certain cogency, but is it entirely accurate? The disturbing and perplexing fact that becomes clear in any study of ideology is that so many people *willingly* surrender themselves to the most bizarre and irrational ideas: the history of anti-semitism is just one case in point.

The Party was organized geographically on a four-tier basis: the *Gaue*, which corresponded roughly to the 34 Reichstag electoral districts, each headed by a Gauleiter appointed by Hitler (there were seven additional *Gaue* for Austria, Danzig, the Saar and the Sudentenland); the sub-districts of *Kreise*, each under a Kreisleiter; and local groups (*Ortsgruppen*) which were further divided into local blocks or street units. A typical *Gaue* was itself divided into a number of administrative sections which dealt with mobilization, internal administration (including publication of circulars, communications, processing of reports and liaison with the office of propaganda), a clemency office, an office for liaison on military matters, a judiciary office and an office of 'special affairs'. At the top level, Party organization was divided into departments dealing with internal matters, and those concerned with state matters including the economy, race, foreign affairs and so on. The Party structure also included a number of very important subsidiary organizations such as the Propaganda Division and the Reich Press Office, the *Deutsches Jungvolk* (young people 10–15) and the Hitler Youth (15–18) for physical education and cultural indoctrination; there were also separate organizations for girls, women, students (surprisingly rather ardent supporters of the regime), civil servants, medical staff, jurists and so forth, and a *Kulturbund* for artists and intellectuals – a special interest of Propaganda Minister Goebbels.

There never was a final resolution of the respective functions of the Party and the Civil Service. As one authority puts it, the 'Party and the civil servants were two organisms existing in a complex state of symbiosis so that it was not always easy to ascertain which one fed parasitically on the other' (Grunberger: 1974, p.82). One suspects that, as in other areas of Nazi organization, for example the *Abwehr* (military intelligence) and the espionage and counter-espionage branches of the SS, Hitler deliberately fostered rivalries so that he alone could be the final arbiter of both policy and practice. It was his version of the divide-and-rule principle. Preferment in the civil service depended very much on social background and educational attainment, whereas the Party's main consideration was seniority: the 'old comrades' who constituted the Party's aristocracy. However, as time went on, it was the bandwagon people, the opportunistic late-comers, the 'March Violets' as they were called (referring to March 1933 when there was a huge influx of members) who eventually landed many of the top jobs. (An SS publication – with an uncharacteristic touch of humour – suggested, that if Hitler had joined the Party later, he would have got much further than he had.) The Party deployed about 100 000 civil servants as honorary political leaders, and adopted a policy of positive discrimination in relation to Party veterans, insisting in 1935 that 10 per cent of the lower and middle ranking appointments should go to those who had joined before September 1930. Prior to 1935 many ward and district officials took over other community tasks and doubled as town mayors and the like. By 1935 it was estimated that Party members occupied 60 per cent of some 52 000 executive posts in state and community agencies, an issue which raised some difficulties between the Party and the civil service and a problem exacerbated by the relatively low pay of Party officials.

A sociological study of the Nazi movement (quoted by Grunberger: 1974, pp.85–6) provides further evidence of the inverse relationship between education and power. This shows that the movement was dominated by poorly-educated Party veterans who rose to control much of the Party machinery and retained that control throughout its history. The strong-arm men (SA and SS) were predominantly of plebeian origin. There were many notable exceptions; the SS, for instance, often recruited some very bright – if unscrupulous – men into its upper echelons. Either these came from the aristocracy who provided one in ten of the higher ranks of the SS while representing less than one per cent of the population as a whole, or they came from academia (see, for example, Carlton: 1992, *Excursus* on The Holocaust and the SS Intelligentsia).

About half the Nazi leadership came from lower middle-class families; their parents were teachers, shopkeepers, artisans, minor officials and so on. Approximately one in four Party administrators were graduates while one in two of those involved with propaganda had a degree. Out of thirty Gauleiter, only seven had anything higher than an elementary education; five had been to university but only three had actually graduated; six of the Gauleiter had been elementary school teachers, ten were clerks/office workers, and one was a labourer. This reflected the general composition of the Party in 1935 when 30 per cent were manual and blue-collar workers, about $19\frac{1}{2}$ per cent were white-collar workers, $12\frac{1}{2}$ per cent were civil servants and 10 per cent were farmers. By 1937, about 20 per cent of the Party membership were Party functionaries of some kind, and well over a third came from the esteemed professions of teaching and the civil service.

The power of Party leaders was considerable. Even the relatively modest block leader constituted an intimidating presence in the tenements under his control. He was able to command confidential files from local tax offices, organize 'voluntary' collections for Party funds and generally act as the Party's eyes and ears in his discrete domain. However, in order to foster better public relations, local Party leaders – somewhat like modern British MPs – were instructed to conduct citizens' surgeries so that they might hear complaints and presumably try to remedy the popular impression that Party functionaries were a privileged élite.

The allegation that Party leaders in particular were a law unto themselves was not entirely unfounded. This was especially the case with those who served in the occupied territories during the war. The Party had its own courts, and it was not that simple for those outside the Party to institute legal proceedings against Party members. But, by the same token, the Party could sometimes be harsh with its own people. It expected more from its own members than from 'outsiders'. Its very important sanction of expulsion could mean considerable disgrace for those concerned, and possibly even dismissal from their non-Party occupations. In the war, many had exemption from military service, but it must be said that on the home front Party members were expected to make supererogatory efforts during emergencies. They were often involved in clearance operations following the extensive damage done by the air-raids as well as welfare work in relation to the homeless and the bereaved. At the same time they were also concerned with the re-allocation of labour, the distribution of food, and the evacuation of refugees when the state in 1944 called for the total mobilization of resources.

In outline, we have followed the fortunes of the Party through the phases of conception and inception to the realization and consolidation of power. But how influential was it? Observers were impressed by the well-organized mass rallies and the general support the Nazis had. But it has been argued that although many thought the Party exerted an 'authoritative radicalizing influence on decision-making ... [it was] ... in fact, increasingly condemned to political sterility' (Hans Mommsen, 'National Socialism: Continuity and Change' in Laqueur: 1979, pp.171–2). It is further argued that political importance resided not in the Party but rather in high ranking officials, such as Martin Bormann of the Party Chancellery, who used their positions as stepping-stones to important government office (Lang: 1979). The Party is thus seen as very much a subsidiary organization which did not seriously attempt to bring about any real integration between the multifarious state organizations. It is even contended that the Party was something of a liability in that its officials, pre-eminently those of Gauleiter rank, persistently created their personal spheres of influence, and survived by a complex and self-interested system of patronage.

This is a well-tried thesis which maintains that Nazism as a system was sustained by a process of negative integration; by a policy of *divide et impera*. The regime was a tangle of cliques, personal independencies and disputed competencies. There were unquestionably leadership rivalries and internal power struggles. There were interminable departmental squabbles which certainly did the regime no good, and the Party was part of this. But is this all it was? A careful appraisal of the nature and functions of the Party especially in the early, formative years of the Nazi movement suggests that it acted as the necessary agency whereby the movement was able to develop its policies and organization. It was permeated – indeed, dominated – by a particular ideology, and it was the vehicle whereby this ideology was mediated to the masses. The ideology was all-encompassing, an organized set of ideas and ideals intended to bring about revolutionary change (Lee: 1987, pp.300–5). Everything was subordinated to it, and society was effectively restructured according to its goals. Hitler had long insisted that all nature was one great struggle between strength and weakness. Thus, eugenic progress could only be made by eliminating that which is inferior, a philosophy that found its ultimate – and horrifying – expression in the death camps.

The key factor, and the one that distinguishes Nazism from fascism (an ill-defined and rather abused term) was that of race. Anti-semitism in particular was not peculiar to the Nazis: it had a long history, especially in Germany and Austria, so it had a specific resonance when tricked out in a somewhat new guise by the Nazi ideologues. Indeed, it might be argued that no movement or set of ideas can flourish unless there is already a certain measure of socio-cultural compatibility. Jews and Jewishness were associated – paradoxically – with both capitalism and communism. It was regarded as a form of infection, something which polluted the world, and something that the 'master race' had a duty to eradicate. This was the heroic ideal which the regime existed to accomplish: its task was to rule and to eliminate the weak. The preservation of the race was the fundamental mission and organizing principle of the Party and of the state.

CHAPTER ELEVEN

Elitism by Economic Status: The Western 'Models' Problem

Economists have sometimes posited that there is such a being as the 'Economic Man', the implication being that we are all economically rational creatures. To what extent are we *all* fundamentally alike? Is it true that whether we are primitives or sophisticates we all have the same basic thought-structures? Some eminent specialists in linguistics (most notably, Noam Chomsky who has spent much of his life trying to discover the kind of mental activity that underlies behaviour) insist that we do all share the same reality, even if our actual life-worlds are different. And it is just these differences that present a problem – or three problems, to be precise:

1. There is first the question of *rationality*. How can we square other pre-modern thinking processes with our own? Can primitives and sophisticates, for example, really identify with each other?
2. Then there is the matter of *comparability*. If others are really so different can they be meaningfully studied and compared?
3. Lastly there is the problem of *modes of analysis*. If others are going to be studied, how is it best done? Can we, for instance, apply modern Western models of economic action to other kinds of society?

Early views maintained that primitive people lived a hand-to-mouth existence, and were therefore unable to make economic judgements. It was thought that their economies were based on the satisfaction of immediate needs, but we now know that this was true only of the very poorest, often nomadic, peoples. Having established this, however, in more recent times the debate about comparability has still continued. Some writers (for example, M. Herskovits), while freely acknowledging the importance of machine technology, insist that practically every economic mechanism and institution known to us is found somewhere in the non-literate world. Yet others, such as Raymond Firth, maintain that the principles of economics which are truly general in their applications are very few, and that most of those which purport to be general have been constructed primarily within the framework of an individualist, capitalist system with its machine technology, monetary exchange and elaborate credit system.

Non-industrial systems certainly were, and in a number of cases still are, characterized by several key features which are now foreign to what we term developed societies, these key features being:

1. *Rudimentary technology*: weaving and pottery are usually the nearest things to mass production to be found along with weapon-making for hunting and warfare, and possibly canoe-making where circumstances require it. In general, there is no great degree of economic specialization. Traditionally, changes were slight and slow, and it is only in relatively recent times with Western contacts that their economic mechanisms have been affected.

2. *Productive units*: these are small; in fact, units are often organized on a kinship basis. There are few wage-relationships, but units frequently have a system of profit-sharing according to a clearly defined scale.

3. *Agents of production*: these are rarely separable and labour is commonly a *social*, rather than a consciously economic activity. In a tribal society, 'capital' might well be supplied by a chief or headman who is, at the same time, just another manual worker.

4. *No constantly expanding market for capital*: capital goods exist (for example, canoes which may take several hundred man-hours to complete) but there is little seeking for fresh avenues of investment.

5. *No widespread entrepreneur system*: there are often enterprising individuals that we may wish to call entrepreneurs who play a part in organizing the flow of goods and services, but again there is little creation – as in the West – of new demands.

6. *Relative inflexibility of the price system*: as Max Weber has argued (Weber: 1968) price systems are of a highly traditionalized type, where considerable resistance is shown by producers and consumers alike to variation or modification in the rates for work. There are, predictably, some exceptions to this; Raymond Firth cites the 'sensitive bargaining system' of Malay fishermen. But there are limits to flexibility: for instance, the traditional 'bride-price' paid in many African societies seems to be more a symbol than an actual economic price. Bride-price tends to be *in*flexible; if it were a price in the economic sense then market value would change with demand and supply but, generally speaking, this is not the case (Firth: 1970).

It was once argued that non-industrial economic systems were different not just because of their lack of technology but also because of the nature of the non-industrialized – particularly primitive –

temperament. In several classic texts the anthropologist, Bronisław Malinowski, did his best to correct such misconceptions. Previously, other writers had suggested either that 'savages' were indolent and irresponsible, or that they were always rational and utilitarian. Malinowski tried to steer a middle course and pointed out that natives were quite capable of arduous work, sometimes of a highly organized nature, and that trade and exchange activities could be complex, regular and often quite elaborate. By comparison with developed societies however, they appeared to be non-rational, irrational, or positively stupid. The underlying assumption was – and probably still is – that in industrialized societies resources are utilized and organized in relation to human wants in the only sensible way.

It is here that we can see the necessarily limited field of application of the principles of economics, as we know them. In non-industrialized societies, the values that informed production, distribution and even consumption were just different from our own. *Labour* could be hard and difficult, though it was often seasonal and therefore irregular. Because of a lack of technology there was also concealed under-employment, that is to say, the individuals engaged were under-employed but the work itself, the immediate task, suffered from over-employment. Often marginal categories of labour were recruited: the young, aged, and even deformed might all be employed. In relatively developed societies, for example, ancient Egypt and Inca Peru, labour was frequently organized on a corvée basis; this was not a form of slavery but rather a kind of tax for those who had little else to give. *Time* too was not greatly recognized, especially in simpler societies. The modern Western framework was not always known, and certainly not always appreciated. *Incentives*, as we understand them, often didn't exist in such societies, certainly not in monetary or profit forms. The deceptive simplicity of, say, traditional Polynesian society could possibly be seen as an affront to our materialism, although it was not perhaps the virtue that it at first appears. After all, island societies, as we have seen, had very little opportunity for accumulation. How does one store wealth (fish?) in these circumstances, especially in such societies where privacy was virtually unknown. It is not that tribespeople were above gain, it was simply just not possible.

In developed pre-industrial societies, this was not the case. Sometimes even temples doubled as treasuries and banks. Accumulation was not only possible, it was also desirable. But even so, other factors such as renown, reputation and prestige mattered as much, and in some instances possibly more, than wealth. In some primitive societies, for instance, it is known that men might refuse to hunt for fear of failure and consequent loss of face. It was also a source of considerable shame if one's family was not provided for, or if one could not find an adequate dowry for one's daughter, or one could not afford the necessary expense of a parent's funeral, or if one could not pay one's debts. In many such societies, esteem was of paramount importance.

In simple pre-industrial societies there was no marked orientation in terms of different classes of work. By and large, work, whether it was building a hut or making a canoe, was seen to be of more-or-less equal value. Nor was there a strong tendency towards the allocation of employment on a social class basis. There were, of course, exceptions. But, in general, work was shared regardless of the status of the worker. This was not so much the case in complex pre-industrial societies where differentiation was much more marked. There is the well-known example of the building of the *Erechtheion*, a temple on the Athenian Acropolis where the workforce consisted of free men (citizens), resident aliens (metics) and slaves. These groups were completely different in terms of status, political and social rights and so forth, yet all received the same daily rate of pay.

There are, therefore, serious limitations on the possible applications of modern economic theory to non-industrialized societies and this can be seen in a number of ways. Consider the assessment of object values: in our kind of society utilitarian objects such as cars can be costed in terms of material and labour (that is, as money). In non-monetary (barter/exchange) economies – even in such highly developed societies as ancient Egypt – this kind of costing seems not to have been possible, although very careful note was kept by overseers of crop yields for taxation purposes. In such societies it was not uncommon to attach considerable value to *non*-utilitarian objects, especially those required for decoration and personal adornment which usually expressed status or rank. But then this is hardly unknown in our kind of society. Non-utilitarian objects such as diamonds still retain an artificial value; yet despite having little intrinsic value, they are easily convertible in terms of cash.

Modern economic concepts are largely foreign to non-industrialized societies whose rudimentary economies have a peculiar rationality of their own. For instance, the modern emphasis on efficiency of production per unit output is difficult to apply to a kin-based economy. The East African Masai, for example, traditionally scorned agriculture as a livelihood because of the belief that the earth gives food by feeding the herds – so why should it be made to contribute twice over? Maximization was not a primary concern. This is exemplified by the account of a Field Officer who advised an African agricultural community to use the chemical fertilizer that he could supply and which would double their yield, and who returned the following year to find that the tribespeople had only cultivated half their land! The concept too of marginal utility rarely applies in kin-based economies where relatives will help one another without any consciousness of gain or loss on either side. This is not to suggest that tribespeople never maximize after the fashion of the West; they do so increasingly. But the tendency has been to maximize leisure rather than profit. Add to all this the fact that the bases of distribution are normally quite different in that they are social as well as economic, and it will be seen that the principles of modern economics which are truly applicable are really very few (Firth: 1970).

The particular feature which vitiates the economic arrangements in both simple and complex pre-industrial societies, and which more than anything else demonstrates a difference of mind-set between them and modern post-industrial society is that of religious ideology. In our highly secularized society there has been a strong tendency towards relegating religion to the rank of a dependent variable (or, as an old acquaintance of mine used to say, 'it just doesn't change the price of oranges, Charlie'). Needless to say, this was far from the case in other places at other times. In some societies certain skills were developed and encouraged while others were deplored, although this had little or nothing to do with supply and demand factors. It was ideology that mattered. As we saw in the Indian caste system, traditional occupational categories were supported by powerful religious sanctions. Such ritual complications tend to baffle the modern observer. Why are certain coveted foods only used for ritual purposes? Why the extravagance of religious feasts in subsistence societies? Why the destruction of valued – even irreplaceable – goods for religious reasons, including human life itself? Indeed, why sacrifice at all? These are all activities which – rightly or wrongly – override what moderns would regard as rational economic considerations. Critics might retort that these were really *in*direct means of trying to ensure material benefits. But although it may be thought that by pleasing the gods, the people might secure fertility, abundance and prosperity, it could be argued that the problem still remains at one remove; why choose such wholly disadvantageous ways of doing this? Other peoples who have been equally devout have found much more 'rational' ways of placating the deities.

In developing countries much has changed with Westernization. To take just two instances: in India media personalities and brewers (once an outlawed occupation for the higher castes) have become wealthy and influential in contravention of traditional caste norms; and even in South Africa, before the establishment of the National Government, certain supermarkets were welcoming both blacks and whites, economic factors being now patently paramount (though as an ideological gesture shoppers had to use different doors). Convergence is undoubtedly taking place and globalization after the Western pattern is now a fact, regardless of the rearguard objections of those who deplore and distrust such changes as symptomatic of a fast-encroaching cultural imperialism.

Why have these differences in development taken place? Why have those peoples who still live in relative poverty not even begun to achieve the standard of living enjoyed by the wealthier nations? Presumably our ancestors all began from much the same starting point but the *speed* at which they developed certainly differed. There were always, of course, more and less favourable climatic conditions with the concomitants of either relative scarcity or abundance of available game (so one can hardly imagine the Esquimaux developing at the same rate as people in the more clement Mediterranean area). Pre-agrarian societies of the hunger-gatherer type were forced to lead a nomadic existence in search of the essentials of life. With the 'agrarian revolution' and with increasing control over nature, settled and eventually urban life became possible. This occurred at different times in different places, the most advanced societies being usually – though not exclusively – found in the great fertile river valleys such as the Nile (Egypt), the Tigris–Euphrates (Iraq), the Hwang-ho (China) and the Indus (Pakistan). These riverine societies were the first to produce an agricultural surplus which in turn made what we now call civilization possible.

With gradual improvements in the quality of life there was a rise in the birth-rate, and though infant mortality – still the bane of the Third World – was still high, population overall increased. Land was the primary resource, and nomadic territoriality gave way to state and communal ownership of land; and plausibly this in turn (according to Marxist theorists) generated the wealth–poverty divide and eventually the class structures which came to vitiate societies. Wealth, or at least the freedom from being almost continually engaged in scratching out a living, made a leisured class possible; and with leisure came time to reflect, time to study and to investigate, and ultimately this bore fruit in terms of written language, the plastic arts, and not least science itself.

After a considerable period of artistic and architectural achievement lasting some 3 000 years, that is from the Egyptian Old Kingdom (the Pyramid Age) to the decline of the Roman Empire in the fifth century of our era, in Europe there was a time of relative dormancy usually known as the Dark Ages. With the revitalization of culture, designated the Renaissance, came the resurgence of reflective philosophy, new social attitudes and theories of the state, the invention of printing, the development of craft-guilds and, not least, voyages of exploration and the rise of the merchant class. In recalling these exploits, some writers – possibly out of an exaggerated desire to promote their own brand of political correctness – have indulged in unwarranted anti-Western revisionism.

One such writer, Erik Dammann, obviously intent on trying to redress the balance in favour of colonized peoples, has rightly emphasized Western injustices to the indigenes but has conveniently omitted the other side of the story. For example, in describing the conquest of Mexico by the Spanish early in the sixteenth century, he concentrates on the architectural marvels of Mexico City (Tenochtitlan), located in the midst of a lake, and on Aztec culture and state organization; and reminds us of the rapacity of Cortés and his tiny army of conquistadores who, aided by tribal levies of some of the Aztec's enemies, conquered and effectively destroyed a civilization (Dammann: 1979, pp.26–30). But in extolling the native virtues of the Aztecs he nowhere sees fit to mention their barbarities: this state was almost continuously at war. Why? Not, as one might expect, for land or for booty – at least not in the conventional sense. War was necessary to secure captives, and captives were wanted for sacrifice: the 'gods were hungry', they required blood to sustain them. So captives were taken to the temples that stood at the summits of their steep, stepped pyramids, were pinioned over 'the stone' by priests who then ripped their hearts from their bodies and offered them – still beating – to the sun or its divine avatars. Sacrifices were made daily, and especially on ceremonial occasions. In fact, the Aztecs had probably the most extensive form of institutionalized sacrifice known to history: for example, at the opening of a temple in 1487, a little before the Spanish arrived, some 4 000 – at a conservative estimate – were sacrificed to the gods. The heads of victims adorned the regularly replenished skull racks, and the tastier portions of the bodies were eaten. Selected victims were flayed and their skins worn by dancing blood-matted priests. There were too other forms of sacrifice, sometimes including women and especially children who were dedicated to Tlaloc, god of rain (Brundage: 1985). To accuse Cortés and the invaders, as some have, of violating Aztec beliefs by 'throwing down the idols', must surely have little justification. One feels instinctively that these horrific practices which were absolutely central to Mexican culture could not be allowed to continue. The imposition of Spanish culture, despite all its cruelties and depredations could hardly have been worse *in the long term* than the one it replaced.

From the seventeenth century onwards in Europe there was a total transformation of systems of production, distribution and exchange from which emerged a large-scale commercial trading network that was international in character. In Britain, the Bank of England (founded in 1694) integrated and enlarged the banking system into a more coherent economic and social institution, and Joint Stock companies developed which facilitated the lending of capital and enabled new trading and commercial ventures to be financed (Harris: 1989, pp.6–7).

All the ingredients were now in place for what we now term the Industrial Revolution: technological development, capital, labour, coal and iron and other essential raw materials, and potential domestic and overseas markets. This explosion in economic activity brought with it the development of large-scale production techniques, and the technical skills and commercial know-how to be able to administer such complex organizations and market their products. Though by no means enviable, the lot of the working population improved considerably. Certainly it was a great deal better than subsistence farming, and more and more people left agriculture and gravitated towards the new industrial conurbations. The system was exploitative and in many ways unjust, but it had overcome the economic 'hump'. Living standards had never been better, and few wanted to return to the old life. Industrial society was here to stay.

But why has this happened in some societies and not in others? Or, more precisely, why has it happened so much more rapidly in some societies than in others? And is it inevitable that all societies will eventually try to follow suit? Theorists concerned with modernization, who see technology as the key to progress, cite substantive factors such as poverty (that is, lack of capital investment), inadequate or non-existent skills and equipment, and – more contentiously – resigned attitudes and a general absence of entrepreneurial get-up-and-go. One might also add a lack of easily exploitable raw materials as sources of potential wealth, poor transport systems, and an inability or unwillingness (as in, say, Cuba) to attract firms and money from the wealthier nations. In one famous analysis written from a free-market economist's point of view, there is a series of well established steps that any relatively undifferentiated society must take in order to modernize (Rostow: 1969): Firstly, it must fulfil the primary conditions for 'take-off', namely an increase in population and the adoption of agricultural techniques which are less labour-intensive and which will free workers for industry; then, with the development of manufacturing, there must be a concomitant development of the infrastructure and an improvement in social facilities; and when (and *if*) heavy industrial development is successful, then consumer goods must be supplied so as to maintain the continued co-operation of the working population.

This is a reasonably commonsensical blueprint for economic growth. Many societies, especially Far Eastern societies such as South Korea, Malaysia and Taiwan, have followed this route. In the words of the social theorist, Talcott Parsons, they have increased the diversity of their social institutions and allowed social values to become more 'generalized', including such values as individual liberty, competition, achievement and so forth. Such a movement, says Parsons, enhances their 'adaptive capacity' (Parsons: 1977). But, leaving aside the disputable 'individual liberty' factor, this formula is something of a counsel of perfection and, according to Rostow, requires a new, able and enterprising economic élite to ensure that the process is got underway. Societies that are unable, for a variety of reasons, to fulfil the basic conditions, are hardly likely to get going in the Western-appointed way. Whether, too, societies characterized by their own traditional values can suddenly adopt a whole new set of Western ideals which extol the benefits of individualism, competition and so on instead of those concerned with community action and tribal loyalty raises issues of both practicality and desirability. What is not greatly explored is what happens if virtually every society *does* industrialize. Few nations can supply *all* their own needs; therefore they must trade, and then we have the intractable problem of cut-throat competition as many try to sell their goods in the same market. Witness, for example, what is happening in the car trade in Great Britain at the present time where foreign importers have now established their own factories and marketing organizations and are vying with one another for an already overcrowded market.

Advocates of the persuasive 'dependency thesis' argue that regardless of what may be seen as the 'backwardness' of simple societies, this condition has been exploited by the West to further its own economic interests. Under colonialism, which could be paternalistic and sometimes oppressive, trading companies were set up to take advantage of cash crops (sometimes grown at the deliberate request of the colonialists) produced by cheap native labour for the benefit of lucrative Western markets. Marx, pre-eminently, and later neo-Marxists have long stressed that from the last century, industrialized nations subjected their colonies to inordinate economic pressure both as suppliers of raw materials and as ready markets for cheap manufactured goods, and still continue to do so, though to less effect. This thesis is not without a certain cogency, especially in regard to capitalist societies (note the neo-colonialism of the USA since the Second World War in relation to Latin America, de Kadt and Williams: 1974). Early in this century, Lenin – not a person normally to excite much admiration among the socially sensitive – acutely observed that monopoly is the essence of imperialism, and that imperialism is really just a form of monopoly capitalism, a term which could be even more appositely applied to the economic system of the one-time Soviet Union.

Few people probably would dispute that development after something like the Western model is desirable. It must surely be a truism to state that people want to be better housed, better medicated, and better educated; poorer nations want to be richer, they want more security for themselves and their children, and they will support the system which brings them these benefits. Otherwise, how can we possibly explain the attractions of the Western example? But can this possibly be achieved without Western help? And exactly what does Western help entail? Does it mean capital intensive industrialization with correspondingly low levels of employment? Does it also mean increasing financial dependency on the West which necessarily involves mounting debts and consequent impoverishment? What appears as a philanthropic gesture can be interpreted as another form of imperialism.

Aid can be both selective and expedient. It is well known that the West is not above unloading unwanted surplus products such as cigarettes on the Third World. These are marketed in high-tar forms at low prices, and the cynic might understandably suspect that this is being done to ensure quicker and more effective addiction to boost further sales. Yet it has to be asked, who are really the principal agents of exploitation? It is known that overseas governments are conspiring in this traffic, even to the point of holding shares in the importing companies or helping to finance indigenous tobacco industries with Western co-operation. This has certainly happened in Uganda, Malawi and Zimbabwe, and especially in Kenya where their exceptional middle-distance running team's high-altitude facilities were 'donated' by the tobacco industry. Since the breakdown of communism in Eastern Europe, some states are being targeted by the West for investment, mainly by the huge American tobacco giants. New Western-financed factories are being set up in Poland and Hungary especially, no doubt in order to offset falling sales in the home market. It must be admitted, therefore, that the West is often guilty of exploitation, but that a number of overseas governments are in the age-old game of exploiting their own people.

Perhaps the West cannot be blamed too much for the way it chooses its friends. It is obviously loathe to aid regimes that are antipathetic to its cause, as for example, in the case of the left-wing Government in Grenada which was ousted by US forces. Complementarily, the West has not been above helping highly-suspect regimes and propping up sundry petty dictators when it suited their long-term strategic interests. Though, to be fair, some of them have become so repressive (like those in Haiti and Somalia) and others have siphoned off so much aid intended for the needy, that the West has lost patience and felt it necessary to intervene in their affairs.

It has been cogently – one might almost say passionately – argued that the one thing we can be sure of is that development *will* take place. It is seen as self-evidently good, and regardless of the disadvantages of industrialization and its consequent cultural changes, it is patently what most people want (Gellner: 1963). But how much of it do they want? In some cases it can be shown that people want *technological* development but are quite sure that this does not have to include certain key features of Western culture. Perhaps the most striking example is Iran (Foster-Carter: 1985, p.6). The late Shah's modernization policies were clearly seen to be un-Islamic, but the revolutionary Government that took over was happy to retain the imported supply of sophisticated weaponry, and is now reported (*Sunday Times*, 5 February 1995) to be negotiating with Germany and North Korea – uneasy bedfellows – for the wherewithal to manufacture its own chemical weapons and delivery systems.

Fundamentalist Islam is nothing if not pragmatic about anything that serves its interests as recent events in Egypt and Algeria have borne out. But it is not alone. Ideology can be flexible when the situation demands it. Similar kinds of opportunism are also the mark of many left-wing Marxist-inspired movements. These often take a purely instrumental approach to the matter of co-operation. It is now well-established that the revolutionary Government of Nicaragua made a temporary alliance with the most notorious (and lethal) of drug-traffickers, the Colombian Pablo Escobar who was killed in 1993. Escobar was also wanted for numerous kidnappings and murders, but the dollar hungry Nicaraguan Government was prepared to overlook these small misdemeanours for a share in Escobar's reputed $4 billion fortune.

The Third World is no one kind of place. It incorporates a wide variety of history, geography and culture, and now its 'constituent' states are at different levels of development. Except in one or two cases, however, notably South Korea and Taiwan, they still lag well behind the West. This unevenness of development may possibly be remedied if the requisite knowledge and technology are diffused by the more advanced nations. As the first Prime Minister of India after decolonization, Jawaharlal Nehru, said, 'It is science alone that can solve the problems of hunger and poverty ... of illiteracy, of superstition and deadening custom and tradition, of vast resources running to waste, of a rich country inhabited by starving people .... The future belongs to science and those who make friends with science' (quoted by Appleyard: 1992, pp.3–4).

No-one surely is any longer unaware of the imperialist depredations of the Europeans, as far as the less developed peoples were concerned. The use of aggressive and opportunistic economic strategies were nothing new even in the days of competitive colonization. Robert Heilbroner writes of the quest for wealth as a 'powerful and protean stimulus', and says that as 'far back as there is history, men have dreamed of wealth' and asks, 'to what heights have they not reached – and to what depths have they not sunk' (Heilbroner: 1956, pp.3–5). Dammann postulates what kind of world it would have been 'without the plunderings of the white man' (Dammann: 1979, pp.43–5) and concludes that all colonized states would have 'made great progress in their development'. Even the Aztecs, he suggests, 'could have grown until their civilization encompassed the whole of the American continent'. He concedes that European material living standards today might have been lower if we had been less imperialistic, but confidently asserts that 'we might well have been a happier people, with a greater capacity for sharing and a richer capacity for enjoying ... life'. This is, of course, well-meaning conjectural nonsense. We are all legatees of a violent and acquisitive past. And who is to say that the human species has changed? One has only to think about takeovers, aggressive marketing – now by one-time dependencies – and, for the common man, the enormous boom in gambling, to realize that the doctrine of the main chance is still with us, albeit in different forms.

The problem of whether the transition from pre-industrial society to post-industrial civilization is 'good' depends very much on the kind of societies in question. Although many anthropologists are concerned to offer the necessary apologia for pre-industrial societies – especially so in the case of their pet projects – they and historians have somewhat dispelled the romantic view of precivilized society, a kind of society which in many ways was not only poor but cruel and thoughtless about the welfare of its people. The world has changed, perhaps *had* to change. But although the techniques of postcivilization at least offer the possibility of a world in which many of the major sources of human misery could be eliminated, there can be no guarantee that this will ever be realized. There are the obvious potential obstacles: war, population growth, technological expansion based on exhaustible resources, and – perhaps most threatening of all – the nature of humans themselves (Boulding: 1964). Nevertheless, the growth of knowledge and the diffusion of that knowledge can work for good or ill. Science and technology plus the promise of better living standards is a heady concoction which few will be able to resist. But the likelihood is that it will just generate new forms of human acquisitiveness and social control.

CHAPTER TWELVE

Elitism by Culture: The Mass Culture Debate

Historians, social scientists and students of society generally are prone to rather tortured debates over the meaning and use of the term 'culture'. The term has had something of a vogue among social scientists. Clyde Kluckhohn, an American social anthropologist, has suggested that culture is a historically derived system of explicit and implicit designs for living which is shared by members of a group. This is highly generalized, as is also anthropologist Raymond Firth's view that culture is the 'way of life' of an organized set of individuals; if society is taken as an aggregate of social relations, then culture is the content of those relations. On this basis, there has to be a gradual process of cultural accumulation whereby new cultural elements are added by invention, discovery and – more contentiously – by cultural diffusion. This incremental complexity can result in the development of influential sub-groups which provide various cultural alternatives for their members. Complementarily, a process of cultural convergence may take place as, for instance, in ethnically differentiated societies, which results eventually in an identifiable configuration of similar cultural features that are reproduced in succeeding generations (an example being the common 'Americanism' of US society). Culture therefore consists of socially created and shared patterns, which are at least in part symbolically formulated and represented, and the evolution of these cultural traits, usually (though by no means always) generates a considerable degree of social integration.

At its most basic level, then, our discussion begins with the nature–nurture argument: is human behaviour genetically or culturally determined? Is it inherent or is it learned? Social science is generally inclined towards the 'learned' position, possibly because the inherent or 'genetic' position seems to smack too much of determinism. Humans – perhaps in their hubris – like to think they are 'free' and self-motivated. This argument, in turn, has given rise to heated discussions about cultural relativism. Are beliefs and behaviour patterns relative to particular societies? Are value-systems comparable? (Non-comparability is regarded as 'commonsense' by Abercrombie, et al.: 1988, though without any evidential support.) And, what is even more contentious in these days of political (and cultural?) corrrectness, are some cultural systems superior to others (Gellner: 1992)?

Culture is sometimes used synonymously with civilization in the sense that both are seen in contradistinction to barbarism. In the Anglo-American tradition, culture is often used loosely to signify the collocation of beliefs, customs and so forth of particular groups, a view that takes into account the widely diversified and pluralistic nature of society. But in what is sometimes termed the German romantic tradition, culture is taken to denote the repository of human excellence and artistic achievement, while civilization has come to mean the process of material development, the precursor and ominous concomitant of the mass society. A similar distinction is made by Herbert Marcuse between material and intellectual culture, and this bears very closely on our present discussion. So is the idea of a coherent or common culture (Western culture, Jewish culture or whatever) problematic? And what of the question of cultures within a culture? Is there such a thing as cultural hegemony, the obvious dominance of one culture over another within the same society? Or are we really thinking here about a dominant ideology like that of, say, faith in the action of market forces and the enterprise economy? Yet, however dominant the ideology and whatever the diversity of modern society, we obviously still have some basis for social consensus.

What is more to the point, can we usefully speak of 'high culture' and 'mass culture'? Some regard this debate as somewhat sterile and outdated. They assert that the division between high culture and low (mass) culture is obsolete because the new social sensibility is 'defiantly pluralistic', and embraces everything from Beethoven to the Beatles, from Shakespeare to Spielberg. It is hedonistically argued that culture (especially art) is not about big truths and universal values, but is simply there to give pleasure. But, to some extent, this cultural pluralism has now given way to what is vaguely (and inappropriately?) called Postmodernism, a variant of the VW Beetle 'it's-so-old, it's-new' type of argument, although in this case 'it's so bad, it's good'. There is a de-emphasis on standards; what matters is understanding the signs and codes of popular culture. According to one observer, 'no longer [do you] have to sweat through *Das Kapital*: you [can] just sit back and deconstruct *Dallas*' (Cosmo Landesman, *Sunday Times*, 14 November 1993).

The underlying issues in this particular discussion are therefore:

1. Can we clearly distinguish a high culture and a mass culture?
2. Are we moving increasingly towards an era of mass culture?
3. If so, how has this culture originated and what are its characteristics?

4.   Is this mass culture detrimental to both individual autonomy and social values?
5.   In what senses is high culture a preserve of an élite?

Let us define our terms. If we concede that culture is that which describes or represents a particular way of life which expresses certain mores and values, then *mass (low) culture* may be said to be that which is characterized by mass production for a mass market using standardized techniques to make standardized products. It is a common culture (some might use the term popular culture) associated with the 'working classes'. *High culture* on the other hand suggests goods/artefacts designed for, and supervised by, a cultural élite. The products are associated with an accepted literary, aesthetic and scientific tradition.

Mass culture, as presently understood, arose in the last century when the Industrial Revolution created the possibility of a mass market. This was the essential pre-condition of its development. There was an increase – albeit modest – in personal income and with time a concomitant increase in personal leisure. These, in turn, led to an increase in demand for cultural products. A particular form of cultural differentiation was thus created by large-scale production, standardization and stereotyping of the product and minimization of cost, all of which resulted in a loss of originality and consequent product inferiority. It became increasingly a matter not of making things up to a standard but down to a price. It is further maintained that lack of education and, to some extent, skills among the working classes made standards of excellence unnecessary, and perhaps still does for most consumers. Theoretically, of course, education is supposed to enhance the levels of sophistication and appreciation for 'better' products. But has it? Is it *cost* that really matters? How many people, for instance, can appreciate – and still less afford – 'great art'? And what constitutes 'great art'? Are these standards simply set by some undefined entity such as the bourgeoisie or the artistic élite? Yet if there are no objective standards upon which categorizations can be made, does this mean that any daub can be a masterpiece? Does it mean that anything that 'expresses' the feelings of the producer (perpetrator?) is *ipso facto* art? Surely, there has to be more to it than this? Surely, we must include the criteria of originality and technical skill, though even here there are apparent contradictions. Isn't talent and technical skill often prostituted for profit? For example, some feel that the 'mature' Picasso was something of a con-man who played on his reputation to produce quickly executed abstracts for exorbitant fees, but he was nonetheless an excellent draughtsman as some of his very early paintings and later sketches demonstrate.

The quality of mass culture was – and again, probably still is – functionally influenced (one hesitates to say, determined) by relatively poor living and working conditions. These encourage(d) escapism and much-sought-after diversion. One has only to think about the massive production of often indifferent films that poured out of Hollywood in the 1930s which makes one wonder just how much all that nostalgia is justified. The films look creaky and artificial to modern eyes yet were often considered to have a certain merit in their own time. People spent long-suffering hours queueing for a sight of their screen idols with whom they presumably wished to identify for a few amaranthine moments. But who is to say that modern television fare is any better than the movie-market productions of yesteryear? Television is a very demanding medium. It devours material at an astonishing rate. Thus, it can be argued, more has to mean less; the more material there has to be for a virtual 24-hour service, the more inferior the material has to be. Perhaps even more so with the threat of ever more channels. British television is still said to be the best in the world, but even here the notorious MFI culture is evident. The justly esteemed *Antiques Road Show*, for instance, which specializes in educating the public about high culture artefacts, has increasingly taken on a 'come-on-down' gameshow appearance in which participants and audiences alike are more interested in the *material* worth of the exhibits than in the exhibits themselves.

It is interesting to see how mass culture apes the high culture, both in its *products* such as, say, cheap clothes that are often little more than inferior reproductions of *haute couture* fashion, and in its *aspirations*, everything from the simple appeal of children's boarding school stories to the antics of the filthy rich in *Dallas*. In this sense, they too may have a vicarious identity function as aspiration-images of the ultimate in consumption patterns. It can, of course, be objected that these are no more than élitist projections which are unrealistic as far as ordinary people are concerned. But does everyone want realism? Isn't there some virtue in presenting normative – albeit idealistic – forms rather than the often sordid substantives of human behaviour, especially in relation to language and violence? As Plato once advocated, give people the good and the beautiful (ideas) as well as the true (the real). But then Plato would have argued – metaphysically – that the ideal *is* the real: all else is simply shadows.

In his many studies of modern society, Arthur Marwick has pointed out that we should make a clear (?) distinction between art and entertainment, both subsumed by the term culture. Art, he argues, 'has the power of revelation and life-enhancement; its producers will be concerned with more than simply producing a marketable commodity, and they will themselves be possessed of gifts denied to the vast majority'

(Marwick: 1991, p.5). He is not contending that there is no place for the analysis and evaluation of popular culture, but maintains it should be distinguished from those products whose main characteristic is immediate appeal, and presumably whose main concern is to make money. In effect, what he (as an authority on modern British culture) and others are saying is that we are the children of two worlds: we can like the products of both, but we should also be able to appreciate the differences between them.

Criticisms of mass culture have been gradually building up over the years. In the last century, intellectuals certainly claimed to know what culture was all about: it was a civilizing influence. Matthew Arnold insisted that it was 'the best that has been thought and said in the world'. Similarly John Stuart Mill, the great high priest of Utilitarianism who gave up the royalties of his book *On Liberty* to finance a cheap edition for the general public, argued – as a liberal – that the quality of culture was damaged by every extension of education. Mass education meant inferior education. In this century, academics such as F.R. Leavis entered the fray with their particular defences of high culture. Leavis took the unpopular view that high culture would always be a minority pursuit. It could never be accessible to the masses because only a suitably trained élite were intellectually capable of appreciating the finer points of music, literature and the like. The intelligentsia, as Karl Mannheim also argued, are the bearers of a high cultural tradition which must be perpetuated from age to age, a view, incidentally, endorsed by T.S. Eliot.

Aesthetic arguments such as these – *arguments based on educated taste* – may have a point. Take the British Booker Prize for literature: this prestigious award is apparently doing nothing for book sales. Nomination used to mean highly increased revenues for the authors and for the publishing houses. For example, sales of Salman Rushdie's book *Midnight's Children* which won the prize in 1981 increased from 3 000 to 20 000. Recent trends, however, suggest that this is no longer the case. According to the press (*Sunday Times*, 2 October 1994), the six novels shortlisted for the nation's most respected award are failing to attract readers or, more significantly, buyers. It is reported that only 1 000 copies of the books on the shortlist had been sold in the previous week, some 75 per cent fewer than those sold in the same week two years earlier. The reason? Elitism, so it is claimed. One marketing director maintained that the year's shortlist did not reflect the public's interests: 'there is an élitist feel to the selection. It is becoming divorced from what people want. I am not advocating a reduction in quality, but less of a distinction between what the public wish to read and what the judges think is art'. There was even the suggestion that anything that had market possibilities had been deliberately excluded from the panel's cogitations. The chairman of the Booksellers Association insisted that 'someone ought to inject some practical experience of bookselling into the judging panel ....' These comments were really not so much a criticism of the panel's thinking as of the panel's composition. It is largely composed of academics and professional critics; representatives of the 'industry' are purposely debarred, because the award is supposed to be above commercial considerations.

The integrity (= standards) versus money problem is suspiciously close to the high culture/mass culture argument. And it raises some pertinent, if awkward, supplementary questions. For instance, what about the situation where high culture and mass culture are reversed? For example, films which were originally made for a mass working-class audience such as, say, the old Charlie Chaplin films, have now become middle-class cult movies. A similar case could be made for jazz which will probably continue only as a minority attraction. This can be compared with the recent commercialization of operatic music, popularized by the 'three tenors' (Luciano Pavarotti, Placido Domingo and José Carreras) whose concerts for the masses have brought them enormous public recognition, as well as joy to their booking agents, and even more to their brokers. This formerly esoteric medium has now been taken up by a wider public, perhaps as a cultural aberration, perhaps as a commercial gimmick – or both.

There have also been *educational criticisms* of mass culture. Richard Hoggart was one of the early critics of what he felt was bad popular culture, and argued that the working class had betrayed their own 'organic culture' for the 'candy-floss' of American television, pop music and cheap novels. As a left-wing educationalist, he maintained that genuine seekers after knowledge were exceptional and untypical of working-class people, and that those who idealized the working class overrated their political sensibilities. But he insisted that to want human beings to be constitutionally different was to fall into a kind of intellectual snobbery. At much the same time, American intellectuals were also inveighing against the soullessness and standardization of modern technological society. Expatriates such as Herbert Marcuse and Theodor Adorno were adding their own indictments to what they saw as the trivialization of European culture in an American context. Intellectuals found it difficult to understand why universal education and the alleviation of much industrial and social misery had not brought that general deepening and enrichment of mind to which revolutionaries and liberals had both aspired. An American sociologist lamented that much of what the egalitarians wanted for ordinary men, they did not seem to want for themselves. But has it ever been different, and has anything really changed? It is instructive to look at the most popular British television programmes for the last few years, shows such as *Neighbours,* *EastEnders* and the seemingly eternal *Coronation Street,* to see that we are still in the throes of a 'culture of mediocrity'.

There are also *socio-political criticisms* of mass culture in that it breaks down the old barriers of class, tradition and taste; that it dissolves once-accepted distinctions, mixing and scrambling everything together into one homogenized culture. Marcuse has argued that mass culture leads to the repression of individuality because it encourages the manipulation of false needs and is therefore a form of disguised exploitation. Art, on the other hand, (and by this he presumably means the products of high culture) can act as a conscious transcendence of alienated existence (Marcuse: 1964). Similarly for Adorno, 'artistic culture' represents one kind of much needed protest (Adorno: 1967). This is not the case, it is argued, with popular music. One has only to note the wealth of many 'protest' entertainers (Marcuse, for example, derogatorily dismisses folk-music as mere 'performances'). 'True' art – whatever is meant by that term – is an expression of personal autonomy which surmounts the prosaic and the banal. These critics argue in a neo-Marxist fashion that the weakening of the traditional socializing agencies (the family, educational institutions and so on) in the wake of rapid technological change has reified culture, insofar as popular values and institutions are now thought to exist beyond human control. Hence they are applying the same logic to culture as Marx applied to the State and Capital. Culture, a human invention, has come to be seen as something over and above human control or correction; culture now exerts a coercive influence on its creators. Adorno further insists that mass culture encourages passivity and conformity: through the mass media in particular, it detaches people from the affairs of the real world by pre-packaging information as entertainment.

Curiously, this kind of criticism comes not only from the radical Left but also from the conservative Right who see this as an age of the anti-individual who welcomes uniformity of belief and conduct. Both see mass culture not as something creative and authentic, but as something with all the necessary ingredients for the possible emergence of new forms of totalitarianism rather than increased democratization. It is not an oppositional movement, challenging conventional taste, but a buying-off of the masses by the modern equivalent of 'bread and circuses', all having the effect of making undesirable social and political conditions more tolerable.

What then can be said for mass culture? One sometimes suspects that high culture advocates may actually resent any advances that mass culture might bring. However, the media, especially television (arguably the main vehicle of mass culture), have an in-built 'Janus factor': while it is undeniably true that much television fare is indifferent in quality and often an insult to the intelligence, it does bring what many would (patronizingly?) see as a necessary diversion to the masses. It is educational as well as entertaining even if programmes are sometimes slanted to portray a particular point of view. The media facilitate greater ease of communication and give greater accessibility to news and information. Indirectly, they also have the potential for more involvement and participation in the general democratic process as well as making some higher cultural elements 'available' to the general public. For instance, the introduction of Classic FM has done much to bring high culture to the masses. For the period March–June 1994 it had a weekly listening audience of over 4.6 million, roughly twice that of Radio 3, the high culture station *par excellence*. The Royal Philharmonic Orchestra, classic FM's 'house-band', now commands £500 000 a year in fees, is heavily booked for concerts at the Royal Albert Hall, and has just secured a lucrative recording contract. Set against this must be the growing popularity of satellite television services which are now in serious competition with the BBC especially over sports coverage. Even such venerated events as the Test Matches and Wimbledon may yet succumb to the financial blandishments of Sky Television.

Commercial populism, as it is sometimes called, is also certainly on the increase. It is taking over the market-place, whether the customers want a package Spanish holiday or a cheap and cheerful Spanish wine at the supermarket. Warehouse clubs offering bottom-line no-frills shopping are growing in popularity. Less expensive own-brand products are gradually overtaking named brands such as Coca-Cola with look-alike alternatives. An intense price-war is taking place where these parvenus of the market-place are challenging the higher values, branded products that have a traditional reputation and are made by well-established organizations. But can the public be blamed, especially in recession-ridden times, if they abjure the traditional and seek out the cheaper options? Fortnum and Mason may be all very well for some but by and large the public will go for value for money.

The divide does exist. It obviously remains to be seen how – indeed if – it will ever be resolved. How far can we safely take the democratization of culture? As one commentator suggests, 'the Purists have three main options if they want to respond. They can follow the BBC's approach [in] … seeking joint ventures with its competition …. They could follow the supermarkets … by becoming more like them …. Or they can stick with their purity, which may be principled but is unlikely to be profitable …. This may be suicide' (*Independent*, 27 September 1994).

It has been said that in matters of taste and discernment the public is almost invariably wrong. This uncompromising view insists that it's not a matter of the two cultures being different; one is unquestionably superior to the other. Keats is better than Dylan and Mozart is better than Madonna. Or are they non-comparable? Some might argue that this is like trying to compare apples and oranges, and that each stands on its own merits. It's all a matter of how much pleasure they give you. And this, in turn, may simply depend upon what kind of a mood you're in. And that's really all there is to it.

It may be that cultural taste and the criteria for assessing it are no longer governed, as some have maintained, by class and status situations. But, then, taste has always been a complex issue. It isn't just a question of education and exposure, important as these are. Our tastes are influenced by a multitude of factors, and it is perhaps presumptuous to suppose that in every area of life one person's taste is as good as any other. It is notoriously difficult to prove it or even to define what 'good taste' is. Some argue that good music, art, literature and so on, have a profundity that is lacking in the products of popular culture; but persuasive as this is, we all know how very easy it is to read into art forms and meanings that aren't there and that their creators certainly didn't intend or – as the poet Robert Browning once indicated – had actually forgotten. Fad and fashion, and not least the desire to be seen as discerning and different can all enter into the equation. As can also a little bravado: the drummer Buddy Rich – regarded by some as the greatest big band drummer ever – when asked by the doctor just before his final operation whether he was allergic to anything, said 'Yes, Country and Western music'.

Sin has been defined as taking the line of least resistance. And it may be that one clue to what is arguably the aesthetic sin is espousing that which is *simple* and *undemanding*. Michael Ignatieff has argued that 'demanding art' is art that requires labour, ingenuity, humour, skill – something that doesn't just entertain or amuse, but which appeals to a fuller range of human emotions. And to this one could add, that which also possesses an intellectual dimension. After all, there is a critical difference in the level of appreciation required for the subtleties of Woody Allen and the slapstick of Norman Wisdom. Even so, the lines can still be blurred. We can all claim that we know what we like, but how is opinion constructed? And on what basis do we choose this rather than that? As Marilyn Monroe (in *Seven Year Itch*) ingenuously observed when listening to a record of the Rachmaninov Piano Concerto, 'That's classical music, isn't it? I can tell – it's got no vocals'.

CHAPTER THIRTEEN

Elitism by Education: The Status of Science Issue

Many years ago, in a famous and controversial Reith Lecture (1959), C.P. Snow pointed to the ever-increasing gulf between what he termed the 'literary intellectuals' and the physical scientists. As a corollary of this, he also emphasized the prosperity of the industrialized societies in comparison with the poverty and unrest in the non-industrialized world. He was particularly critical of those literary intellectuals who were ignorant of scientific concepts, and even more impatient with those who were unaware that such matters are important. The divide still exists: and, despite government edicts about a necessary balance in school curricula, the division between the physical scientists and others is likely to increase rather than decrease because knowledge itself – especially scientific knowledge – is increasing, and no one student can possibly become a specialist in everything.

The primary aim of all academic disciplines is arguably the search for truth. But this begs the question, is truth 'out there' to be discovered or is truth socially constructed? With certain qualifications, science assumes the former while the arts and social sciences – again with qualifications – assume the latter. Complementarily, we must also ask if there are not various kinds of truth: objective truth, subjective truth and so forth? The arts/humanities which, generally speaking, are discursive and intensely subjective, are, one suspects, just a little envious of the exactitude and objectivity which are attainable in the sciences. The social sciences too which, in a sense, bridge the gulf between the arts and the sciences are perhaps also guilty of science-envy. In Economics and Psychology, in particular, there are laudable attempts to emulate the physical sciences, but without anything like the same degree of success. But then it is usually less difficult to get the mechanics right than to get people right.

How then is a science to be defined, by its aims, its content, its capacity for measurement and prediction, or its method? These are the factors which are said to distinguish and mark it off from other disciplines. It is not (*contra* Giddens: 1991) just that its ideas are open to mutual criticism and revision by other members of the scientific community, true as this is. Other academic disciplines do exactly the same thing; one has only to look at any learned journal to see how many arguments go on within any particular 'trade'. It is rather that science involves careful testing of hypotheses and ideas, and – as Karl Popper rightly argues – advances propositions that are *open to falsification* by further experimentation. Science starts with an impertinent question, and hopefully comes up with a pertinent answer.

However, we have to recognize that this ideal of a science is itself subject to certain qualifications. The work of Thomas Kuhn (1970) on the nature of 'everyday science' contends that scientists necessarily work with certain paradigms, that is, ways of seeing the world which dictate what kinds of scientific work should be done and what kinds of theory are therefore acceptable within the scientific community. Over time there are what he terms 'paradigm shifts'. Models change and consequently the nature of scientific discourse alters. (Note, for example, the current debate in cosmological circles over the Hubble Constant and the conflicting theories regarding the speed of the 'fleeing galaxies' and the age and origins of the universe.) Everyday, routine science produces a series of anomalies which result in one paradigm being necessarily discarded for another. In effect, what Kuhn is saying is that yesterday's scientific certainties are the relics of today, but that, if anything, this is not to the detriment of science. Wasn't it Alexander Pope who once said that it was no shame for a man to change his mind? It simply shows that he is a wiser man today than he was yesterday.

The anxiety that is expressed especially outside the scientific community is that society is increasingly succumbing to control by a scientific élite. Science is now the acknowledged explanatory paradigm and scientists are the masters of the knowledge of how the world works. Furthermore, the esoterica of science are advancing so rapidly that the public cannot possibly keep abreast of its practitioners. Ordinary people cannot understand what it's all about. There are two distinct universes of discourse, and inevitably misunderstanding leads to mistrust. But is this mistrust justified? Surely we have nothing to fear from science, *per se*. The *practice* of science can only lead to qualified 'truth'. What we have to fear is the wrongful and dangerous *applications* of scientific discovery – something we have all seen in weaponry, in environmental pollution, improperly tested drugs, and so forth.

Robert de Ropp has suggested that it's all rather like the legend of Prometheus and his brother Epimetheus. Prometheus 'the man of foresight' risked the wrath of Zeus in order to bring fire from heaven to benefit mankind and was punished for his presumptuousness and defiance of the gods. To make matters worse, his good intentions were annulled by the foolish meddling of Epimetheus and his wife Pandora who between them unleashed all kinds of evil in the world which no one could control. 'Today the great challenge is no longer the discovery of new scientific laws. Perhaps we already know too much for our own good. The challenge is rather to prevent [those without foresight from bringing] ruin to us all' (de Ropp: 1972, p.xiii).

In contrast to those who have an abiding distrust of science and its seemingly unassailable position in Western culture, there are those who have a touching faith in science to solve all the world's ills, given time and resources. However, as John Casti points out, there are a number of popular fictions as to what constitutes scientific activity:

1. *The primary goal of science is the accumulation of facts.* But, as has already been intimated, the mere cataloguing of data is not enough. A fact is relatively unimportant until it can be correlated with other facts which may then give rise to a theory to account for those facts. So, for example, it is one thing to be aware that there is a particularly acute drugs problem, say, in Edinburgh, but quite another to have some kind of a theory that will go some way towards explaining *why*; or to know that Britain, with all its sophisticated methods of conception control, has a very high incidence of teenage pregnancies hardly helps unless we can adduce reasons to account for what impressionistically is a rather strange phenomenon.

2. *Science is concerned primarily with solving practical and social problems.* This is far from the case. Science is mainly about understanding; it is a matter of theory and application. Science is not technology, although it does, of course, inform technology.

3. *Scientific knowledge is truth.* Again, as we have seen, science does not claim to be able to provide ultimate, unchanging explanations. In fact, the whole purpose of science is, as it were, to supersede itself. Science is an empirical pursuit and experience is never complete. Therefore, by definition, the work of science is never done; it is, in Popper's phrase, an unending quest.

4. *Science distorts reality in that it doesn't take into account the full range of human experience.* But how can it? Science like other disciplines must specialize; it can't know everything about everything. As in other disciplines, its practitioners must select the materials that are susceptible to investigation by the methods that science has designed. These are said to follow the established procedure of observation–hypothesis–experiment–theory and laws (if any). If experiments don't confirm the initial hypothesis then new hypotheses are formulated, and the process starts over again.

Whether this is the correct sequence is still a matter of debate. Popper insists that scientists are mistaken in thinking that the scientific process begins with observation. He insists that every observation presupposes a theory; that everything observed must assume in advance a way of thinking about it. Theories are derived from other theories or vestigially from previously conceived ideas. So induction is something of a myth; it does not exist. Indeed, Popper goes further and argues that how scientists arrive at a theory has no necessary bearing on its logical or scientific status. The 'act of creation', as Arthur Koestler called it, may take place in any number of ways. Popper agrees: it could be by a flash of inspiration, in a dream or a dream-like state, or even through some kind of misunderstanding or serendipitous mistake (see Magee: 1973, p.32). For Popper, there is no more 'logic' to the creative act in the sciences than there is in the arts. Every discovery contains an 'irrational element' – a kind of creative intuition or inspired guess, a view corroborated by Einstein in his correspondence with Popper. Observation is selective: it first needs an interest, a focus, a point of view – pre-eminently, a *problem*.

It is also characteristic of science that its claims are normally verified by the well-tried practice of publishing results in reputable academic journals. This often generates considerable debate, and constitutes a form of necessary – and salutary – peer group assessment. All disciplines have their reception systems, criteria whereby other disciplines are deemed worthy of credence and therefore inclusion within the scientific domain. Science is particularly impatient with those disciplines that peddle what it regards as pseudo-science. It regards as inadmissible those who are guilty of anachronistic thinking such as the resuscitated creationists, and those that are prone to 'seek mysteries' of the Bermuda Triangle or lost Atlantis type. It is critical too of those who appeal to myths to buttress their arguments or who use ancient lore as a guide to some current 'reality'. Pseudo-scientists are said to have a casual approach to evidence, and have a tendency to confuse quantity with quality. They also propound irrefutable hypotheses: ideas which by their very nature are not open to falsification, and which they are unwilling to revise (Casti: 1989, pp.59–60). But it should always be appreciated that pseudo-science (which carries with it implications of trickery and fraud) may be confused with heterodox science, heretically 'alternative' ideas and hypotheses, for which there is sufficient – albeit inconclusive – evidence to warrant further investigation such as studies of the paranormal (Carlton: 1988).

The criteria, whereby a science is said to be a science, have found their way into other disciplines, particularly the social sciences. One can see this especially in the scientization of sociology. There are expectations that ideally sociology should have similar applications; that it should be a kind of social engineering and produce 'results'. In short, that it should have a practical payoff. This has been criticized, for example, by Peter

Berger, on *moral grounds* because it is arguable what kinds of application are legitimate; on *practical grounds* because there exists an abiding temptation to produce quick and inferior results; on *plausibility grounds* that sociology is different in kind from the natural sciences, and can never copy them convincingly despite its often esoteric language and – one suspects – waning cult of quantification; and on general *disciplinary grounds* because the attempt to ape the natural sciences has inevitably led to the vulgarization of the discipline (Berger and Kellner: 1982).

A great deal of emphasis is put on the *processes and procedures* of science, but much less on the motives of the scientists themselves. Science is supposed to be value-free, but this is hardly the case. One practitioner readily admits that 'scientists usually think of science as one area of life in which ideologies play no role. Nevertheless, there is a collection of beliefs and ideals about the practice of science that the scientific community clings to with such universal tenacity that it is difficult to describe it as anything other than an ideology – the ideology of science' (Casti: 1989, pp.10–15).

Correct as this judgement may be, scientific knowledge itself is not static: it is subject to change as its practitioners come increasingly to understand the world we inhabit, their changing paradigms being necessarily influenced, as we have seen, by what is regarded as acceptable within the scientific community. Their knowledge is regarded as exemplary knowledge, and they have come to be regarded by many with an almost superstitious respect, as children might see a stage magician. They are now a kind of scientific aristocracy, and although criticism exists, for example by keen environmentalist groups, most people will probably give them the benefit of the doubt, and blame rather their employers (as in, say, the thalidomide case) or their political masters. In academia, jealousy has been occasioned by over-funding; money always seems to be available for scientific projects. Scientists' influence with government as consultants has also often given rise to 'scientization of politics' allegations, not least because of the way scientists abrogate to themselves the knowledge of what is and what is not 'true' or worthwhile knowledge. This claim – or presumption – to be the custodians of scientific canons has generated anew the debate about the hegemony of the physical sciences. The issue has been raised particularly by sociologists that science is really one form of 'social construction', although their argument once 'deconstructed' seems to be more about sensitivity concerning the scientific status of sociology than it is about science *qua* science.

In the most banal sense, science has to be a social construction insofar as most forms of human activity are socially constructed. But this is not quite what the sociologists mean. They are more concerned with the 'ambiguities' of the scientific enterprise, and the age-old philosophical debate of whether 'truth' is discovered or imposed. They are adopting a Kantian stance (somewhat surprising in this so-called Postmodernist academic climate) that 'we see things not as they are, but as we are'. Many sociologists (for example, Steven Yearley, a professed 'moderate constructionist') argue not only that scientific and technical knowledge is shaped by commercial and political priorities, but that 'even the status of the facts of science is believed to be constructed by the activity of scientists' (Yearley: 1988, p.13). That is to say that, not only are the applications of scientific endeavour open to question but so are the motives and concerns which underlie that endeavour and which inevitably affect its operation.

Radical theory of this kind has been quite influential. Its advocates see 'truth', especially scientific 'truth', as an optional and gratuitous concept; and the very idea of scientific progress is superfluous as progress is unmeasurable. Kuhn actually asserts that there are no certain methods or methodological rules for evaluating scientific theories, although he does suggest that a good theory should be:

- *consistent*, with no internal contradictions, and consistent with currently accepted theories;
- *inclusive*, in that it extends beyond the particular observations and laws that it was formulated to explain;
- *simple*, insofar as it brings order to the phenomena in question; and
- *fruitful*, in perhaps disclosing new phenomena, or phenomena that were not previously understood.

Persuasive and straightforward as these points are, critics could maintain that if he is to be consistent, there is no possible way to justify *this* particular selection of criteria. It is arguable whether for the thorough-going relativist there can be any real objectivity or rationality in science. This is the point at which Kuhn and Popper diverge because Popper maintains that when the time comes to adopt a new paradigm this can be – and usually is – done rationally and logically.

Of course, scientists must be sceptical and all claims should be carefully scrutinized for invalid arguments and errors of fact. They should, ideally, adopt an attitude of detachment and conduct their work with impersonal efficiency; admittedly, a counsel of perfection. Furthermore, there should be a high degree of accessibility of the knowledge thus acquired, especially if it is in the public interest. Inevitably, the approach to their work will be determined by their fundamental beliefs about the nature of things. In other words, their basic philosophy of science. Are they relativists, or are they instrumentalists for whom reality is simply the readings on their monitors? Or are they realists; do they believe that 'out there' objective reality exists? What, too, of the 'rivals' in the humanistic disciplines? How do they view the scientific pursuit of knowledge? There are those who espouse various shades of relativism, others who believe that we must be wary of any so-called scientific 'fact' which may easily be modified or entirely refuted in the near future, while others accept that there is a real world out there that has yet to be understood.

In the recent past (1994) the question of the 'true' nature of science caused something of a furore at a meeting of the British Association for the Advancement of Science. Natural scientists were aghast at the idea that their work was being interpreted as a 'social construct' by some sociologists. Lewis Wolpert, an embryologist at the University of London, accused sociologists of being hostile towards science and confusing the public by denying that there is such a thing as scientific truth. 'You would think that the sociologists and philosophers would have helped to illuminate the nature of science .... The great disappointment is that not only have they failed to illuminate it but they have actually obfuscated it' (quoted in *The Times Higher Education Supplement*, 16 September 1994). Concerning one particular research programme at the University of Edinburgh on the sociology of scientific knowledge, he added that all the results were either 'trivial, obvious or wrong'.

Related issues concern how scientists work, the nature of scientific discourse, the scientists' alleged 'closed shop' and the criteria for project funding (always a sore point with Humanities academics who feel that they almost invariably lose out in the money stakes); in short, a synoptic view of the whole culture of science (see the work of Michael Mulkay: 1990). This all seems to be fair game. But what physical scientists find particularly baffling are allegations that the public should have greater access to scientific policy-making because science is 'not an especially truth-seeking activity' (Steven Fuller, also quoted in the *Times Higher Education Supplement*). One detects just a hint of science-envy when Professor Fuller complains that 'there are very few people [presumably including himself] who have the authority in society to contest what scientists say. Scientists tend to be believed. We are reviving the silenced voices'. In order to tip the balance, he goes on to cite the example of the development of vaccines in the nineteenth century which made such a difference to public health, and argues that the reduction in the incidence of certain diseases was brought about largely because of environmental changes. 'Scientists like to portray a magic bullet, but sociologists are also pointing out that there were improvements in public hygiene. It is very typical of the myopic attitude of scientists. They don't realize what else is going on'. If he has been quoted correctly, for scientists these are brash, irritating statements. What is more, the vaccines argument is quite fallacious. It is, of course, quite correct to point to the contributions made to public health by advances in hygiene and sanitation, but, as Eva Etzioni-Halévy (1985: p.98) argues, this too was related to scientific developments especially concerning the nature and effects of micro-organisms of which the public were previously unaware.

Richard Dawkins of New College, Oxford, has also inveighed against the social construction thesis. He concedes that the acquisition of scientific knowledge has a social dimension, but insists that this should in no way detract from the scientific endeavour, *per se*. He makes the point that if, for example, Darwin was inspired by Victorian economics when he thought of natural selection, it cannot affect the primary question of whether life does in fact evolve. He argues that, by and large, Western science works and that to take extreme relativist views about, say, the comparative merits of Western medicine and witchcraft practices is 'deeply silly'. Cultural relativism may shed some light on different social customs and other peoples' thought processes, but it doesn't alter the 'facts'. Pragmatism and rationality usually go hand in hand.

It has to be admitted however that, for some, science has given way to scientism, the adulation of science as the only and ultimate guarantor of human happiness. This soteriological view of science has its critics, not least among the scientists themselves. Albert Einstein warned against the reification of science when he insisted that concepts which had proved useful to scientists can easily assume such great authority over us that we forget their terrestrial origins and accept them as unalterable facts. Science is not the only rational paradigm or the sole source of our salvation. Like all human pursuits, it too has its failings. Science has brought undoubted advances in affluence, health and longevity for more people than ever before. Its knowledge and the application of that knowledge have therefore made a substantial contribution to the general welfare of society. Unfortunately, the effects of science have not always been beneficial or benign. This, of course, has not been the intention of science but the unforeseen consequences of applied science rather than pure research. Often its applications have neutralized the overall achievements of science. The development of sulphamides in the 1930s and the introduction of antibiotics during the Second World War made a considerable difference to recovery rates and to life expectancy. Yet we know too that drugs have been marketed prematurely without sufficient testing procedures, with calamitous results. The introduction of thalidomide and its tragic aftermath would be a case in point as would also be the ambiguous effects of valium, the most prescribed drug in the world. Under pressure to enhance the prestige of the drug company concerned and not least to speed up the profit-making possibilities, research chemists have produced drugs whose effects have sometimes been harmful and in some cases actually deleterious. Indeed, some research has indicated that in both the USA and the United Kingdom more people die each year from prescribed drugs than from road accidents, and that a similar level of casualties may occur in other countries where pharmaceutical products are widely used (Melville and Johnson: 1983).

Yet more worrying is the fact that many micro-organisms are proving resistant to the present range of drugs. Even those drugs which worked initially are being foiled in their operations by the development of new strains of bacteria and viruses. This is particularly evident in the Third World where there is a high incidence of disfiguring diseases such as leprosy, and often fatal diseases such as malaria. Even diseases that were once regarded as curable are not always succumbing to conventional antibiotics: cholera, typhoid and gonorrhoea are on the increase, especially in countries where health programmes are often unavoidably underfunded. The benefits of medical research still far outweigh its disadvantages but, as one authority contends, 'as medical science is advancing, drugs are multiplying. And as drugs are multiplying and as prescription and intake are proliferating, their harmful as well as their beneficial effects must necessarily multiply as well' (Etzioni-Halévy: 1985, p.104).

The link too between science and military requirements is well attested. The development of ever more weapons of mass destruction has undoubtedly been accelerated by wartime necessity, and this has been particularly so during the Cold War period with the production of more sophisticated nuclear armaments, supplemented by chemical and biological weapons of sinister efficiency. We have become only too aware that despite attempts by the 'great powers' to restrict their numbers and to reduce testing, that such weapons are proliferating among smaller and indeed poorer nations. It is now a status symbol to be in 'the club', even if you can't afford it. Some states (notably India and Pakistan) which still have desperate poverty, are nevertheless insistent that they must have these weapons even if it means buying in the technology and the know-how. The fact that it is now estimated that in a future full-scale war there is enough nuclear and biological weaponry to destroy the planet really says it all.

This is, of course, all quite apart from the dangers posed by possible nuclear accidents. It has been reported that the US Pentagon has admitted that in 1961 a B52 bomber jettisoned two 24 megaton bombs before it crashed. One bomb broke on impact, contaminating the area with plutonium, and the parachute on the second bomb and a single safety switch prevented an explosion 1800 times more powerful than the Hiroshima bomb. And then there is always the possibility of a terrorist chemical/nuclear threat with subsequent intimidation and blackmail ... the potential scenarios are horrifying, but they are possible and even likely. So they must be contemplated.

Science has also taken us into the space-age beginning, needless to say, not with the early Russian Sputnik but with the highly controversial development of the V2 (revenge weapon) rocket by Werner von Braun and his team at Peenemunde during the Second World War. It is interesting, in retrospect, to note that the Allies were able to develop the atomic bomb but not a rocket delivery system, while the Germans had the delivery system, but without the bomb with which they would unquestionably have won the war. Ever since there has been serious controversy regarding the on–off space programmes, especially in the USA. Ingenious as the technology is, and awe-inspiring as space exploration has been, people still question the financial wisdom of the whole enterprise. In the USA, for example, it is calculated that the Apollo programme cost 40 billion dollars, which prompted the retort from Dwight Eisenhower that to spend this kind of money to reach the moon was 'just nuts'. Many felt that the money could have been better used elsewhere. One estimate was that it would have given a ten per cent rise to every teacher in the country; financed Ph.D research programmes for 50 000 new scientists and engineers; built ten new medical schools; endowed faculties for the 53 nations that had joined the UN since its founding; created three large charitable organizations; and still have $100 million left over (reported by de Ropp: 1972, p.227). Whether it was all in the interests of science, or whether it was a moon-race for national prestige, is still a matter of some debate.

So is science socially contingent? In summarizing the central argument, it is important to reiterate that scientific knowledge is distinct from the circumstances surrounding its production. The idea that the sociology of science can, as it were, deconstruct the relations between scientific knowledge and the cultural factors concerned with its production must be critically questioned. Robert Merton (1979) has argued that a clear distinction must be made between the *cognitive identity* of science, its paradigms, methodology and so forth, and its *social identity*, that is, its institutional arrangements.

No one seriously contends that science presumes to present us with a definite representation of a uniform (or otherwise) reality. It is surely uncontentious that in some circumstances the 'findings' of science have been coloured by the ideology of the scientists in question. This was certainly the case in Soviet Russia and the influential views of the biologist T.D. Lysenko whose maverick ideas were accepted as the last word on inheritance and genetics. Or again, the firmly held beliefs of eminent German academics which 'confirmed' Nazi race theory. These and other suspect – indeed, dangerous – ideas have been the products of science, but it has also taken the *researches of other scientists* finally to refute them. Furthermore, one must never forget the many top-class scientists (including Albert Einstein) who were either banished by, or fled from, such regimes because they could not accommodate such political ideologies within the compass of what they saw as the rationality of science.

To have formulated preconceptions does not rule out the impartiality of the scientific quest. Of course, scientists conceptualize about the world of nature, and the extent to which these concepts are the products of human beings means that they are necessarily social constructs. But this does not have to mean (as Kuhn) that such concepts do not enable scientists to arrive at 'real' knowledge of the world. And to maintain (as Mulkay) that the physical world could be analysed perfectly adequately by abandoning the language and presuppositions of science in favour of some other form of interpretation seems to make little sense. *What* other form of interpretation? And how would this be superior?

All science proceeds by a process of trial and error. Science does not claim to be all-wise and all-knowing, and if there are those that think otherwise they have certainly been badly advised. Meanings created by scientists in their interpretation of the world have to be partial and inconclusive; that is in the very nature of the discipline. Empirical enquiry is never finished; verification and modification of theories is what science is all about. Experience is ongoing and therefore every scientific theory has to be a proposition of high generality, but that generality has been high enough to give us our modern technological society with all its many taken-for-granted benefits.

So despite the many doubtful aspects about the scientific enterprise, where would we be without it? Every time we switch on a light, start the car or need dental treatment, we have to be thankful for science. We tend to forget that for most people for most of history life has indeed been 'nasty, brutish and short'; that for most of the time our forebears were cold and hungry, with little to ease their pain and discomfort. The age of science and technology which has brought us so many advantages constitutes but a tiny fragment of the human occupation of the planet. The immeasurable rise in living standards compared with only a century or so ago testifies to science's so taken-for-granted effectiveness. The planet still has plenty of problems, but if scientists can't solve them, who can? Our future must largely – and critically – depend on science, even though scientific knowledge is the preserve of a highly specialized, though not always well-intentioned, élite. But there must be limits. Just because something becomes technically feasible should it therefore be put into operation? Humans were once slaves of nature, must they now become servants of technology?

And what of those uncharted domains, of the cosmos, of mind and consciousness, that still need to be explored? There are anomalies in physics, unanswered questions about the origins of the universe, the whispers of creation; paradoxes of quantum theory; in the continuing enigmata concerning energy fields; and not least the puzzling historical synchronicities in art and culture. These are well documented (for example, by Laszlo: 1993) but still not explained. And how will they ever be explained without the aid of science? The questions are as fascinating as the answers are elusive. Yet despite all the debates about the nature of science and the validity of its methods, the quest must surely go on. We all want a better world, and the ongoing search is a reflection of the congenital curiosity of the human species.

Postscript

It has to be assumed that now readers have successfully negotiated the seemingly tortuous intricacies of élite theory, they can be excused for thinking that it is all little more than academicized common-sense. However, it is to be hoped that some of the various exemplifications of the theory have added some colour to its rather pallid complexion. Readers may be excused for thinking that the initial discussion is reiterative. So many writers are effectively saying the same things, albeit in somewhat different ways. By so doing, their differentiae become the stuff of new reputations. In this writer's estimation, at least, no-one has added much of substance to the work of the earlier theorists, Weber, Mosca and Pareto, although some applications of the theory have been especially enlightening (for example in relation to Stalinist Russia and Nazi Germany; see Conquest: 1990 and Bullock: 1991).

The key issues that have concerned us are how élites come to be élites; how élites are maintained and perpetuated; and, most fundamental of all, whether we *must* have élites. Our studies have suggested that whether we like them or not élites are a ubiquitous phenomenon. Just about every society, certainly every developed society, has élites of some kind or another. Elites do not have to be of the political variety; they may be, and often are, intellectual or cultural élites who exert influence rather than power.

Arnold Toynbee, perhaps this century's greatest historian, attempted to depict uniformities in the growth and decline of civilizations, and saw the origin and growth of civilizations as a process dominated by a pattern of challenge and response. The challenge, which may be one of natural forces such as a climate change, or perhaps the threat of either revolution or invasion, is said to be met by an intelligent élite which is able to respond to the challenge. Indeed, Toynbee argued that all growing civilizations have a 'creative minority' which is followed by the majority of the people. This élite is able to shape the unique 'style' of the civilization which develops in qualitative rather than quantitative terms. But eventually it is faced with a challenge that it is unable to meet. It is regarded as an inexorable law that the creative minority will find it impossible to avoid the inevitable decline, which may continue for centuries (Toynbee cites the case of the Roman Empire). During disintegration, the creative minority, in its impotence, becomes a *ruling élite*, and fruitlessly tries to stem the tide by repression; but all to no avail. For Toynbee, nothing fails like success.

What happens when a society tries to do without an élite? And here we should not think in terms of a small, tribal community such as, say, the traditional Bushmen where leadership was a purely nominal affair, but rather of a relatively sophisticated community as could be found in many of the city-states (*poleis*) of classical Greece. Athens – to take an obvious example from our previous discussion – would be one such state. We have seen that the Athenians, often held up as exemplars to posterity, experimented with a democracy that was so radical that councillors were not elected but chosen by lot for a year, and were not allowed to hold office more than twice. There was no executive, and every district was represented on every steering committee and then only served for a tenth of the year (even this ephemeral body chose a new chairman every day). Similar procedures operated with nearly all the offices of state, even the law courts. To our way of thinking it was participation gone wild. But it did give everyone a chance to make their contribution to the running of the state at least once in their lifetime, that is, of course, unless they were women, minors, resident aliens (metics) or slaves.

People since have regarded this system either as an exciting innovation in politics, a noble failure, or – perhaps a few – as an unmitigated disaster. Certainly, it is debatable whether it worked – or worked *that* well. Or, indeed, whether it can really be classed as a democracy at all, at least as far as we have come to understand the term. It was decidedly not the personification of political virtue. In what we have come to regard as 'human relations' it was certainly no better than more hierarchically organized city-states and, at times, it could be a great deal worse. As with participatory systems generally, there were times when disputation was so rife that Athens' social equilibrium (which was most unstable) was punctuated by – albeit temporary – counter-experiments in oligarchy. It would appear that 'open' systems have been just as prone to ambitious *coups* as their 'closed' and more repressive counterparts.

The whole issue of élites and élitism is very much bound up with that of social ranking and, in the social sciences especially, the question of social ranking is a prime topic. Indeed, observers of the social science scene might be forgiven for assuming that sociology in particular is obsessed with the matter of class. Underlying this concern with class are the same basic questions. Why do societies have ranking? Do they have to? And if they do, and if they must, on what bases should this ranking take place? Sociologists distinguish between *social stratification* and *social class*. The term social class, in its strict Marxian usage, denotes one's proximity to the ownership of the means of production and the differential relationships that this involves. Social class, therefore, has an economic base and is related to differential access to capital. *Social stratification*, on the other hand, is a more inclusive term than social class and denotes ranking based on a variety of criteria, education, life-style, voting behaviour and so forth, not just economic criteria. Stratification normally relates to the formal rankings in society whereas *social differentiation*, an even wider term, relates to the more informal distinctions we make such as those concerning age, sex, race and religion – or, not infrequently, some combination of these.

The additional co-ordinate for studying stratification (and one which is most closely associated with Max Weber) is that of *status*, and status with its strong connotation of esteem is very much associated with certain types of élite. The relationship between status and class tends to be close, particularly in modern societies, but – as we shall see – it is not an inevitable or even necessary connection. Status is bound up with conceptions of honour and prestige which may have little, if anything, to do with wealth. The association of class position and status is much more a feature of advanced societies where wealth is seen as a reward for entrepreneurial success, and where money is related to industriousness, ability and especially investment and risk. In former societies, there might even be an inverse relationship between wealth and status. Indeed, there was sometimes a positive correlation between status and *poverty*, as, say, in the case of some Hindu gurus and Buddhist monks. Having said this, however, there is no doubt that in several cultures in both the present and the past there have been notable examples of a connection between ritual status and political power, as our discussion of élite types has already shown. The irony is that where there are no 'natural' or obvious bases for social distinctions, they are often contrived for the purpose. Criteria are 'designed' – indeed, tailor-made – so as to fit would-be élites for their position in society.

In broad terms, therefore, we can say that social position (including élite status) is a function of the necessary role differentiation in society. The more complex the society, the more division of labour there will be, and the more complex will be the differentiation of status roles. Thus evaluation of these roles will lead to differential ranking and this, in turn, will result in differential rewards for those concerned. Such a scheme is neat, persuasive, and just a little simplistic. It is *not* to argue that every person gets his dues, or that some people are not grossly overpaid, but in a very broad sense this is how many systems work. Elites and inequality do exist, and will continue to exist as long as people evaluate tasks, property, artefacts and achievement unequally.

Elite formation is itself subject to certain condition. Elites come in various forms and with markedly different orientations. Some élites are of a strongly *traditionalist* type and have a high resistance to change, and traditionalism has often taken a military or sacerdotal form. In transitional situations, for instance, the main objective of religious élites is often to gain full official recognition by the state and possibly obtain positions of influence and administrative importance in the state hierarchy. There is too an understandable desire for autonomy and the assurance of state protection. In these circumstances, as in modern Saudi Arabia, there is often an 'understanding' – a *modus vivendi* – between the élite and the state whereby the power of the rulers is supported and legitimated by religious sanctions. This may be compared with the situation in which the religious élite *is* the state, where state policy and religious imperatives are inextricably intertwined, as in modern Iran.

Endorsement of the governmental apparatus is much more likely to be found in military élites, if, indeed, the military élite is not also the ruling élite, as in modern Iraq where state ideology is the special preserve of the military junta. In this case, it does not require the recognition of the state – it hardly needs to recognize itself – but rather the explicit or tacit approval of the people in whose name it, theoretically, runs the country. Military élites of this kind are wont to protest that their rule is purely temporary and their measures, which may well be oppressive, are simply an expedient in order to give the country some degree of stability. There is often some truth in this, but it does give rise to a certain cynicism, considering that it has always been one of the well-tried fictions of totalitarian systems.

Elites, on the other hand, may have a positively *adaptive* orientation, and will tend to adopt a much greater degree of acceptance of, or tolerance towards, new institutional goals, and even participation in new cultural, social and political orders. This, again, is particularly evident in some transitional societies where élites have been prepared to work within new institutional frameworks (Eisenstadt: 1973). Probably most élites come into this category. It is the way of compromise, and usually acceptable compromise.

Adaptive élites may be compared with *transformative* or modernizing élites. These are often highly cohesive groupings with a strong sense of self-identity, and may comprise an oligarchy within a monolithic party. Not unusually, they are coercive élites with the will and the ability to get things done, albeit ruthlessly where necessary. The situation with coercive élites is rather complex (for an ideal-type analysis, see Runciman: 1974). On the one hand, they may be intent on destroying the symbols and structures of a society once they seize power, and on the other, they may wish to retain certain key elements of the old order in an attempt to assure some measure of continuity with former traditions. This was typically so within Nazi Germany in 1933.

For those who despise or, at least, distrust élites, it is worth bearing in mind that both democratic and non-democratic systems facilitate the formation of élites. These may be relatively autonomous (and therefore quite powerful) bodies within a democratic society, representing a multiplicity of different interests. Competition within such a system may be *intra*-élite rather than inter-élite in nature, and can, of course sometimes work to the citizens' advantage. In the political sphere, however, critics argue whether elections are anything more than an opportunity to express people's opinions on the performance of *past* governments. It may give the people no real control over *future* events. In fact, elections are said to serve chiefly as a 'symbolic exercise designed periodically to reaffirm a common belief in democracy to give symbolic reassurance to the masses ... a ritual ... to befuddle the public and legitimize the power of the élite' (Etzioni-Halévy: 1989, p.16). A less cynical view is that a principal function of democracy, with all its admitted faults, is that it sustains an interplay between élites, and that this is a salutary activity. After all, democracy probably emerged as the result of a struggle for control of resources as much as a conflict between classes. Thus in democratic systems some major élites (for example, craft guilds) enjoy a certain independence from the ruling élite, and have a measure of success in achieving certain rights and liberties for their members. Thus, it has been argued that in Western-style democracies the power of the state (the ruling élite) is limited by the countervailing power of other élites (Etzioni-Halévy: ibid., p.xi).

Elites, it would seem, are an inevitability. Like them or not, they are here to stay. We all like to disparage authority, especially if it is repressive or indifferent. And in some ways we like it even less if, as is so often the case, it is also inexcusably inefficient. What so often concerns us is the *raison d'être* of any élite's existence. Why is it here, why and how was it formed, and what is the basis of its authority? Can we have confidence in such people, respect their credentials and their judgements, or feel that they have a right to say what they do? Because only then can we honour their decisions. Our problem is that we cannot always feel that we can trust those who presume to be our betters, especially when we sense that the grounds of their authority are often suspect or actually spurious. This is pre-eminently the case with politicians, who have no formal training for their work. Yet the public still insists on putting them into power while, at the same time – according to surveys – consistently ranking them alongside advertising executives and door-to-door salesmen. This has always been the problem with élites, how to sort out the ambitious and the self-seeking from those who genuintly want to serve. Perhaps those who comprise such élites are not even sure themselves. But then, when was anything ever done out of a pure motive?

Bibliography

Abercrombie, H., Hill, S. and Turner, B., *Dictionary of Sociology* (2nd edn), Penguin, Harmondsworth, 1988.

Abercrombie, N. and Ward, A. (eds), *Social Change in Contemporary Britain*, Polity Press, Cambridge, 1992.

Ablin, D. and Hood, M. (eds), *The Cambodian Agony*, Sharpe, New York, 1987.

Adas, M., *Prophets of Rebellion*, Chapel Hill, University of Carolina Press, N. Carolina, 1979.

Adas, M., *Machines as the Measure of Man*, Cornell University Press, Ithaca, New York, 1989.

Adkins, A., *Moral Values and Political Behaviour in Ancient Greece*, Chatto & Windus, London, 1972.

Adorno, T., *Prisms: Culture, Criticism and Society*, Spearman, London, 1967.

Albrow, M., *Bureaucracy*, Macmillan, London, 1970.

Allen, T. and Thomas, A., *Poverty and Development in the 1990s*, Open University and OUP, Oxford, 1992.

Andreski, S., *Latin American Politics*, Doubleday, New York, 1970.

Andrewes, A., *The Greek Tyrants*, Hutchinson, London, 1976.

Angelucci, O., *The Secret of the Saucers*, Amhurst Press, Amhurst, Wisconsin, 1955.

Appleyard, B., *The Pleasures of Peace*, Faber, London, 1989.

Appleyard, B., *Understanding the Present*, Picador Books, London, 1992.

Arendt, H., *The Origins of Totalitarianism*, Meridian, New York, 1958.

Axtell, J., *The European and the Indian*, OUP, New York, 1981.

Barkun, M., *Disaster and the Millennium*, Yale University Press, New Haven, 1974.

Basham, A., *The Wonder that was India*, Fontana Collins, London, 1971.

Baynes, N. and Moss, H. (eds), *Byzantium*, OUP, Oxford, 1961.

Beaglehole, J., (ed.), *The Journals of Captain Cook on his Voyages of Discovery* (vols. I, II and III), Cambridge University Press, Ithaca, New York, 1989.

Bell, D., *The Coming of Post-Industrial Society*, Heinemann, London, 1974.

Bendix, R., *Max Weber: an Intellectual Portrait*, Heinemann, London, 1960.

Berger, P. and Kellner, H., *Sociology Reinterpreted*, Penguin, Harmondsworth, 1982.

Berkhofer, R., *The White Man's Indian*, Alfred Knopf, New York, 1978.

Beteille, A. (ed.), *Social Inequality*, Penguin, Harmondsworth, 1969.

Bitterli, U., *Cultures in Conflict*, Polity Press, Cambridge, 1989.

Bloor, D., *Knowledge and Social Imagery*, University of Chicago Press, Chicago, 1991.

Boahen, A., *African Perspectives on Colonialism*, Johns Hopkins University Press, Baltimore, 1987.

Bohannan, P., *African Outline*, Penguin, Harmondsworth, 1966.

Bose, N.K., 'Caste in India', *Man in India*, **31** (107–23), 1951.

Bottomore, T., *Sociology*, Allen & Unwin, London, 1962.

Bottomore, T., *Elites and Society*, Basic Books, New York, 1964.

Bottomore, T., *Sociology as Social Criticism*, Allen & Unwin, London, 1975.

Boulding, D., *The Meaning of the Twentieth Century*, Allen & Unwin, London, 1964.

Bowle, J., *A History of Europe*, Heinemann, London, 1979.

Brandon, W., *The American Heritage Book of Indians*, Dell, New York, 1961.

Brockman, J. and Rosenfeld, E., *Real Time*, Picador, London, 1973.

Brower, D., *The World in the Twentieth Century: the Age of Global War and Revolution*, Prentice-Hall, Englewood Cliffs, New Jersey, 1988.

Brown, M., *After Imperialism*, Heinemann, London, 1963.

Browning, R., *The Byzantine Empire*, Weidenfeld & Nicolson, London, 1980.

Brundage, B., *The Jade Steps*, University of Utah Press, Salt Lake City, 1985.

Brundage, J. (ed.), *The Crusades: Motives and Achievements*, D.C. Heath, Boston, 1964.

Brym, R., *Intellectuals and Politics*, Allen & Unwin, London, 1980.

Bullock, A., *Hitler and Stalin: Parallel Lives*, HarperCollins, London, 1991.

Burridge, K., *New Heaven, New Earth*, Blackwell, Oxford, 1969.

Caldwell, M. and Tan, L., 'Cambodia in the South East Asia War', *London Monthly Review Press*, London, 1973.

Calvert, P., *The Concept of Class*, Hutchinson, London, 1982.

Carlton, E., *Ideology and Social Order*, Routledge & Kegan Paul, London, 1977.

Carlton, E., 'Science, Pseudo-science or Suprascience: the anomalous position of Parapsychology', *Self and Society*, **XVI** (3), May/June 1988.

Carlton, E., *War and Ideology*, Routledge, London, 1990.

Carlton, E., *Occupation: the Policies and Practices of Military Conquerors*, Routledge, London, 1992.

Casti, J., *Paradigms Lost*, Sphere Books, London, 1989.

Catlin, G., *North American Indians*, Penguin, Harmondsworth, 1989.

Chafetz, S., *Feminist Sociology: an Overview of Contemporary Theories*, Peacock, Itasca, Illinois, 1988.

Chandler, D., 'A Revolution in Full Spate: Communist Party Policy in Democratic Kampuchea', in Ablin, D. and Hood, M. (eds), *The Cambodian Agony*, 1987.

Chapman, B., *Police State*, Macmillan, London, 1970.

Charles, N., *Gender Divisions and Social Change*, Harvester Wheatsheaf, Hemel Hempstead, 1993.

Clarke, A.C., *Voices from the Sky*, Pyramid Books, New York, 1967.

Claster, J. (ed.), *Athenian Democracy*, Holt, Rinehart & Winston, New York, 1967.

Cohen, D., *The Ancient Visitors*, Doubleday, New York, 1976.

Cohn, N., *The Pursuit of the Millennium*, Harper, New York, 1961.

Collier, J., *Indians of the Americas*, Mentor Books, New York, 1948.

Comaroff, J. and Comaroff, J., *Of Revelation and Revolution*, University of Chicago Press, Chicago, 1991.

Connerton, P. (ed.), *Critical Sociology*, Penguin, Harmondsworth, 1976.

Connor, S., *Postmodernist Culture*, Blackwell, Oxford, 1989.

Conquest, R., *The Great Terror*, Hutchinson, London, 1990.

Coulton, G., *Medieval Panorama*, Fontana, London, 1961.

Cruikshank, M. (ed.), *Lesbian Studies*, The Feminist Press, New York, 1982.

Curthoys, A., *For and Against Feminism*, Allen & Unwin, Sydney, Australia, 1988.

Dammann, E., *The Future in our Hands*, Pergamon Press, Oxford, 1979.

Daniken, E. von, *Gold of the Gods*, Souvenir Press, London, 1972.

Dank, M., *The French against the French*, Cassell, London, 1978.

Davidson, B., *Africa in History*, Paladin, London, 1974.

Davies, J., *Democracy and Classical Greece*, Fontana, Glasgow, 1978.

Deaux, K. and Wrightsman, L., *Social Psychology in the 80s* (4th edn), Brooks/Cole, Monterey, California, 1984.

Debo, A., *The Road to Disappearance*, University of Oklahoma Press, Oklahoma, 1967.

de Crespigny, A. and Minogue, K., *Contemporary Political Philosophers*, Methuen, London, 1976.

de Kadt, E. and Williams, C. (eds), *Sociology and Development*, Tavistock, London, 1974.

Dely, G. (ed.), *Readings in Popular Culture*, Macmillan, London, 1990.

D'Emilio, J. and Freedman, E., *Intimate Matters: a History of Sexuality in America*, Harper & Row, New York, 1988.

de Reuck, A. and Knight, J. (eds), *Caste and Race: Comparative Approaches*, Churchill, London, 1967.

de Ropp, R., *The New Prometheans*, Delta Books, New York, 1972.

Djilas, M., *The New Class*, Thames & Hudson, London, 1957.

Driver, H., (ed.), *The Americas on the Eve of Discovery*, Prentice-Hall, Englewood Cliffs, New Jersey, 1964.

Dumont, L., *Homo Hierarchicus*, University of Chicago Press, Chicago, 1970.

Dunant, S., *The War of the Words*, Virago, London, 1994.

Dworkin, A., *Pornography: Men Possessing Women*, Putnam, New York, 1979.

Dye, T. and Zeigler, L., *The Irony of Democracy* (7th edn), Brooks/Cole, Monterey, California, 1987.

Ehrenreich, B., Hess, E. and Jacobs, G., *Remaking Love: the Feminization of Sex*, Doubleday, New York, 1986.

Eisenstadt, S.N., *Tradition, Change and Modernity*, John Wiley, New York, 1973.

Eisenstein, H. and Jardine, A. (eds), *The Future of Difference*, G.K. Hall, Boston, 1980.

Elias, N., 'Problems of Involvement and Detachment', *British Journal of Sociology*, 7, 1956.

Ellis, W., *Alkibiades*, Routledge, London, 1989.

Epstein, C., *Deceptive Distinctions*, Yale University Press, London, 1988.

Erickson, C., *The Medieval Vision*, OUP, New York, 1976.

Etzioni-Halévy, E., *The Knowledge of Elite and the Failure of Prophecy*, Allen & Unwin, London, 1985.

Etzioni-Halévy, E., *Fragile Democracy*, Transaction Publishers, New Brunswick, New Jersey, 1989.

Ewers, J., *The Blackfeet*, University of Oklahoma Press, Narman, Oklahoma, 1958.

Fendon, E., *Early Tahiti as Explorers Saw It*, University of Arizona Press, Tucson, Arizona, 1981.

Festinger, L., *When Prophecy Fails*, Harper, New York, 1956.

Fine, J., *The Ancient Greeks*, Belknap Press, London, 1983.

Finley, M., *The Ancient Greeks*, Pelican, Harmondsworth, 1971.

Finley, M., *Aspects of Antiquity*, Penguin, Harmondsworth, 1972.

Finley, M., *The Ancient Economy*, Chatto & Windus, London, 1973.

Firestone, S., *The Dialectic of Sex*, Bantam Books, New York, 1970.

Firth, R., *Human Types*, Sphere Books, London, 1970.

Fisher, N., *Social Values in Classical Greece*, Dent, London, 1976.

Fitzhardinge, L., *The Spartans*, Thames & Hudson, London, 1980.

Fontaine, C., 'Teaching the psychology of women: a lesbian feminist perspective', in M. Cruikshank (ed.), *Lesbian Studies* (pp.71–82), The Feminist Press, New York, 1982.

Foreman, G., *The Five Civilized Tribes*, University of Oklahoma Press, Oklahoma, 1972a.

Foreman, G., *Indian Removal*, University of Oklahoma Press, Oklahoma, 1972b.

Forrest, E., *The Snake Dance of the Hopi Indians*, Tower Books, New York, 1969.

Forrest, W., *A History of Sparta*, Hutchinson, London, 1971.

Foster, H., (ed.), *Post Modern Culture*, Pluto Press, London, 1983.

Foster-Carter, A., *The Sociology of Development*, Causeway Press, Ormskirk, 1985.

Freid, G.L. and Higley, J., *Elitism*, Routledge & Kegan Paul, London, 1980.

Friedrich, C. and Brzezinski, Z., *Totalitarian Dictatorship and Autocracy*, Praeger, New York, 1965.

Galbraith, K., *The New Industrial State* (2nd edn), Penguin, Harmondsworth, 1972.

Gellner, E., *Thought and Change*, Weidenfeld & Nicolson, London, 1963.

Gellner, E., *Postmodernism, Reason and Religion*, Routledge, London, 1992.

Gershuny, J., *After Industrial Society?*, Macmillan, London, 1978.

Gerth, H. and Mills, C. Wright, *From Max Weber*, Routledge & Kegan Paul, London, 1948.

Ghurye, G., *Caste and Race in India*, Routledge & Kegan Paul, London, 1933.

Giddens, A., *Sociology*, Polity Press, London, 1989.

Goffman, E., *The Presentation of Self in Everyday Life*, Doubleday, Garden City, New York, 1959.

Goldman, J., *Ancient Polynesian Society*, Chicago University Press, Chicago, 1970.

Good, T., *Above Top Secret*, Sidgwick & Jackson, London, 1987.

Good, T., *UFO Report 1991*, Sidgwick & Jackon, London, 1991.

Gorovitz, S., 'John Rawls' in A. de Crespigny and K. Minogue, *Contemporary Political Philosophers*, Methuen, London, 1976.

Gould, H., *The Hindu Caste System: the Sacrilization of a Social Order*, Chanakya Publications, New Delhi, 1987.

Gould, J. and Kolb, W. (eds), *Dictionary of Social Sciences*, Tavistock, London, 1964.

Gouldner, A., *Enter Plato: Classical Greece and the Origins of Social Theory*, Routledge & Kegan Paul, London, 1955.

Greenleaf, W., *Oakeshott's Philosophical Politics*, Longmans, London, 1966.

Gross, E. and Pateman, C., *Feminist Challenges: Social and Political Theory*, North Eastern University Press, Boston, 1986.

Grunberger, R., *A Social History of the Third Reich*, Penguin, Harmondsworth, 1974.

Gutteridge, W., *The Military in African Politics*, Methuen, London, 1969.

Hallgarten, G., *Devils or Saviours*, Oswald Wolff Books, Oxford, 1960.

Hamilton, B., *The Medieval Inquisition*, Arnold, London, 1981.

Haralambos, M., *Sociology: Themes and Perspectives*, University Tutorial Press, Slough, 1980.

Harding, S., *Feminism and Methodology*, Indiana University Press, Bloomington, Indiana, 1987.

Harris, G., *The Sociology of Development*, Longman, London, 1989.

Hartman, B., *Reproductive Rights and Wrongs*, Harper & Row, New York, 1987.

Hayter, T. and Watson, C., *Aid: Rhetoric and Reality*, Pluto Press, London, 1985.

Hebdige, D., *Hiding in the Light: on Images and Things*, Routledge, London, 1988.

Heilbroner, R., *The Quest for Wealth*, Eyre & Spottiswoode, London, 1956.

Hewison, R., *The Heritage Industry: Culture in a Climate of Decline*, Methuen, London, 1988.

Hibbert, C., *Africa Explored*, Allen Lane, London, 1982.

Hill, M.A., *A Sociology of Religion*, Heinemann, London, 1973.

Hoffnung, M., 'Motherhood: contemporary conflict for women' in J. Freeman (ed.), *Women: a Feminist Perspective* (pp. 157–75), Mayfield, Palo Alto, California, 1989.

Hultkrantz, A., *Religions of the American Indians*, University of California Press, London, 1980.

Hulton, J., *Caste in India*, OUP, London, 1951.

Irwin, C., *Fair Gods and Stone Faces*, W.H. Allen, London, 1964.

Jameson, F., 'The Politics of Theory: Ideological Positions in the Postmodernism Debate', in P. Rainbow and W. Sullivan (eds), *Interpretive Social Science: A Second Look*, University of California Press, Berkeley, California, 1987.

Jarvie, I., *Concepts and Society*, Routledge & Kegan Paul, London, 1972.

Jarvie, I., *The Revolution in Anthropology*, Routledge & Kegan Paul, London, 1987.

Johnson, H., *Sociology: a Systematic Introduction*, Routledge & Kegan Paul, London, 1964.

Johnson, P., *A History of the Modern World*, Weidenfeld & Nicolson, London, 1983.

Jones, A.M.H., *Athenian Democracy*, Blackwell, Oxford, 1957.

Jones, E. and Pitman, T., 'Towards a general theory of self-presentation', in J. Suls (ed.), *Psychological Perspectives on the Self*, Hillsdale, Erlbaum, New Jersey, 1982.

Jouvenel, B. de, *On Power*, Liberty Fund, London, 1993.

Kamenka, E., *Bureaucracy*, Blackwell, Oxford, 1989.

Kamenka, E. and Krygier, D., *Bureaucracy: the Career of a Concept*, Edward Arnold, London, 1979.

Karnow, S., *Vietnam: a History*, Penguin, Harmondsworth, 1983.

Keller, S., *Beyond the Ruling Class*, Random House, New York, 1963.

Kiernan, B., 'Conflicts in the Kampuchean Communist Movement', *Journal on Contemporary Asia*, **10**, 1980.

Klapp, O., *Models of Social Order*, Mayfield Publishing, Palo Alto, California, 1973.

Kuhn, T., *The Structure of Scientific Revolutions*, Chicago University Press, Chicago, 1970.

Lang, J. von, *Bormann*, Weidenfeld & Nicolson, London, 1979.

Lantenari, V., *Religions of the Oppressed*, Mentor, New York, 1965.

LaPière, R., *A Theory of Social Control*, McGraw-Hill, New York, 1954.

Laqueur, W. (ed.), *Fascism*, Penguin, Harmondsworth, 1979.

Lasswell, H. and Lerner, D. (eds), *World Revolutionary Elites*, MIT, Cambridge, Massachusetts, 1965.

Laszlo, E., *The Creative Cosmos*, Floris Books, Edinburgh, 1993.

Lee, S., *The European Dictatorships*, Routledge, London, 1987.

Lenski, G., *Power and Privilege*, McGraw-Hill, New York, 1966.

Lerner, D., *The Passing of Traditional Society*, Free Press, New York, 1964.

Lipset, S., 'Value Patterns, Class and Democratic Polity: the US and Great Britain', in K. and J. Tunstall (eds), *Sociological Perspectives* (pp.320–30), Penguin, Harmondsworth, 1971.

Lyndon, N., *No More Sex War*, Sinclair-Stevenson, London, 1992.

Mack Smith, D., *Mussolini's Roman Empire*, Peregrine, Harmondsworth, 1979.

Macksey, K. and Woodhouse, W., *The Penguin Encyclopedia of Modern Warfare*, Viking Penguin, London, 1991.

McLoughlin, J., *The Demographic Revolution*, Faber, London, 1991.

Magee, B., *Popper*, Fontana, London, 1973.

Mannheim, K., 'The problem of the intelligentsia: an inquiry into its past and present role' in E. Mannheim and P. Kecskemeti (eds), *Essays in the Sociology of Culture*, Routledge & Kegan Paul, London, 1956.

Marcus, G. (ed.), *Elites*, University of New Mexico Press, Albuquerque, New Mexico, 1983.

Marcuse, H., *One Dimensional Man*, Routledge & Kegan Paul, London, 1964.

Marwick, A., *British Society since 1945* (revised edn), Penguin, Harmondsworth, 1990.

Marwick, A., *Culture in Britain since 1945*, Blackwell, Oxford, 1991.

Meir, C., *The Political Art of Greek Tragedy*, Polity Press, Cambridge, 1993.

Melville, A. and Johnson, C., *Cured to Death*, Stein & Day, New York, 1983.

Menger, H., *From Outer Space to You*, Sauceran Books, Clarksburg, West Virginia, 1959.

Mennell, S., *Sociological Theory* (2nd edn), Nelson, Walton-on-Thames, 1980.

Merton, R., *Social Theory and the Sociology of Knowledge*, Allen & Unwin, London, 1979.

Michels, R., *Political Parties: A Sociological Study of the Oligarchical Tendencies in Modern Democracy*, Free Press, New York, 1962.

Mies, M. et al., *Women: the Last Colony*, Zed Books, London 1988.

Mills, C. Wright, *White Collar: the American Middle Classes*, OUP, New York, 1951.

Mills, C. Wright, *The Power Elite*, OUP, New York, 1956.

Moore, B., *Social Origins of Dictatorship and Democracy*, Beacon Books, Boston, 1966.

Moorehead, A., *The Fatal Impact*, Mead & Beckett, Sydney, 1987.

Mosca, G., *The Ruling Class*, McGraw-Hill, New York, 1939.

Mulkay, M., *Sociology of Science*, Open University Press, Buckingham, 1990.

Nava, M., *Changing Cultures*, Sage, London, 1992.

Nelson, G., *Cults, New Religions and Religious Creativity*, Routledge & Kegan Paul, London, 1987.

Oakeshott, M., *Rationalism in Politics and other Essays*, Methuen, London, 1962.

O'Hanlon, R., *Caste, Conflict and Ideology*, CUP, London, 1985.

Oldenbourg, Z., *Massacre at Montségur*, Weidenfeld & Nicolson, London, 1961.

Oliver, D., *The Pacific Islands*, CUP, Cambridge, 1951.

Olivier, R. and Fage, J., *A Short History of Africa*, Penguin, Harmondsworth, 1969.

Ollenburger, J. and Moore, H., *A Sociology of Women*, Prentice-Hall, Englewood Cliffs, New Jersey, 1992.

Orlov, D., *The History of the Nazi Party*, David & Charles, Newton Abbot, 2 vols, 1971 and 1973.

Pareto, V., *The Mind and Society*, Dover Press, New York, 1973.

Parsons, T., *The Social System*, Free Press, New York, 1951.

Parsons, T., 'The Distribution of Power in American Society', *World Politics*, **X** (123–43), 1957.

Parsons, T., *The Evolution of Societies* (ed. Jackson Toby), Prentice-Hall, Englewood Cliffs, New Jersey, 1977.

Pilger, J., *Heroes*, Pan, London, 1989.

Pilger, J., *Distant Voices*, Vintage Books, London, 1992.

Plamenatz, J., *Ideology*, Pall Mall, London, 1970.

Plotnicov, L. and Tuden, A. (eds), *Essays in Comparative Stratification*, University of Pittsburgh Press, Pittsburgh, 1970.

Popper, Sir K., *The Open Society and its Enemies* (Vols. I and II), Routledge & Kegan Paul, London, 1966.

Powell, A., *Athens and Sparta*, Routledge, London, 1988.

Prewitt, K. and Stone, A., *The Ruling Elites*, Harper & Row, London, 1973.

Putnam, R., *A Comparative Study of Elites*, Prentice-Hall, Englewood Cliffs, New Jersey, 1976.

Pym, C., *The Ancient Civilization of Angkor*, Mentor, New York, 1968.

Quinton, A., 'Karl Popper' in A. de Crespigny & K. Minogue, *Contemporary Political Philosophers*, Methuen, London, 1976.

Randles, J., *UFO Study*, Robert Hale, London, 1981.

Rawls, J., *A Theory of Justice*, Oxford University Press, Oxford, 1972.

Reitlinger, G., *The SS, the Alibi of a Nation*, Arms & Armour Press, London, 1981.

Revill, J., *World History*, Longmans, London, 1962.

Rice, T.T., *Everyday Life in Byzantium*, Batsford, London, 1967.

Roberts, J., *The City of Sokrates*, Routledge & Kegan Paul, London, 1984.

Roberts, J., *Triumph of the West*, Little, Brown, New York, 1986.

Roberts, M., *Caste Conflict and Elite Formation*, CUP, London, 1982.

Rostow, W., *The Stages of Economic Growth*, CUP, Cambridge, 1969.

Runciman, Sir S., *Byzantine Civilization*, Methuen, London, 1975.

Runciman, W., 'Towards a Theory of Social Stratification' in Frank Parkin (ed.), *The Social Analysis of Class Structure*, Tavistock, London, 1974.

Said, E., *Culture and Imperialism*, Chatto & Windus, London, 1993.

Sartre, J.P., *Being and Nothingness*, Methuen, London, 1957.

Schlenker, B., *Impression Management: the Self-concept, Social Identity, and Interpersonal Relations*, Brooks/Cole, Monterey, California, 1985.

Scott, J. (ed.), *The Sociology of Elites* (Vol. 1), Elgar, Aldershot, Hampshire, 1990.

Service, E., *Profiles in Ethnology* (3rd edn), Harper & Row, New York, 1978.

Shawcross, W., *Sideshow,* Fontana, London, 1980.

Shawcross, W., *The Quality of Mercy: Cambodia, Holocaust and Modern Conscience*, Simon & Schuster, New York, 1984.

Sheehan, B., *Seeds of Extinction*, University of North Carolina Press, Williamsburg, Virginia, 1973.

Shils, E., 'Centre and Periphery', in P. Worsley et al. (eds), *Introducing Modern Sociology*, Penguin, Harmondsworth, 1970.

Shirer, W., *The Rise and Fall of the Third Reich*, Pan Books, London, 1964.

Sihanouk, N. and Burchett, W., *My War with the CIA*, Penguin, Harmondsworth, 1979.

Silverberg, J. (ed.), *Social Mobility in the Caste System in India*, Mouton, The Hague (den Haag), 1968.

Sinfield, A., *Literature, Politics and Culture in Postwar Britain*, Blackwell, Oxford, 1989.

Snyder, L., *Hitler's German Enemies*, Robert Hale, London, 1991.

Soustelle, J., *Daily Life of the Aztecs,* Penguin, Harmondsworth, 1961.

Southern, R., *Western Society and the Church in the Middle Ages*, Penguin, Harmondsworth, 1970.

Spicer, E., *A Short History of the Indians in the United States*, Van Nostrum, New York, 1969.

Story, R., *The space-gods Revealed*, New English Library, London, 1977.

Story, R., *Guardians of the Universe?*, New English Library, London, 1980.

Taylor, C. and Sturtevant, W., *The Native Americans*, Salamander Books, New York, 1991.

Tetlock, P., 'Pre- to post-election shifts in Presidential rhetoric', *Journal of Personality and Social Psychology*, 1981.

Thapar, R., *A History of India* (Vol.1), Penguin, Harmondsworth, 1976.

Thion, S., 'The Pattern of Cambodian Politics', in D. Ablin and M. Hood (eds), *The Cambodian Agony*, Sharpe, New York, 1987.

Thompson, J., *Studies in the Theory of Ideology*, Polity Press, Cambridge, 1928.

Thrupp, S. (ed.), *Millennial Dreams in Action*, Mouton, The Hague (den Haag), 1962.

Thucydides *The Peloponnesian War* (trans. Rex Warner), Penguin, Harmondsworth, 1972.

Timasheff, N., *Sociological Theory: its Nature and Growth*, Random House, New York, 1957.

Tomasek, R., (ed.), *Latin American Politics*, Doubleday, New York, 1970.

Tong, R., *Feminist Thought: A Comprehensive Introduction*, Westview Press, Boulder, Colorado, 1989.

Toynbee, A., *Science in Human Affairs*, Columbia University, New York, 1968.

Toynbee, A. and Ikeda, D., *Choose Life: a Dialogue*, OUP, Oxford, 1976.

Turner, H. (ed.), *Reappraisals of Fascism*, Franklin Watts, New York, 1975.

Underhill, R., *Red Man's America*, University of Chicago Press, Chicago, 1971.

Vaillant, G., *The Aztecs of Mexico* (revised edn), Doubleday, New York, 1962.

Vickery, M., *Cambodia 1975–1982*, South End, Boston, 1982.

Wallace, A., *The Death and Rebirth of the Seneca*, Vintage Books, New York, 1972.

Washburn, W., *The Indian in America*, Harper & Row, New York, 1975.

Weber, M., *The Theory of Social and Economic Organisation*, Free Press, New York, 1957.

Weber, M., *The Religion of India: the Sociology of Hinduism and Buddhism*, Free Press, New York, 1962.

Weber, M., *Economy and Society*, Bedminster Press, New York, 1968.

Weech, W., *History of the World*, Odhams, London, 1946.

Weiss, J., *The Fascist Tradition*, Harper & Row, New York, 1967.

Wheeler, Sir M., *The Indus Civilization* (3rd edn), CUP, Cambridge, 1968.

Wilkinson, R. (ed.) *Governing Elites*, OUP, New York, 1969.

Wilson, B. (ed.) *The Social Impact of New Religious Movements*, Rose of Sharon Press, New York, 1978.

Wilson, E.O., *Sociobiology: the New Synthesis*, Harvard University Press, Cambridge, Massachusetts, 1975.

Wilson, J., *Equality*, Hutchinson, London, 1966.

Wood, E. and Wood, W., *Class Ideology and Ancient Political Theory*, Blackwell, Oxford, 1978.

Worsley, P., *The Trumpet Shall Sound*, Shocken, New York, 1957 (and 1968).

Worsley, P. et al. (eds), *Introducing Modern Sociology*, Penguin, Harmondsworth, 1970.

Wright, R., *Stolen Continents: the Indian Story*, TSP, Uxbridge, 1994.

Yearley, S., *Science, Technology and Social Change*, Unwin Hyman, London, 1988.

Zacour, N., *An Introduction to Medieval Institutions*, Saint James Press, London, 1976.

Index

Abelard, Peter 129
Abercrombie, N., Hill, S. & Turner, B. 181
Ablin, D. & Hood, M. 116, 118, 121
Adair, J. 82
Adas, M. 100, 108
Adorno, T. 186, 187
Adrian IV 130
Aegean islands 45
Africa 7, 75, 93ff., 103, 104, 111–12, 178
Albigenses 131ff.
Albigensian Crusade 134ff.
Alexander (the Great) 16, 45, 69
Algeria 179
Ali, Noble Drew 111
Alkibiades 51, 53
Allen, Woody 22
America, see USA
American Indians 3, 10, 72ff., 108ff.
Andreski, S. 12
Andrewes, A. 54
Angelucci, O. 113
Angkor 112, 116–17, 119
Antiphon 53
Apaches 74
Appleyard, B. 179
Arabs 66, 93, 112
Aragon 134, 139
Arapaho 73
Arendt, H. 12
Aristophanes 45, 51
Aristotle 20, 23, 45, 57, 58
Armenians 73
Arnold, M. 185
Arnold of Brescia 129–30
Aron, R. 4, 21
Aryans 35, 40, 41, 74, 160
Ashanti (of the Gold Coast/Ghana) 7, 97
Asia Minor 35, 45, 46, 52–3, 66
Assassination(s), see Atrocities
Athens 1, 15, 18, 45ff., 63, 151, 172, 203

Atlantis 105
Atrocities 15, 51, 53, 56, 63–4, 66–7, 72ff., 77–8, 83ff., 88, 94, 99, 102, 103, 104–5, 106–7, 109, 120, 122ff., 132–3, 136ff., 163
Augustine 130
Austria 167
Authority (types) 60–62
Axtell, J. 86, 87
Aztecs 76, 99, 109–10, 175, 180

Bantu 104
Barkun, M. 108, 111
Basileius 131
Bayer 64
Beatles 182
Becket, Thomas 142
Beethoven, L. von 182
Belgium/Belgians 93, 94, 96
Bell, D. 7
Bendix, R. 38
Benedictine Order 127
Berger, P. & Kellner, H. 193–4
Berkhofer, R. 87, 88
Beziers 137
Bitterli, U. 98, 99, 102–3
Blackfeet 80
Black Power 111
Boers 93
Bogomils 131
Bohannan, P. 93–4, 95
Booksellers' Association 186
Bormann, M. 167
Bottomore, T. 2, 4, 5, 11, 36, 44
Boulding, D. 180
Bowle, J. 130, 131
Brahmins 33, 34, 35ff.
Brahmanas 35
Bram 138
Braun, W. von 199
Britain/British 80–81, 83, 86, 95, 175, 177, 184, 185
Browning, Robert 189
Brundage, B. 175

Brym, R. 11
Buddhism 14, 37, 39, 108, 116, 123, 204
Bulgars 66
Bullock, Sir A. 202
Bureaucracy 11, 21, 44, 59ff., 164ff.
Burridge, D. 109
Bushmen 203
Byzantine/Byzantium (Constantinople, Istanbul) 59ff., 131

Caesar, Julius 16
Caillie, R. 94
Callitrates 52
Calvert, P. 4
Cambodia (Kampuchea) 14, 116ff.
Cameroons 96
Carcassonne 137–8
Carlton, E. 11, 13–14, 15, 51, 54, 56, 73, 89, 165, 193
Carthage/Carthaginians 102
Caste system 33ff., 173
Casti, J. 192, 193, 194
Castro, Fidel 11
Cathars, see Albigenses
Catlin, G. 72, 74, 75, 79
Chafetz, S. 146
Chandler, D. 124
Chapman, B. 163
Charles, N. 151
Cherokees 77, 81
Cheyenne 73, 74
Chinese, China 7, 11, 61, 98, 100, 116, 119–20, 122, 124–5, 126, 174
Choctaws 81
Chomsky, N. 169
Chuckchee 10
Clarke, Arthur C. 114
Class 3ff., 11, 45ff., 100–101, 102, 103, 144, 203–4
Claster, J. 52
Cluny/Cluniacs 127–8
Cohn, B. 39
Cohn, N. 115
Collier, J. 77
Colonialism 90ff., 117–18, 175, 177, 179
Columbus 75, 76, 87
Comaroff, J. & Comaroff, J. 90
Commanches 73

Communist/Communism 7, 10, 19, 25, 62, 118ff., 161, 162, 178
Conquest, R. 10, 202
Constantine 64–5
Constantine of Mananalis 131
Cook, Captain 100–101, 102
Cortes, H. 99, 109, 175
Coup d'état, see also Revolution, 11, 14, 15, 65, 66, 112, 119, 124, 161, 203
Creeks 80ff., 84–5, 86
Crete 15
Cruickshank, M. 145
Crusades 66
Cuba 11, 125, 176
Cults 104ff.
Culture 181ff.
Curthoys, A. 153

Dahl, R. 6, 7
Dahomey 7
Dammann, E. 175, 179–80
Danes 93
Daniken, E. von 112
Dank, M. 15
Davidson, B. 96
Davies, J. 57
Dawkins, R. 197
Delos 47
de Kadt, E. & Williams, C. 176
Democracy 1ff., 7ff., 15, 17ff., 45ff., 54, 88, 203, 206
D'Emilio, J. & Freeman, E. 147
de Montford, Simon 136ff.
de Reuck, A. & Knight, J. 40, 42
de Ropp, Robert 191–2, 199
de Torres, L. 98
Diseases 72, 73–4, 86, 99, 100, 103, 198
Djilas, M. 62
Dodderidge, J. 82
Dominic 141
Dravidians 40
Driver, H. 76
Dunant, S. 153
Durkheim, E. 110
Dutch 93
Dworkin, A. 144

Education 27
Egypt 7, 13, 49, 61, 65, 70, 74, 76,

98, 105, 116, 171, 172, 174, 179
Ehrenreich, B., Hesse, E. & Jacobs, G. 147
Einstein, A. 193, 197, 200
Eisenstadt, S.N. 205
Eisenstein, H. & Jardine, A. 144
Election 104ff.
Elias, N. 9
Eliot, T.S. 185
Elites (Theories) 1ff.
   and definitions 2ff.,
   and values 7ff.,
   and intellectuals 9ff.
   and ideology 12ff.
   and aggression 15ff.
   and personality factors 16ff.
   and social democracy 17ff.
   and ethics 21ff.
   and caste 33ff.
   and social differentiation 45ff.
   and bureaucracy 59ff.
   and race 72ff.
   and moral right 90ff.
   and millenarianism 104ff.
   and conquest 116ff.
   and ecclesiastical authority 127ff.
   and gender 143ff.
   and political parties 156ff.
   and economic status 169ff.
   and mass culture 181ff.
   and education 190ff.
   see also specific categories:
      ideology, democracy, race,
      religion, ethics etc.
Ellis, W. 51
Engels, F. 82
England/English 75, 77, 78, 93, 136, 139
Ephors/Ephorate 54
Epstein, C. 149–50
Escobar, P. 179
Esquimaux 104, 174
Ethics 21ff., 101
Ethiopia 111
Etzioni-Halévy, E. 197, 198, 206
Ewers, J. 79

Farben, I.G. 64
Feminist/feminism, see Sex/sexuality
Festinger, L. 113
Fifth Monarchy Men 106

Finley, M. 151
Firestone, Shulamith 144
Firth, R. 169, 170, 173, 181
Fontaine, C. 146
Ford, G. 122
Foreman, G. 84–5
Forrest, E. 110
Foster-Carter, A. 179
Francis of Assisi 140
Frederick Barbarossa 130
Frederick (of Prussia) 63
Freisler, R. 162
French/France 4, 62, 75, 83, 84, 86, 93, 95–6, 107, 117–18, 119, 120, 123, 131ff.
French Revolution 28, 160
Freud, S. 17
Freidrich, C. & Brzezinski, Z. 160
Fromm, E. 17
Fulani 96
Fuller, S. 196–7

Galbraith, K. 92–3
Gandhi, M. 43
Garvey, Marcus 111
Gellner, E. 31, 88, 91, 178
Gender, see Sex/sexuality
Genghis (Chingis) Khan 9
Germans/Germany 30, 60, 63–4, 93, 96, 117, 156ff., 182
Gerousia 54
Gestapo, see Nazis
Ghost Dance 108, 114
Ghurye, G. 33
Giddens, A. 7, 31, 156, 190
Goebbels, J. 157, 165
Goering, H. 161
Goffman, I. 17
Good, T. 114
Gorovitz, S. 22
Gouldner, A. 3
Grattan, J. 73
Greece/Greek 1, 3, 11, 18, 22, 35, 45ff., 64, 65, 74, 98, 112, 151, 179, 203
Greenleaf, W. 24, 25, 27, 29
Gregory VII 128
Gregory IX 141
Grenada 178
Gross, E. & Pateman, C. 143
Grunberger, R. 165

Gutteridge, W. 15
Guyana 104–5, 115

Habermas, J. 194
Haile Selassie 111
Haiti 178
Hamilton, B. 132, 141
Haralambos, M. 6
Harappa 35
Harding, S. 143
Harris, G. 175
Hartman, B. 148
Hawaii 92, 102
Hayek, F. 23–4
Hebdige, D. 90
Heilbroner, R. 179
Helots 56
Henry II 142
Henry, Claudius 112
Herero 96
Heresy 127ff.
Herskovits, M. 169
Hill, M. 108
Himmler, H. 136
Hindenburg, P. von 159–60
Hinduism, see also Caste, 116, 204
Hirohito 9
Hitler, A. 28, 63, 157ff.
Hobbes, T. 24
Hobsbawm, E. 115
Ho Chi Minh 118
Hoffnung, M. 148
Hoggart, R. 186
Homosexuality 26, 55, 144, 146,
    153, 161
Honorius III 140
Hopi 109ff.
Hultkrantz, A. 110
Hulton, J. 34
Hungary 178
Huns 65
Hunter, F. 6
Hurons 83, 84
Hussites 129
Huxley, A. 18, 40, 105

Ictinus 52
Ideology, see also Religion, 12ff.,
    15–16, 24ff., 42, 57, 74, 78, 95,
    100, 104ff., 123ff., 127ff., 157ff.,
    173ff., 179, 182, 193, 200

Ignatieff, M. 189
Inca 97
Indian/India 7, 15, 33ff., 96, 98, 116,
    198
Indonesia 42
Indus Valley culture 35, 41, 174
Infanticide 102
Innocent II 129
Innocent III 134, 136, 139, 140
Innocent IV 142
Inquisition 140, 141–2
Intellectuals 9ff., 15, 18, 19
Iran (Persia) 14, 15, 35, 46ff., 53, 57,
    65, 69, 131, 133, 179, 205
Iraq 205
Ireland 75
Iroquois (including Onandagas,
    Mohawks, Oneidas, Senecas,
    Cayugas and Tuscororas) 77, 80,
    82ff.
Irwin, C. 76
Islam 13, 14, 37, 38, 39, 41, 65–6,
    96, 131, 136, 179
Isokrates 57
Israel 66, 112, 136
Italy (and Italian Colonial Empire)
    35, 66, 94, 127, 128, 129, 131,
    162

Jackson, A. 82
Jamaica 111, 112
Japanese/Japan 92, 98, 100, 117–18,
    122
Jarvie, I. 91, 108
Jefferson, T. 82
Jerusalem 65
Johnson, H. 44
Johnson, P. 123, 124
Jones, E. & Pitman, T. 17
Jones, J. (Temple Cult) 115
Jouvenal, B. de 22
Judaism/ Jews 74, 98, 104, 115, 136,
    137, 158, 161, 164, 168, 182
Justinian 65, 69–70, 134

Kamenka, E. 59, 64
Kant, I. 195
Karnow, S. 119, 120
Keller, S. 20, 21
Kennedy, Helena 151
Kennedy, J. 30

Khmers 112, 116ff.
Kibbutzim 106
King, Martin Luther 111
Kissinger, H. 125
Kitchener 93
Klapp, O. 18
Kleisthenes 45, 46
Kleon 51
Kluckhohn, C. 181
Koestler, A. 193
Krupps 64
Kshatriyas 34
Kuhn, T. 191, 195, 200
Kwakiutl 10

Lang, J. von 167
Languedoc 137ff.
Lantenari, V. 114
Laos 120, 125
LaPière, R. 44
Laqueur, W. 167
Lasswell, H. 8, 11
Latin 35
Latin America 12, 176
Lavaur 138
Lazzlo, E. 201
Leavis, F.R. 185
Lee, S. 17, 167
Lenin 28, 124, 176
Lenski, G. 14, 15–16, 127
Leo IX 128
Leopold of Belgium 94
Lerner, D. 8, 11
Lévi-Strauss, C. 149
Lipset, S. 5, 7
Locke, J. 24
Lollards 129
Louis, Prince of France 140
Lovedu 41
Lundberg, F. 7
Luther, M. 9
Lyndon, N. 143, 152
Lysenko, T. 200

Machiavelli 2
Mack Smith, D. 94
Magee, B. 17, 193
Magellan, F. 98
Mahomet II 67
Major, J. 4
Malawi 178

Malaysia 176
Malinowski, B. 170
Mandans 74, 75, 79
Manichaeus/Manicheans 130ff.
Mannheim, K. 11, 20, 185
Manu 35
Mao Tse-Tung 28, 123, 124, 125
Maori 103
Marcus, G. 1, 6, 7
Marcuse, H. 182, 186, 187
Marmande 140
Marwick, H. 184–5
Marx/Marxist 3, 5–6, 19, 20, 21, 24,
    25, 42, 60, 62, 106, 107, 124,
    143, 144, 158, 174, 177, 179,
    187, 203–4
Masai 172
Massacre, see Atrocities
Maslow, A. 8
Matabele/Mashona 41, 93
Mather Cotton 87
Maya 76, 109
McKenney, T. 82
McLoughlin, J. 152–3
Melos 51
Melville, A. & Johnson, C. 198
Menger, H. 113
Mennell, S. 31
Menominee 10
Mesopotamia, see also Iraq, 35, 61,
    74
Merton, R. 199
Metics (resident aliens) 48, 172
Mexico 99, 109, 175
Michels, R. 2–3, 157
Mies, M. 144
Military 12, 15, 40–41, 47–8, 52,
    55ff., 69, 70, 109, 116ff., 136ff.,
    161, 163, 166, 198, 205
Mill, J.S. 28, 185
Millenarianism 104ff., 130
Mills, C. Wright 3–4, 6, 7, 29
Minoan(s) 15
Moctezuma II 109
Models (ideal types) 59ff.
Mohenjo-daro 35
Monarchy 64ff., 116, 156
Monroe, Marilyn 189
Montanus 130
Montsegur 142
Moore, B. 11

Moorehead, A. 100–101
Moravians 81
Mosca, G. 1, 2, 4, 6, 7, 13, 202
Muggeridge, M. 30
Muhammed, Elijah 111
Mulkay, M. 196, 200
Mungo Park 94
Muslims, *see* Islam
Mussolini, B. 9, 162

Nama 96
Napoleon 16
Natchez 80
Nazi(s)/Nazism 9, 10, 30, 60, 63–4,
    73, 104, 106, 136, 156ff., 200,
    202, 205
Nehru, J. 179
Nelson, G. 108
Nicaragua 179
Nigeria 96
Nixon, R. 121–2, 125
Normans 66, 68
Norseman 179
North Korea 179

Oakeshott, M. 23ff., 152
Oldenburgh, Z. 135, 136
Oligarchy 2ff., 46, 52–3, 54ff.
Oliver, R. & Farge, J. 94
Ollenburger, J. & Moore, H. 143,
    144, 147, 148
Orlov, D. 164
Orwell, G. 105
Ottomans 9, 65, 67
Outcastes (scheduled caste) 34, 36, 43

Pakistan 35, 174, 198
Palestinians 112
Pareto, V. 1, 2, 6, 7, 13, 202
Parsons, T. 4, 7–8, 29, 91, 176–7
Paulicans 131
Peasants' Revolt 129
Pequots 84, 87
Perikles 47, 51
perioikoi 55–6
Peru, *see also* Inca, 13, 99, 116, 171
Personality factors 16–17, 150–51
Pharmaceuticals 197–8
Phidias 52
Philip of France 136ff., 140
Phillips, Melanie 154

Philosophy 23ff.
Phoenicia/Phoenicians 76
Picasso 183
Pilger, J. 124, 125, 126
Plato 11, 18–19, 20, 25, 45, 48, 53,
    58, 105, 130, 184
Plotnicov, L. & Truden, A. 39
Plutarch 45
Poland 178
Political correctness 153–4
Pol Pot 119, 122, 123ff.
Polybius 128
Polynesia 72, 100ff., 171
Pope, Alexander 191
Popper, Sir K. 17, 18–19, 21, 24, 191,
    192–3, 195
Population control 148–9
Pornography 147
Portuguese 93
Postmodernism 182ff., 195
Prewitt, K. & Stone, A. 21–2
Prostitution 37, 87, 124, 147
Protestantism 29, 101–2, 107, 134
Prussia 63
Puranas 35
Putnam, R. 20
Pym, C. 116
Pythagoras 149

Quakers 80, 87
Quayle, D. 126
Quinton, A. 22

Race 33ff., 74ff., 144, 167ff.
Randles, J. 114
Ras Tafari (Jamaica) 110ff., 114
Rawls, J. 22–3
Raymond of Toulouse 134ff.
Reitlinger, G. 63–4
Religion 9, 10, 13–14, 36ff., 65ff.,
    77, 78ff., 81, 86, 95, 97, 98–9,
    101, 102, 104ff., 116ff., 123,
    128ff., 162, 173ff., 204
Renaissance 174
Revill, J. 130
Revolution 11, 13, 15, 52–3, 61, 62,
    117, 123, 157ff., 159, 161
Rhodesia (Zimbabwe) 41
Rice, T. 69
Rich, Buddy 189
Rig-Veda 35

Roberts, J. 91
Roberts, M. 40
Robert the Pious 132
Roman Catholicism 9, 127ff.
Rome/Romans 54, 61, 64–5, 68, 69,
    70, 74, 130ff., 156, 174, 202
Rostow, W. 176, 177
Rousseau, J.J. 24
Runciman, W. 67, 205
Rushdie, Salman 185
Russia 11, 13, 28, 62, 119, 125, 160,
    176, 200, 202

SA (stormtroopers), see Nazis
Samos 52–3
Sanskrit 35
Saracens 66
Sartre, J.P. 17, 29
Saudi Arabia 205
Schlenker, B. 16
Science/scientific development 174,
    179–80, 190ff.
Scott, J. 2, 6
Sects 130ff.
Selby, H. 10
Seminoles 85–6
Seneca Indians 77
Service, E. 101
Sex/sexuality 37, 39, 43, 130, 131,
    143ff.
Shakespeare, W. 29, 182
Shaw, B. 29
Shawcross, W. 116, 117, 125
Sheehan, B. 82, 84
Shils E. 8
Shiva 35
Shoshones 73
Shudras 34, 40
Siam/Siamese 117
Sicily 50, 51
Siemens 64
Sihanouk 117–18, 119, 122, 126
Sinhalese 39
Sioux 108
Slaves/slavery 18, 26, 37, 48, 49–50,
    93, 111, 128, 172
Smith, J., Captain 98
Snake Dance 109ff.
Snow, C.P. 190
Snyder, L. 161
Social work 27

Sociology 193–4, 194–5, 196, 203–4
Sokrates 18, 50, 52, 54, 103, 155
Solon 46
Somalia 178
Sophists 52
South Africa 41–2
Southern, R. 134
South Korea 92, 176, 179
Soviets, see Russia
Spanish America 42, 73, 80, 93,
    109–10, 175
Spanish/Spain 65, 93, 97, 175, 188
Spartans/Sparta 18, 42, 45ff., 77, 151
Spielberg, S. 182
Spicer, E. 81, 83
Sri Lanka (Ceylon) 39
SS, see Nazis
Stalin 10, 62, 160, 161, 202
Stanley, H.M. 94
Story, R. 112
Sudan/Sudanese 93
Suleiman 9
Swazi 7
Syria 65

Tahiti, see Polynesia
Taiwan 176, 179
Tartars 67
Taylor, C. & Sturtevant, W. 73, 84
Television 149, 184, 186ff.
Tetlock, P. 17
Teutonic knights 160
Thapar, R. 34, 37
Thatcher, M. 126
Thebes/Thebans 56
Theodora 65
Thera (Santorini) 15
Thompson, J.W. 127
Thrupp, S. 112
Thucydides 45, 53, 56, 91
Timur (Tamerlane) 9
Tito, Marshal 62
Tlaloc 175
Tobacco industry 178
Toltecs 109
Tomasek, R. 12
Tong, R. 145
Totalitarianism 17ff., 28, 156ff., 205
Toulouse 138–9, 140
Toynbee, Sir A. 202–3
Trades Unions 17, 25

Tupinamba 76
Turks, *see also* Ottomans, 66, 73, 98
Tyrannies 46, 54, 57–8

UFOs 113–14
Uganda 178
Underhill, R. 78
United Kingdom 8, 16, 26, 27, 28, 63
USA 4, 6, 16, 41–2, 72ff., 103, 111,
    112, 118–19, 120ff., 176, 178,
    181, 198–9
Uta-Naphistim 35
Utilitarianism 18, 22, 40, 185
Utopias 19, 25, 105

Vaillant, G. 109
Vaishyas 34
Vandals 65
Venetians 66–7
Vichy regime 15, 117–18
Vietcong 119, 120, 122
Vietnam/Vietnamese 117, 119ff.
Vishnu 35

Waldo/Waldensians 132
Wallace, A. 77
War 4, 12, 15, 18, 49, 50, 51, 56,
    64ff., 77, 78, 81ff., 93, 102, 109,
    117ff., 136ff., 152, 157–8,
    163ff., 176, 198
    (Second World War) 1, 7, 9, 22,
    122, 197, 199
Washburn, W. 76, 80
Watchtower Society 105
Weber, M. 3, 5, 12, 38, 39, 42, 44,
    59ff., 108, 170, 202, 204
Weech, W. 128
Wheeler, Sir M. 35
Whitehorn, K. 154
Wilkinson, R. 10
Wilson, E. 150
Wilson, J. 19, 20
Witchcraft 132
Wolpert, L. 196
Wood, E. & Wood, W. 58
Woodcock, G. 25
Worsley, P. 104, 108, 115

Xenophon 45
Xhosa 104

Yearley, Stephen 195
Yugoslavia 62
Yurok 10

Zimbabwe, *see also* Rhodesia, 178
Zoroastrianism 130
Zulu 7, 41